PENGUIN BOOKS

LITERARY DEMOCRACY

Larzer Ziff is the author of *Puritanism in America: New Culture in a New World*, *The American 1890s: Life and Times of a Lost Generation*, *The Career of John Cotton: Puritanism and the American Experience*, and numerous articles in the field of American literature. He is also the editor of The Penguin American Library edition of *Selected Essays* by Ralph Waldo Emerson. Larzer Ziff is currently Caroline Donovan Professor of English at Johns Hopkins University.

Larzer Ziff

Literary Democracy

The Declaration of Cultural Independence in America

PENGUIN BOOKS

For Joel Ziff
and
for Abigail Ziff

Penguin Books Ltd, Harmondsworth,
Middlesex, England
Penguin Books, 625 Madison Avenue,
New York, New York 10022, U.S.A.
Penguin Books Australia Ltd, Ringwood,
Victoria, Australia
Penguin Books Canada Limited, 2801 John Street,
Markham, Ontario, Canada L3R 1B4
Penguin Books (N.Z.) Ltd, 182–190 Wairau Road,
Auckland 10, New Zealand

First published in the United States of America by
The Viking Press 1981
Published in Penguin Books 1982

LIBRARY OF CONGRESS CATALOGING IN PUBLICATION DATA
Ziff, Larzer, 1927–
Literary democracy.
Includes index.
1. American literature—19th century—History
and criticism. 2. Literature and society—United
States. 3. United States—Civilization—1783–
1865. I. Title.
PS201.Z5 1981b 810′.9′003 82-3706
ISBN 0 14 00.6199 1 AACR2

Printed in the United States of America by
Offset Paperback Mfrs., Inc., Dallas, Pennsylvania
Set in Linotron Old Style # 7

ACKNOWLEDGMENTS
Time and facilities for the preparation of this book were provided by fellowships from the John Simon Guggenheim Memorial Foundation, the American Council of Learned Societies, and Yaddo, all of whom I thank most sincerely. I am indebted to Linda Ziff for the valuable suggestions made as a result of her close reading of the initial draft, and to Malcolm Cowley for his perceptive comments on later stages. Parts of chapters Sixteen and Seventeen first appeared in *New Perspectives on Melville*, ed. Faith Pullin (Edinburgh, 1978), and *The Yearbook of English Studies* (Vol. 8, 1978), ed. G. K. Hunter and C. J. Rawson; I thank the editors and the Modern Humanities Research Association for permission to reprint. Chapters Two and Sixteen appeared originally in *Democracy*.

Table of Contents

Preface

This book narrates the life and times of those writers who established American literature as a distinct way of imagining the world. Although they inherited the English language and with it British literary conventions, these writers, in their achievement, declared the independence of American culture. They discovered that America meant more than a new setting for time-honored forms; it meant a new way of perceiving reality. They not only developed new subject matter and experimented with new language within the older language but also invented the new forms demanded by such unprecedented material.

The principal writers who established the literary independence of America were Edgar Allan Poe, Ralph Waldo Emerson, Nathaniel Hawthorne, Henry David Thoreau, Walt Whitman, and Herman Melville. Their careers centered in the era that began with the great panic in 1837 and ended with the outbreak of the Civil War, the period, therefore, with which this book is concerned. But since the story of how a major American literature made a sudden emergence must also be the story of the culture that nurtured the great writers, their careers are considered within the social contexts that contained them and are contrasted with the highly informative careers of their significant contemporaries.

For the sake of certain aesthetic interests, literature may be thought of as separate from society, just as for the sake of certain scientific interests, mass may be considered in isolation from the field in which it exists. But just as mass is finally inseparable from its field of force because it is fundamentally an intense form of the energy that surrounds it, so, I believe, literature is a particular concentration of cultural forces continuous with, rather than apart from, society. Accordingly, in treating literature and society I am not so much concerned with literature as a mirror of society—which it is only from a limited and simplified point of view—as with literature as a unique and intense social form.

In *The Flowering of New England* and *The Times of Melville and Whitman,* Van Wyck Brooks provided enduring pictures of many aspects of the period that I now revisit. He was concerned primarily with recapturing the flavor of the world the writers inhabited, and he offers incomparable impressions of the furniture in their houses, the sights in their streets, and the notions that circulated in their newspapers and in the counting houses. He was not concerned, as I am, with the process by which the details of the world—especially its cultural anxieties—worked their way into the form and texture of literature. His discussion of the writings centers, rather, on the way they mirror their society, and he treats them as additional artifacts of a rich and crowded scene. My history is not so packed with the details of the material culture as is Brooks's, in part because I am the beneficiary of his work and proceed from it, in greater part because I discuss what existed only insofar as I see it influencing literature. Unlike Brooks's, my history constantly moves between the world observed and the creative processes of the writers who inhabited it, justifying description of the former by exhibiting its subtle effects on the latter.

F. O. Matthiessen's *American Renaissance* remains the standard work on the purely literary quality of the writings of the period. Subtitled "Art and Expression in the Age of Emerson and Whitman," his book analyzes the way in which the major writers (Poe excluded) fused form and content. Concerned with the aesthetics of American Romanticism, it does not deal with the cultural context of the works it examines. Since I am tracing a history, I do not engage in extended textual explications, as did Matthiessen, although my own conclusions benefit greatly from his work. But I do speak in some detail about language and form as they reflect the state of the culture, and in this way I cross into Matthiessen's terrain on my different errand.

This book, then, differs from Brooks's works in its demonstration of certain precise connections, literary as well as biographical, between the American democracy and its first great body of imaginative writing. It differs from Matthiessen's in its exposition of the social origins of great writing. No previous work on the period turns on the two equally valued focal points of the common concerns of the society and the distinct literary achievement of its writers.

Emerson said that each age must write its own books: "The books of an older period will not fit this." Ours is the postwar age of America the superpower. In it American literature is a common commodity on the shelves of foreign bookstores and is to be found in the curricula of such widely differing institutions as Moscow University and the University of Oxford. But despite the historical and critical activity that has accompanied the global interest in American literature, the present age has not written its book about the period in which American literature achieved its definition. Strictly speaking, ages do not write books; people do—and that is my excuse for writing this one.

The generation of American writers born immediately after the Revolution was raised in a period when the new republic was discovering that it neither could be nor needed to be a democracy. The French Revolution seemed to underline to Americans the anarchy that would follow if they did not restrict the franchise and consolidate authority. Tribal allegiance to royal Britain pulled more powerfully than ideological allegiance to republican France. The consequent conservatism of the Federalist period is manifest in the writings of its major authors despite the differences in their specific political views.

Washington Irving (b. 1783), James Fenimore Cooper (b. 1789), and William Cullen Bryant (b. 1794) all followed English literary models that were conservative in their reflection of English society. Although these Americans wrote about their own nation, they were constrained by adherence to their models to trim their work to foreign dimensions. They furnished it, for example, with subtle social manners, or ancient monuments, or a rustic folk rooted in Old World lore. A good deal of what they observed in their society failed to register in their writing because they had no precedent for regarding it as worthy of being presented. America was made to fit literature before literature was made to fit America.

The achievement of Irving, Cooper, and Bryant was impressive, and they greatly influenced writers of the following generation. What might have been expected from such beginnings was a gradual, cautious growth. As a result of it, the concerns of American society would become available to American literature to the extent that English literary tradition provided conventions in terms of which they could be expressed. American writers would develop those themes that were suggested by the preexisting forms. So much for expectations. The slow growth indeed occurred, but unpredictably and dramatically it was surpassed by the sudden appearance of a native literature that was startling in content and radically original in form. A land that in one generation had quite on schedule produced Irving, Cooper, and Bryant did not in the next produce Longfellow, Lowell, and Holmes alone. Without warning it also yielded Poe, Emerson, Hawthorne, Thoreau, Whitman, and Melville. Suddenly there were American books of the first rank, not by prevailing provincial standards but by the standards of world literature.

The boundaries that mark the following discussion of this literary quickening have immediately recognizable reference to events of political history: 1837 was the year of the great panic and 1861 was the year in which the Civil War began. But they mark a distinct literary era also. Emerson, first in time and foremost in contemporary reputation among the major writers, owed his first attentive audience partly to a financial disaster. His idealism seemed particularly appealing after the collapse of the material world in 1837. That same year, Hawthorne ended his isolation and his anonymity by publishing his first book and announcing in it that he was opening an intercourse with the world. In that year also Edgar Allan Poe left Virginia for New York and the world of national magazines. The year of the panic was a notable year of literary outsettings: Melville made his first voyage and Thoreau graduated from Harvard. Although the connection between financial collapse and this myriad of beginnings is not precise, neither is it, as I show, mere accident.

The year 1861 saw the last months of the old America. The Civil War was followed by the patching together of a new nation, a clear continuation of the old republic and yet a distinctly different entity. Poe did not live to see the outbreak of the war, nor did Hawthorne and Thoreau live to see the end of it. Emerson lived through it, only to admit to himself that his creative energies were spent, while

Whitman came through splendidly, but in the process inescapably changed direction, so that all who chronicle his career speak validly of the "later Whitman" to distinguish his postwar accomplishments from the revolutionary explosion of *Leaves of Grass* in its first three editions. And Melville, by war's start, had lapsed into a near-silence that lasted till he died; for some thirty years he published no fiction. More obviously than the opening year, the terminal year of this history marks a political and a literary crossroads.

Enclosed within the framing dates are the remarkable 1850s when *The Scarlet Letter, Moby-Dick, Walden,* and *Leaves of Grass* appeared hard on the heels of one another. They were only the most notable of a range of outstanding books that included others by the same authors, as well as Stowe's *Uncle Tom's Cabin* and Emerson's *English Traits*. That decade is rightly seen as unparalleled, yet the high point then attained is connected to the stirrings that began around 1837 and cannot be accounted for unless such connection is made.

Of the seventeen chapters that follow, twelve center on the major writers: Emerson, Poe, Hawthorne, Thoreau, Whitman, and Melville in that order, save that Melville also serves as a prologue. In these chapters, a good deal of consideration is given to the relationship of those major authors to the writings of lesser authors of the day and especially to its dominant cultural concerns. The remaining five chapters, unevenly spaced between those on the major figures as the subjects require, are devoted to the views of the Boston literati, dominant socially and powerful in the world of letters; the landscape of social nightmare that complemented the terrain of Poe's aesthetic nightmares; the career of Margaret Fuller, representing the condition of women and also representing a class of gifted persons who wrote only because their society afforded them no outlet for the direct action for which their talents were better suited; the remarkable concurrence of slack sentiment and tough-minded Calvinism in the most popular novel of the period, indeed of the century, *Uncle Tom's Cabin;* and George Washington Harris's viciously antisentimental but equally Calvinistic complement to that outlook, which opposed it sectionally and, more important, on the level of class warfare. Each chapter takes its rise from a thematic concern that runs through both literature and society. In the chapters on major writers the responding voice of the culture can be heard, and in those more broadly concerned with the culture the major writers' voices are also present.

The period under discussion is evoked as a whole in the early chapters and then explored in terms of the major figures and the major concerns that animated it. This affords a better sense of the era, I believe, than does a methodical year-after-year survey. For the bare facts of chronology, the Annals below may be consulted.

Rather than affirming a center for the book I have claimed twin focuses, literature and society. Rather than affirming a mirror relationship between the two I have claimed a causal relationship. Explanation is certainly in order. At the beginning, therefore, let us look at the first book of an author who did not know that he was an author when he underwent the experience he there fictionalized, and who was so far from intentionally writing of his America that he regarded the exoticism of his subject as its major appeal. Nonetheless, the work finds its form and force because in it the cultural concerns of the new literary democracy find theirs.

Annals

From the Great Panic to the Civil War

1837: Administration of Martin Van Buren; major financial panic.
Burton's Gentleman's Magazine (1837–40)
United States Magazine and Democratic Review (1837–49)
Cooper, *Gleanings in Europe* (1837–38)
Emerson, "The American Scholar"
Hawthorne, *Twice-Told Tales*

1838: Wilkes expedition departs to explore Pacific Ocean and South Polar regions.
Martineau, *Retrospect of Western Travel*
Tocqueville, *Democracy in America* (first American edition)
Cooper, *The American Democrat*
Whittier, *Ballads and Anti-Slavery Poems*
Emerson, "The Divinity School Address"
Poe, *The Narrative of Arthur Gordon Pym*

1839: Antislavery view enters politics with formation of Liberty party by moderate abolitionists.
Longfellow, "Hyperion"; "Voices of the Night"
Poe, *Tales of the Grotesque and Arabesque*

1840: William Henry Harrison defeats Martin Van Buren in presidential election. Population, 17,069,000 (to nearest thousand).
The Dial (1840–44)
Dana, *Two Years Before the Mast*

1841: Harrison inaugurated; at his death, John Tyler becomes president (1841–45).

New York Tribune founded
Cooper, *The Deerslayer*
Emerson, *Essays, First Series*
Poe, "The Murders in the Rue Morgue"

1842: Webster-Ashburton treaty establishes northeastern border of United States.

Dickens, *American Notes*
Cooper, *Wing-and-Wing*
Longfellow, *Ballads and Other Poems*
Poe, "The Masque of the Red Death"
Hawthorne, *Twice-Told Tales* (enlarged edition)

1843: Beginnings of political nativism (American Republican party).

Prescott, *The Conquest of Mexico*
Poe, "The Gold-Bug"; "The Black Cat"
G. W. Harris begins publishing sketches in *Spirit of the Times*.

1844: Senate rejects Calhoun's treaty for annexation of Texas; James K. Polk, first "dark-horse" candidate in history, defeats Henry Clay in presidential election; "Fifty-four forty or fight."

Dickens, *Martin Chuzzlewit*
Cooper, *Afloat and Ashore*
Emerson, *Essays, Second Series*
Lippard, *The Monks of Monk Hall,* reprinted (1845) as *The Quaker City*
Fuller, *Summer on the Lakes*

1845: Presidency of Polk (1845–49); annexation of Texas; nineteen-volume report of Wilkes expedition; General Zachary Taylor's force moves into Texas; "Manifest Destiny."

Cooper, *Satanstoe*
Poe, *The Raven and Other Poems*
Fuller, *Woman in the Nineteenth Century*
G. W. Harris, "The Knob Dance" (his first vernacular tale)

1846: Oregon boundary settled at 49th parallel; Mexican War (1846–48); "Republic of California" declared under Bear Flag; Wilmot Proviso prohibits extension of slavery into territories gained from Mexico.

Holmes, *Poems*
Emerson, *Poems*
Poe, "The Cask of Amontillado"; "The Philosophy of Composition"
Hawthorne, *Mosses from an Old Manse*
Melville, *Typee*

1847: Battle of Buena Vista; Vera Cruz expedition; capture of Mexico City.

Prescott, *The Conquest of Peru*
Longfellow, *Evangeline*
Melville, *Omoo*

1848: Discovery of gold at Sutter's Mill; Seneca Falls Convention for women's rights; Zachary Taylor defeats Lewis Cass and Martin Van Buren (Free-Soil) in presidential election.

Lowell, *The Biglow Papers; A Fable for Critics; The Vision of Sir Launfal*
Poe, *Eureka*
1849: Presidency of Taylor (1849–50).
Parkman, *The Oregon Trail*
Ticknor, *History of Spanish Literature*
Longfellow, *Kavanagh*
Poe, "Annabel Lee"; "The Bells"; "Eldorado"
Thoreau, *A Week on the Concord and Merrimack Rivers*; "Civil Disobedience"
Melville, *Mardi; Redburn*
Death of Poe

1850: Death of Taylor, and Fillmore's presidency (1850–53); Compromise of 1850 (Webster's March 7th speech; Fugitive Slave Law).

Harper's Monthly Magazine (1850–)
Whittier, "Ichabod"; "Songs of Labor"
Emerson, *Representative Men*
Hawthorne, *The Scarlet Letter*
Melville, *White-Jacket;* "Hawthorne and His Mosses"

1851: Public reception accorded Louis Kossuth is the last widespread indication of United States sympathy with the spirit of the revolutions of 1848.

Parkman, *The Conspiracy of Pontiac*
Simms, *Katharine Walton*
Hawthorne, *The Snow Image; The House of the Seven Gables*
Melville, *Moby-Dick*

1852: Franklin Pierce defeats Winfield Scott and John P. Hale (Free-Soil) in presidential election.

Hawthorne, *The Blithedale Romance*
Stowe, *Uncle Tom's Cabin*
Melville, *Pierre*

1853: Presidency of Pierce (1853–57); Perry reaches Japan; New York and Chicago linked by railroad.

Putnam's Monthly Magazine (1853–57)
Lippard, *New York: Its Upper Ten and Lower Million*

1854: Kansas-Nebraska Act; founding of Republican party; reemergence of Know-Nothing party, now called American party.

G. W. Harris, "Sut Lovingood's Daddy, Acting Horse" (first Sut Lovingood tale)
Thoreau, *Walden*
Death of Lippard

1855: Armed skirmishes break out in "bloody Kansas"; John Brown arrives in Osawatomie.

Irving, *The Life of George Washington*
Simms, *The Forayers*
Longfellow, *The Song of Hiawatha*
Whitman, *Leaves of Grass*
Melville, *Israel Potter*

1856: James Buchanan defeats John C. Frémont (Republican) and Millard Fillmore (Know-Nothing) in presidential election.

Kane, *Arctic Explorations*
Motley, *The Rise of the Dutch Republic*
Simms, *Eutaw*
Emerson, *English Traits*

Stowe, *Dred*
Whitman, *Leaves of Grass* (second edition)
Melville, *The Piazza Tales*

1857: Presidency of Buchanan (1857–61); Dred Scott decision; commercial and financial panic (August).
Atlantic Monthly (1857–)
Harper's Weekly (1857–1916)
Melville, *The Confidence-Man*

1858: Lincoln-Douglas debates; Republican party success in state and congressional elections; transatlantic cable.
Longfellow, *The Courtship of Miles Standish*
Holmes, *The Autocrat of the Breakfast-Table*

1859: John Brown's raid on Harpers Ferry; Jefferson Davis calls for repeal of law prohibiting importation of slaves.
Stowe, *The Minister's Wooing*

1860: Lincoln defeats Stephen Douglas, John C. Breckenridge, and John Bell in presidential election; South Carolina secedes; population, 31,443,000.
Whittier, *Home Ballads*
Holmes, *The Professor at the Breakfast-Table*
Emerson, *The Conduct of Life*
Hawthorne, *The Marble Faun*
Whitman, *Leaves of Grass* (third and enlarged edition)

1861: Presidency of Lincoln; ten more states secede; Fort Sumter fired upon (April 12).

Chapter One

The Reluctant Spark: Melville Among the Typees

In 1841, Herman Melville, twenty-two years of age, signed aboard the *Acushnet* as a common seaman and sailed from New Bedford, Massachusetts, for the Pacific Ocean, there to kill whales. His enlistment was a matter of defeat if not despair. He had already been unsuccessful at schoolteaching and in commerce and had failed in other attempts to attach himself to one or another enterprise that promised to grow with the rapidly expanding country.

He came from a prominent family—indeed, two prominent families. His mother was a Gansevoort, descended from Dutch settlers in the Upper Hudson River Valley, a community that had retained feudal practices in land management until after the American Revolution, even as its church had retained the full predestinarian strain of orthodox Calvinism long after New England churches began to dilute it. The Melville grandfather had been a general in the Revolution and was a distinguished figure on the streets of Boston, in clothes and manner a living intrusion of the eighteenth century into modern times. When the Continental army decisively reversed the course of the Revolution by defeating General Bourgoyne at Saratoga, the men involved were a combination of British New Englanders such as the Melvilles and Dutch New Yorkers such as the Gansevoorts.

Herman Melville, then, had some claim to being one of the gentry, even in democratic America. But distinguished descent and long residence in the land were not sufficient to ensure competence, let alone prominence, in that commercial society, and Melville's father had entered trade and ended bankrupt, dead in spirit and finally dead in body while Herman was a boy. And so, as Melville noted, a whaling ship was his Harvard College and his Yale.

But although going to sea was an emphatic announcement of the rupture that the young man felt had opened between him and his society, it was also a signaling of the nature of the self that was now afoot on its own career. Melville was an inlander, and many another inlander in his day also set forth in retreat from the town of his upbringing and the conditions of his life, seeing his retreat, however, as an advance. He went west to start life over, to begin the world anew, as a common phrase had it. Implicit in this venture was the necessary repetition by the new westerner of the history—from clearing to farm to village—that his native region had undergone. In the repetition, however, he would be the original settler. In exchange for enduring seclusion, hardship, and provincialism in the new land he would acquire the wealth that those who had lived before him in his birthplace had already appropriated. He would make history rather than remaining its victim.

To choose the sea, in contrast, was to choose a confinement with others of the same, bottommost economic class, a confinement so intense that an intimacy well beyond that of the tightest rural village was inescapable. With economic distress in common, the members of the crew had as differences their backgrounds: a wide range of countries and countrysides, religious beliefs and practices, native tongues, learning, and lore, backgrounds that had shaped them before dispossessing them and sending them to sea. The society before the mast was naive and superstitious, but it was also cosmopolitan beyond any cross-cultural mix that could be achieved by the expatriated man of wealth.

Not only did the seaman reject the provincial privacy that the movement westward on the continent implied, he also denied the commitment to the future, the starting life again. Going to sea was a truce with history, an acceptance of the conditions that had brought the seaman to his lowly situation, and a gesture of unwillingness to reopen the matter. He encapsulated himself in what history had made him and in that capsule set sail.

"Shall I not have intelligence with the earth? Am I not partly leaves and vegetable mould myself?" Thoreau asked these questions in the solitude of Walden Pond. The election of the sea was the election of wind and wave, natural intelligences like leaf and mould, to be sure, and yet so different in texture as to define another kind of man.

When the *Acushnet* touched at the Marquesas Islands in the South Pacific, Herman Melville abandoned his ship, spent a month roaming the islands, then signed aboard another whaler, which took him to Oahu. After more beachcombing, he went into service aboard an American man-of-war on the Peruvian station, and finally returned home. There he was encouraged to write up the account of the adventures he talked about in so lively a fashion. The result was *Typee,* published in 1846, based on his scant month's stay on one of the Marquesas, but spun into a fictionalized narrative of a four-month residence. It quickly became a popular book in England and America.

In *Typee,* Melville describes his flight inland from his ship in search of the Happars, a tribe that he had been told was extremely amiable to strangers. But he blunders in his flight and instead is taken in by the Typees, the other remote tribe, enemies of the Happars and men with a reputation for savagery and cannibalism. During his stay with them he can never rid himself of his fear of their reported cannibalistic practices although, in fact, he experiences only comfort at their hands. Food is abundant without toil; sex is abundant without guilt; and each day is spent in the gratification of the senses.

A great part of the popularity of the book came from its being the first entertainingly written account of South Sea island culture. It is a direct ancestor of the experiences and accounts of such as Robert Louis Stevenson and Paul Gauguin. As opposed to earlier reports by navigators and missionaries, which spoke of the islands in terms of opportunities to be seized, work to be done, and profits to be taken in exchange for benefits conferred, Melville's narrative yields to island life and revels in it because the implicit contrast is not with high civilization so much as with cribbed confinement in the forecastle of a noisome vessel.

A particularly American aspect of *Typee*'s appeal stemmed from the fact that America, too, had its savages, Indian tribes that had been decimated or forcibly removed from their lands as Europeans advanced westward from the Atlantic seaboard. Some American thinkers and writers had warned that the whites, in their treatment of the Indians, were not only committing a grave social injustice but also being unfair to themselves. If the promise of America was to be fully realized, they argued, it meant not just enormous space and resources for exploitation and Europeanization. It meant, rather, a chance to escape from the determinations of European history and to learn anew how to live. The principal instructors should be nature and the native Indians, who lived their daily lives in response to nature's rhythms.

"They inveigh against the governments of Europe, because, as they say, they favour the powerful and oppress the weak," Frances Trollope wrote of the Americans in 1832. "You will see them one hour lecturing their mob on the indefeasible rights of man, and the next driving from their homes the children of the soil, whom they have bound themselves to protect."[1]

But there was a humanitarian response to this humanitarian indictment; it asserted that the continental expansionism annihilating the Indians grew from the needs of the crowded masses of Europe, who were pressing for release into a new dignity; and that the Indians, when they saw the light, would adhere to and benefit from this historical necessity. Longfellow addressed the solitary mournful Indian chief accordingly:

> Ah 'tis in vain that with lordly looks of disdain
> thou dost challenge
> Looks of disdain in return, and question these walls
> and the pavements,
> Claiming the soil for thy hunting-grounds, while
> down-trodden millions
> Starve in the garrets of Europe, and cry from its
> caverns that they too
> Have been created heirs of the earth, and claim its
> division![2]

As for the nascent counterexpansionist interest in Indian culture, Daniel Webster spoke for the necessary continuity of political democracy when he wrote: "I ought to say that I am a total unbeliever in the new doctrines about the Indian languages. I believe them to be the rudest forms of speech; and I believe there is as little in the languages of the tribes as in their laws, manners, and customs, worth studying or worth knowing."[3] *Typee,* concerned as it was with another primitive culture, one that could be contemplated without the guilt and practical objections that were constantly raised when the Indians were under discussion, was, therefore, an attractive work. It was not directly about the Indian problem, although brief reference was made to it, but that problem gave a latent force to the author's narrative and the reader's experience of it.

Melville described the society and the daily life of the Typees as a version of paradise. He was especially taken by the absence of labor, money, and guilt, seeing that habits he thought were natural to mankind when he grew up in America were, in fact, culturally determined and baneful. He saw that savagery was a term applicable to the Europeans' colonial and missionary activities in the Pacific rather than to the people they practiced upon. The young author, discovering for himself what social theorists had for centuries been speculating upon, did not hesitate to point up the obvious ironies: "When I consider the vices, cruelties, and enormities of every kind that spring up in the tainted atmosphere of a feverish civilisation, I am inclined to think that so far as the relative wickedness of the parties is concerned, four or five Marquesan islanders sent to the United States as missionaries might be quite as useful as an equal number dispatched to the islands in a similar capacity."[4]

Although he does not base his admiration for Typee society on an extended comparison between that society's economic conditions and those that characterized American civilization in general and had coerced his life in particular, Melville's account comprehends such contrasts fully. At one point he considers the single non-Edenic element of Typee life, the lone factor that, seemingly, tells against the perfection of that society and indicates that those islanders, too, are cursed. It is the absence among them of any easy means to kindle fire. Each time a flame is required, and of course it is almost constantly required for cooking, the islander must engage in a frenzy of labor, in striking disproportion to all other aspects of his life.

Melville describes the process in detail as his friend Kory-Kory performs it. The islander takes a six-foot length of wood some six inches in thickness, props it up at a forty-five-degree angle, mounts it, and then, taking a smaller stick in both hands, vigorously rubs it up and down against the large log he is astride.

> At first Kory-Kory goes to work quite leisurely, but gradually quickens his pace, and waxing warm in the employment, drives the stick furiously along the smoking channel, plying his hands to and fro with amazing rapidity, the perspiration starting from every pore. As he approaches the climax of his effort, he pants and gasps for breath, and his eyes almost start from their sockets with the violence of his exertions. This is the critical stage of the operation; all his previous labours are vain if he cannot sustain the rapidity of the movement until the reluctant spark is produced. Suddenly he stops, becomes perfectly motionless. His hands still retain their hold of the smaller stick, which is pressed convulsively against the farther end of the channel, among the fine powder there accumulated, as if he had just pierced through and through some little viper that was wriggling and struggling to escape from his clutches. The next moment a delicate wreath of smoke curls spirally into the air, the heap of dusty particles glows with fire, and Kory-Kory, almost breathless, dismounts from his steed.[5]

The analogy between this process and that of the male's behavior in sexual intercourse is obviously and, one assumes, consciously evoked by Melville. The specific diction of the passage—"furiously along the smoking channel," "approaches the climax," "all . . . vain if he cannot sustain," "pressed convulsively," "little viper . . . wriggling and struggling to escape," and the climactic product issuing "spirally" with its alliterative suggestion of "sperm"—indicates a high concern on the author's part to stress the parallel.

But the provocation of the passage lies deeper. Why does Melville, who seems to luxuriate in the sensual pleasures of Typee society and to defend them against the strictures of civilization, use the greatest of those pleasures as an analogy for hard work? The immediate response, it would seem, is that he himself comes from a world in which the curse of labor and the wearing of the fig leaf had a coordinate commencement. Whatever his express enjoyment of Typee life may be, he cannot overcome his sense of Adam's shame, his guilt.

But this supposition, although to the point, will not finally suffice. For what the awakening Melville is here further expressing, with not so full a consciousness but with convincing power, is—in our terminology, not his—the connection between the alienation of labor in modern industrial society and the alienation of the self from the self. "What a striking evidence does this operation furnish of the wide difference between the extreme of savage and civilised life," he writes. "A gentleman of Typee can bring up a numerous family of children, and give them all a highly respectable cannibal education, with infinitely less toil and anxiety than he expends in the simple process of striking a light; whilst a poor European artisan, who through the instrumentality of a lucifer performs the same operation in one second, is put to his wit's end to provide for his starving offspring." [6]

Industrialization has brought about the convenient match, affordable by all, and also the poverty-stricken matchmaker, struggling with incessant cheerlessness. For him, sexual intercourse is a matter of a joyless instant unattended by the full engagement of the self, while getting a living for himself and the consequences of such instants is a matter of a lifetime dogged by anxiety. The savage on his island labors at his lovemaking because it is the complete expression of a self that need not withhold stamina for the externally imposed demands of getting a living at his job; his world stands ready to embrace the consequences. Melville seems consciously to have given his description of the firemaking a sexual content. But the telling force of the passage does not derive from this conscious purpose; indeed, were this the principal source of its strength it would differ little from the more popular passages of deliberate titillation devoted to bare-breasted nymphs found elsewhere in the book. Rather, what elevates this passage into its full expressiveness is the source that suggests the analogy. The author is here in touch with his own culturally created complexities, and their pressure upon him fuses an image of honest labor as sexual act in contrast with exploited labor as guilt-ridden sexuality.

If Melville had reason to question the organization of American life when he described the life of the Typees in such images, he nevertheless saw no reason to question the explicit democratic ideal of egalitarianism on which American life was presumably organized. The islanders, he says, were "governed by that sort of tacit common-sense law which, say what they will of the inborn lawlessness of the human race, has its precepts graven on every breast."[7] The statement is in the key of Thomas Paine. To view savagery as inherently lawless is really to view democracy as ultimately unworkable. Undemocratic forms of authority require the doctrine of natural depravity, as Paine perceived when he asserted that "the palaces of kings are built on the ruins of the bowers of paradise."[8] If American civilization has gone wrong, so wrong as to disinherit the young such as Melville, it has done so by allowing adverse experiences to detach its social system from its foundation on a belief in the inborn goodness of all men; it has stopped halfway along its track and instead of accepting the unleavened bread of the wilderness has returned for the yeast of natural depravity with which to bake the loaf of democracy.

"It is to this indwelling, this universally diffused perception of what is *just* and *noble,* that the integrity of the Marquesans in their intercourse with each other is to be attributed,"[9] Melville says. Manifestly, he is referring to a political government among the islanders which can be lax because harmony arises from the possession of common virtues. But "integrity . . . in their intercourse" is a phrase which connects politics with sexual behavior even as he had earlier connected economics with it. The view of human nature that does not fear lawlessness and makes democracy possible is one that must be equally fearless about all forms of natural human behavior, including sexuality. The placing of physical love behind the curtain in America is an indication of blockages between the body politic and the human body, of which, in a persistent, classical image, it is the enlargement. European societies, as Hawthorne, for one, observed, even though in their arbitrary class divisions they channel sexual expression, do at least recognize a necessary correspondence between natural desires and social forms. Nonmarital intercourse between the gentleman and the woman of the lower classes is not merely permitted but made possible and sanctioned by the class system. But democracy, in proclaiming one class made up of all, cannot accept that this means an unconstrained sexual as well as social mingling. As a result it drives sexuality from the threshold of expression to the darker places of the mind. Thus, with the obliteration of the social divisions of European society, America opened psychic divisions within its young.

"I will frankly declare, that after passing a few weeks in this valley of the Marquesas, I formed a higher estimate of human nature than I had ever before entertained," says Melville. And then he adds, "But alas! since then I have been one of the crew of a man-of-war, and the pent-up wickedness of five hundred men has nearly overthrown all my previous theories."[10]

Why, then did he leave this paradise? On the surface of the narrative his answers are adequate to the adventures described. He missed home and friends; he could never free himself from the notion that, despite their amiable conduct toward him, he was among cannibals and might become their victim. But such casually proffered explanations are not adequate to the deeper level of his perception of the virtues of Typee culture. He had arrived there with a wounded leg, whose throbbings resisted medication but vanished once he entered fully into the activities of that society. It is symbolic of the psychic wound visited upon him by civilization and of the wholeness that can be reclaimed by submission to the natural—specifically, it symbolizes the malfunctioning of the sexual organ inhibited by arbitrary social codes and its restoration in a sexual environment that knows no guilt. There are reasons to stay more powerful than the expressed reasons for departure.

He tells us the principal cause of his leaving was his loneliness. Despite the constant companionship of the natives, he says, "There was no one with whom I could freely converse; no one to whom I could communicate my thoughts; no one who could sympathise with my sufferings."[11] His meaning, clearly, is not merely linguistic. The tongue is a difficult one and he is making but slow progress in it. But even had he attained the comprehension of a professor of South Seas philology, his complaint would have stood, for it is related to a deeper cultural factor, the life from which language grows.

Earlier, when he wished to illustrate his contention that with the Typees "one tranquil day of ease and happiness follows another in quiet succession," he described one of his days among them because, as he said, "the history of a day is the history of a life."[12] And here, of course, even though Melville represents it as the source of happiness, we locate the source of his troubled mind. The Typees have no history and accordingly have no language; no means, that is, of communicating thoughts and sufferings that are the products of history. Melville by the time of his arrival in their society is the result of history; his aching leg is the symbol of its alienating force. Despite his contempt for every influence of modern history upon the South Seas—the imperial bloodletting and the ruthless Christianizing—and despite his own victimization at the hands of American history—family bankruptcy and life aboard a foul ship worked by the dregs of society—he cannot step out of historical time into the timeless round of the Typees, tranquil and happy as it is.

The sameness of Typee life is a feature of its mythic nature. Among them time is reversible. They know all universal history and in their rituals periodically reenact it, relive the breakthrough of the sacred into the world they inhabit. They can repeatedly claim the origin of their reality. Their time is cosmogonic.

But Melville is the product of chronological time and is not obliged to know the whole of universal history. For him time is irreversible, and rather than reenact what cannot ever be again he uses language to explain his temporal location.

Hence his fear of cannibalism, which he insists upon keeping alive in himself although he is never threatened by it. The rituals that alarm him are affirmations by the Typees that they are living in mythical time, and for him to yield to them would be to lose his identity, to be swallowed up. Whether or not the Typees are literal cannibals, they are certainly figurative cannibals and are devouring Melville's historical identity. They keep urging him to get tattooed, and he jests with the reader that if he submits he will lose face. But it is not a jest; if he submits he will lose the image that he recognizes when he looks into the mirror of his mind.

In his most intense moment of isolation among those who feel for him but do not understand him, he speaks of exotic birds, "purple and azure, crimson and white, black and gold," who visit the valley of the Typees. But, he mourns, they do not sing, "alas! the spell of dumbness is upon them all."[13] Their brilliant appearance fills him with melancholy rather than cheer. It tells him, we may infer, that perfect, beautiful, uninhibited, free-flying, gorgeous natural existence, submission to the timeless, is submission to silence. Mythic time needs no language; the gesture is all.

And Melville, finally, opts for history and for language, knowing full well the pain he must resume. As the importunities for him to be tattooed increase and his resistance stiffens, his leg begins to throb again. His historical self is returning. And so he flees into the sea. The Typees furiously swim after his boat to pull him back into their time, and in that moment the act of violence that he had feared throughout finally takes place. But it is the reverse of what he had imagined, for he is the perpetrator. In terror at being dragged back he seizes a boathook and gouges the throat of the Typee who is closing upon him, and thus escapes with reddening water in his wake.

Melville's subsequent works were to be haunted by similar images of history fighting free of myth with all the passion of a lover who must resist the love that will engulf him: Benito Cereno locked in a combat with Babo that extends beyond Babo's death; Ishmael floating to survival on the coffin of Queequeg. And in his final work he restated the link, unbreakable as he saw it, between history and language. Billy Budd, the mythic man destroyed by history, is perfect in every respect save one—he has a speech impediment.

These concerns also shaped Melville's greatest contemporaries. Their America was making history in a linear projection of Europe westward, and yet their America had no history of its own other than this European thrust. They were stirred by the powerful, murky possibility that their true history might be natural history, the mythic tale of man remade by a new environment, rather than the historical tale of man civilizing the wilds. Those such as Hawthorne and Melville who chose language and history while responding to the lure of mythic possibility became, for the most part, novelists, although the forms they achieved were different from those of the English novel, even as the formlessness of the society that they chose to express was different from the structured system that was English society. Those such as Emerson and Thoreau who chose myth and the expression of a sense that in America the world could be made to create itself each day were accordingly attracted to silence as the ultimate language, even as they employed language to persuade their countrymen that their lives were not irreversible, and drew that language from a theory of its inherence in natural forms. Fiction for them was an outmoded vehicle, a conveyance in which traditional societies could be seen on their outings, and they sought genres commensurate with the new prophetic voices in which they spoke.

Typee, written by a relatively uneducated and unreflecting young man who was endeavoring to fictionalize his exotic escapades and bring them to the attention of others in a bluff and hearty tone resonant of landlessness, was, after all, rooted in the soil of America. Beyond its author's realization, the book gained its expressiveness from what nourished it more than from what it manifested. That this nourishing humus, American culture, now contained such fertile force was apprehended neither by him nor by his contemporaries. But the fertile elements had been assembled and would soon be feeding an American literature.

Chapter Two

Sloven Continent: Emerson and an American Idea

In January 1841, the month that Herman Melville boarded the *Acushnet* in New Bedford, Ralph Waldo Emerson, fifty miles to the north, delivered a new lecture. "I will not inquire into the oppression of the sailors," he said. "I will not pry into the usages of our retail trade." Instead he concentrated on the larger proposition that the system of trade on which the prosperity of his country was based was so general a system of selfishness that "we eat and drink and wear perjury and fraud in a hundred commodities."[1]

Emerson was then thirty-seven years old and in the full swing of the powers that had gathered in him after the collapse of his first, singularly mediocre career. The heir of a clerical lineage, he had dutifully attended Harvard and was graduated without distinction. He prepared for the Unitarian ordination, which he received in 1829, and with his first pulpit took also a wife, whom he buried less than two years later. He then resigned his pulpit and, with the help of gifts from family and friends, set out to travel in Europe in order to discover his true relation to the world. Once back in America, he was able to realize about $1200 per annum from his wife's legacy, and he used it to remain apart from the mainstream of life in his commercial community. He remarried, but his reluctance to return to the ministry came, he knew, not just from a hesitation to share in a body of religious beliefs but from a positive refusal to become part of business. The church, he felt, was but a branch of commerce. "If you do not value the Sabbath, or other religious institutions," he remarked, "give yourself no concern about maintaining them. They have already acquired a market value as conservators of property."[2]

Emerson sat in Concord: he thought, observed, read, wrote in his notebooks, and then wrote from them for publication. He began to give lectures—occasional lectures and series of lectures—which were soon after to find printed form and to convince readers. By 1841, the year in which his *Essays, First Series* was published, he had acquired a piercing if restricted fame. First young easterners and then other Americans became aware that apart from the magnetic field lying between the polarized interests of State Street, Boston, and the capital at Washington—between the positive force of trade fighting free of restrictions and the negative force of the people's government seeking to control rather than to yield to business—there existed another pasture, commonly called Concord, in which character was attempting a separation from the minutiae of American reality in order to discover whether the ultimate meaning of such petty details indeed necessitated that they should exist precisely as they did. It was not a pasture with fit fodder for many, and those who browsed in the actual, geographical Concord showed misshape rather than symmetry to the dispassionate observer.

Nathaniel Hawthorne, too, resided there, but in the physical rather than the spiritual township, as he insisted with such vehemence that at times he appeared to be trying to convince himself. Looking about him he wrote:

> Never was poor little country village invested with such a variety of queer, strangely dressed, oddly behaved mortals, most of whom took upon themselves to be important agents of the world's destiny, yet were simply bores of a very intense water. Such, I imagine, is the invariable character of persons who crowd so closely about an original thinker, as to draw in his unuttered breath, and thus become imbued with a false originality. This triteness of novelty is enough to make any man, of common sense, blaspheme at all ideas of less than a century's standing; and pray that the world may be petrified and rendered immovable, in precisely the worst moral and physical state that it ever yet arrived at, rather than be benefitted by such schemes of such philosophers.[3]

But Hawthorne's skeptical glance at the glassy-eyed and bearded who came to the actual village of Concord to be near Emerson does not diminish the symbolic power the word "Concord" exerted on the many who never visited it. To them "Concord" meant that within America there could be a place in which man established his identity with those truths that hid behind appearance, and so worked upon his destiny rather than remaining its mute and willing victim. Emerson's modest rentier's income had been invested to give his country a native equivalent of what magnificent fortunes had supplied in other lands in such splendid institutions as court and monastery: a place where thought and imagination could be exercised in relative freedom from immediate consequence, a center of intent both culturally revolutionary and politically powerless. Once this Concord entered into the consciousnesses of young Americans in fenceless Illinois and in paved Brooklyn, it did not much matter what grotesque spectacles and fuzzy proclamations assailed the eyes and ears in the lanes of Concord, Massachusetts. Trade and politics were not the inevitable shapers of America's career; thought and imagination also existed and could be made to count.

American life had inhibited the American writer. Its lack of social density and its high geographical mobility deprived him of a sure location inside or outside the world of his fellows, and without such a growing place his art was stunted. His countrymen lacked a common history and were thus a people without a lore. Characteristic native scenes were of so recent a beginning they stood forth in jagged two-dimension. Time must pass, it seemed clear, before such raw outlines could deepen and in the mellowing lend resonating value to the house, the shop, the street. Many lives would have to be lived in these locations before the landscape had a lore. The so-called nature poets of England, who apparently turned away from the existence of historical associations, actually relied enormously upon them. Their woodland scenes were punctuated by the smoke ascending from the thatched roof of the peasant; their wildflowers grew in the clefts of ruins.

Emerson's awareness of this threadbare, native condition affected the first formulations he drew from sources such as Greek philosophy, Oriental scriptures, and post-Kantian thought, and gave them their American coherence. He felt the force of idealism because it explained to him that those phenomena that seemed America's shortcomings were, in fact, its most powerful enablers. With a natural environment that was as yet largely unhistoricized, Americans could think beyond appearance and see that the afflatus that moved in each man was identical with that which flowed in nature. The selfsame divinity thrust forth its features in both. What appeared to be an objective nature was in reality merely mediate, an assemblage of commodities and symbols for the sustenance of human life and the conveyance of human thought. Each day brought with it this perpetual revelation so that history, when set in the scale against man's diurnal opportunity to reclaim his relationship to the universe, was negligible. Those older cultures, proud in the possession of time's accumulations, were, in truth, encumbered. Within them, social tradition and artifact had been transmitted for so long so unthinkingly that they had attained the fatal status of objective realities. They were coercing men, whereas all the value they had ever possessed they had acquired from men, who had so imbued them as an expression of the divine flux within the human soul. History was the cursed arresting of such divinity in forms, and the adherence to the forms as if they were the force itself. America was blessed in its native poverty of such forms, freed from the idols that were worshipped in place of the dynamic god.

But America had at least one idol—money—and those who knew its potency, not just bankers and planters but writers and theorists also, were unmoved by the early Emerson manifesto, *Nature,* published in 1836. The actual, they felt, had its own rules of conduct and one had to attune oneself to them to succeed. On the level of petty trade, Emerson's belief that truth did not reside in appearance was wickedly parodied by everyday experience. A man who worked in a barter store near Danbury, Connecticut, for example, recalled:

> The hatters mixed their inferior furs with a little of their best, and sold us hats for "otter." We in return mixed our sugars, teas and liquors, and gave them the most valuable names. . . . Our cottons were sold for wool, our wool and cotton for silk and linen. . . . The customers cheated us in their fabrics; we cheated the customers in our goods. Each party expected to be cheated, if it was possible. Our eyes and not our ears, had to be

our masters. We must believe little that we saw, and less that we heard.[4]

Tocqueville saw beyond such crooked penny-catching to the larger matter and did not hesitate to declare that trade was the romance of the moderns and America was the modern nation of nations, so that in America heroism was to be located in trade, not in artistry or war. In their bold and zestful commercial dealings, he said, Americans were not following calculation but an impulse of their natures. This, however, was not what Emerson meant by the heroism of nature, and his idealistic message was, it seemed, apart from the realities.

Then, in 1837, the sway of the actual broke down. Its rules were exposed as blind superstitions; the reality built up from the tiny maxims of Benjamin Franklin, the confident speculations of the China merchants, the style of the great plantation owners, and the daring of the dealers in western lands was fractured, and through the cracks there opened the space through which Emerson's light could shine. The panic of 1837 silenced the shouts of national confidence and in the hush Emerson's voice was heard. In the 1840s the economy recovered and growth became the dominant feature of American life. The tonnage engaged in foreign trade soared within twenty years to the highest point reached before World War I: the 2,818 miles of railroad that existed in 1840 were so rapidly increased that by 1853 Chicago, St. Louis, and the northwest branch of the Missouri had been reached.[5] But 1837 was remembered, and ever thereafter there were listeners for Emerson's message.

Henry Varnum Poor, for example, believed that man's mind was stronger than institutions and that it could be made to control the chaos of the investment market. First as editor of the *American Railroad Journal* and then as agent for the investor, he sought to systematize the financial market through written analysis of new investment opportunities and was stirred to his undertaking by Emerson's ideas.[6]

Freeman Hunt of Quincy was formed by the panic of 1837 and the voice of Emerson, which sounded then in his native region. In 1839 he founded his *Merchant's Magazine and Commercial Review* in New York, a journal that served Karl Marx, among others, as the best source of information on the American economy, and in it printed echoes of the self-reliant doctrine he had heard:

> Sit not with folded hands, calling on Hercules. Thine own arm is the demi-god. It was given thee to help thyself. . . . There is an equality in all, and the resolute will and pure heart may ennoble either [the study, office, counting-room, workshop, or furrowed field].
>
> But no duty requires thee to shut out beauty, or to neglect the influences that may unite thee with heaven.[7]

Emerson's address, "The American Scholar," was his melodramatic entry onto the stage of American life. More than sixty years after the United States had declared its political independence, here at long last, observers felt, was the declaration of intellectual independence. That address was delivered to a highly specialized audience, the members and guests of the Phi Beta Kappa Society at Harvard. But it was delivered in August of the panic year of 1837, the worst year the United States of America had ever experienced, and the audience that heard it or read it had been opened to its meanings. Before Emerson reached the platform in August the price of cotton had fallen by almost one half; mobs had demonstrated repeatedly in the streets of New York and, in response to the inflated prices of food and fuel, had looted the city's flour warehouses; the major banks had suspended specie payments; and the sale of public lands in the West had fallen by some 82 percent. The panic not only affected the subsistence of hundreds of thousands; it broke the merger of political and economic interests that had slowly but promisingly been developed in the earlier years of the decade. Then George Bancroft, Jacksonianism's optimistic theorist, had made strong anticapital pronouncements, and craft-centered trade societies had been engaged in political action as well as the strike to gain both economic ends and such social benefits as the extension of free education. The panic pulverized cooperative enterprise as well as individuals, and Emerson spoke from amid the ruins of American morale.

He spoke, however, as founder-member of the only party that had won ground in the panic—the idealists. While both Democrat and Whig, both worker and entrepreneur, both farmer and industrialist, both southerner and northerner, had suffered a common defeat that swallowed the smaller skirmishes they had gained or lost against one another, Emerson noted with some grim satisfaction that this, in sum, meant the American commitment to the actual existence of a practical world that ruled affairs by discernible laws was now exposed for the fiction that it was. Assertions of the primacy of inborn values and affirmations of the individual's ability to control his destiny rather than submit to it could, in the breakdown of the economy, no longer be dismissed as crackpot. Emerson told his notebook in May 1837: "Prudence itself is at her wit's end. Pride and Thrift & Expediency, who jeered and chirped and were so well pleased with themselves and made merry with the dream as they termed it of philosophy & love: Behold they are all flat and here is the Soul erect and unconquered still."[8]

An audience was now prepared to listen to such declarations as "Let there be worse cotton and better men,"[9] because the seemingly inescapable laws that compelled better cotton and worse men had proved to be mere superstitions that had destroyed both cotton and men. With his Harvard address in the offing, Emerson told himself: "Let me begin anew. Let me teach the finite to know its Master. Let me ascend above my fate and work down upon my world."[10] The party of the idealist was now possible, a party that must always be the party of one, because by definition it had to be the emergence of one plus one plus one rather than of a group responding to external circumstances or submitting to a collective will. The head was not made to serve the feet.

Emerson began his address with the old fable of the beginning, in which the gods divided man into men so that he might be more helpful to himself, "just as the hand was divided into fingers, the better to answer its end."[11] That, he asserted, should serve as a reminder that there is "One Man," not doctors, professors, farmers, and shopkeepers, but one man. Each is an original unit, "a fountain of power." Unfortunately, American society in its geographical, social, and economic divisions has amputated man from his trunk, severed him from his instincts, and in the streets one sees walking monsters, "a good finger, a neck, a stomach, an elbow, but never a man."

He set out to teach original man how to reclaim himself. First, he must learn from nature, so abundant around him that at times its very plenitude hid what it was: "the opposite of his soul, answering to it part for part. One is seal and one is print. Its beauty is the beauty of his own mind." Therefore, the maxim "Know thyself" and the maxim "Study nature" are one and the same.

Next the American must gain a right sense of the influence of the past. Emerson praised noble books, the past's chief means of access to the American present, but praised them for their capacity to transmit the living voice of their authors—the manifestation of the same flux that moved through the reader—rather than for any aesthetic stasis they achieved. Books worked, when they worked, just as nature did, answering the spirit within man with the corresponding spirit within creation. When authorial stamina broke down or when the authorial pen was deflected from the line of force, books—and even the greatest were not exempt—were valueless. The sacredness of great writing stems from the act of thought kinetically present in it, not from the text itself. The poet chanting is divine, the chant is not. When men come to read the writings themselves rather than to respond to the spirit moving in them they fall into the same corruption as occurs when love of a saint's life is debased into worship of his statue.

"I had better never see a book," said Emerson, "than be warped by its attraction clean out of my orbit, and made a satellite instead of a system." He saw this to the bottom: "The discerning will read, in his Plato or Shakespeare, only that least part,—only the authentic utterances of the oracle,—all the rest he rejects, were it never so many times Plato's and Shakespeare's. Every thing that tends to insulate the individual,—to surround him with barriers of natural respect, so that each man shall feel the world is his, and man shall treat with man as sovereign state with a sovereign state,—tends to true union as well as greatness." The union of selfish interests in America had proved false; the American Union itself would be so unless men could base it on individual identities.

The past had protested, and today again we might well protest, that utterance is not separable from its manner; that its authenticity stems not from inherent content but from the realization achieved by form. Emerson was not immune to such effects. But to yield to them was for him to exchange original potency for borrowed aids. It showed a modesty that was ultimately cowardice, as respect for inherited wisdom facilely became avoidance of self-awareness. Unless a man had firmly fixed in him the prime truth that he was in his wholeness as original as any other man who is or has been—not as good or as smart or as handsome, but as integrally original—he was condemned to a reduction of the divine intent. History did not make men except insofar as men lost sight of themselves; men made themselves, and the sunrise each morning brought news to the corresponding soul that this was so.

Emerson was advocating the mythic nature of our existence, the constant possibility for man to be in touch with his creation and in living along that channel to determine his daily reality. Man is not the creature of history, and a year in which history went all wrong, 1837, served to underline the proposition that it was not history that was at fault but those who lived history rather than their own lives.

Approaching the great American brag—that the country produces men to match its geographical sublimity—Emerson put the emphases where he knew that they belonged:

> Public and private avarice make the air we breathe thick and fat. The scholar is decent, indolent, complaisant. See already the tragic consequences. The mind of this country, taught to aim at low objects, eats upon itself. There is no work for any but the decorous and complaisant. Young men of the fairest promise who began life upon our shores, inflated by the mountain winds, shined upon by all the stars of God, find the earth below not in unison with these, but are hindered from action by the disgust which the principles on which business is managed inspire, and turn drudges, or die of disgust, some of them suicides.

The remedy was clear: plant yourself on your instincts and the world will come round.

His message in "The American Scholar" was in conflict with the way in which American democracy had imagined itself, specifically opposed, it seemed, to Jacksonianism's assertion of the people against property. Emerson's sympathies were against property, but the weapon with which he opposed it was not the people; it was the person. He was thereby caught in a tangle from which he persistently sought to extricate himself without snapping the strands of truth.

On one hand, America's redemption resided in man's individual spiritual enterprise, but the most visible correlative of this was the economic enterprise of the entrepreneur. As much as he despised the belly-serving of the capitalist, Emerson could not back down from the logic that provided the enterprising money-maker as a symbol of self-realization. "The harvest," he was compelled to admit from his philosophy, "will be better preserved & go farther laid up in private bins, in each farmer's corn barn, & each woman's basket, than if it were kept in national granaries." Planting oneself on one's instincts meant individual not collective effort, as he wrote in his journal: "Take away from me the feeling that I must depend upon myself, give me the least hint that I have good friends & backers there in reserve who will gladly help me, & instantly I relax my diligence & obey the first impulse of generosity that is to cost me nothing and a certain slackness will creep over my conduct of affairs."[12]

On the other hand, the materialism of private economic enterprise was also the very reverse of the idealism that alone gave the key to life:

> The Rich & the Poor. Alas the poor are the poor of these rich . . . they also sought to be rich & their grief now is not that the rich are rich, but that themselves are not. They load these last with every name of opprobrium; they tell all their selfishness & grieve that they themselves are not able to be as selfish & worthless. The rich also are no better; they are the rich of these poor.[13]

How to break into this herding of avarice and restore the constituent particles to their true identities? Democracy as demogoguery kept them in their massed condition through appeals to interest rather than to reason. "The Best are never demoniacal or magnetic but all brutes are,"[14] he insisted. And what the politicians did was to assert unreasoning attraction on the sheer magnetic force of the mob. If he was to liberate them into the custody of their reason, he must believe that they had reason, and counter to the mode of public harangues adapted to an assumed popular ignorance, he had to proceed from the proposition that "the people know as much & reason as well as we can do."[15]

A contradictory mood told him that the mob was "the emblem of unreason; mere muscular & nervous motion, no thought, no spark of spiritual life in it."[16] But was that, after all, contradictory? The point was that there was no mob in reality, only thinking beings, and that the apparent mob was mere symbol of a falsehood fostered in malice or in ignorance by the politicians and the press.

One day in 1838 George Bancroft, seeking to impress Emerson with the power that resided in the press, talked of the *Boston Globe*. It had, Bancroft said, a circulation of 30,000, and since each copy was read by ten persons its editorial articles were read by 300,000 persons. He pronounced this awesome fact, Emerson recalled, with "deepmouthed elocution." But Emerson felt that he replied badly to Bancroft when he muttered that he wished that if they wrote for so many they could write better, and thus let the matter lapse. What he should have told Bancroft but told his notebook instead was: "What utter nonsense to name in *my* ear this *number,* as if that were anything. 3,000,000 such people as can read the Globe with interest are as yet in too crude a state of nonage to deserve any regard."[17] To deserve any regard, that is, because of their sheer number. As individuals each should be brought rapidly to outgrow his nonage.

His wrestlings with the monster, mob, the phantom of unreason conjured up from the body of reasoning Americans, arrived finally at this conclusion:

> Concert, men think, is more powerful than isolated effort & think to prove it arithmetically with slate & pencil: but concert is neither better nor worse, neither more nor less potent than individual force. . . . Let there be one man, let there be truth & virtue in one man, in two men, in ten men, then can there be concert; then is concert for the first time possible; now nothing is gained by adding zeroes, but when there is love & truth, these do naturally & necessarily cohabit, cooperate, & bless.[18]

Ten years after the great panic Emerson traveled to England to lecture at the invitation of the Mechanics' Institutes of Lancashire and Yorkshire. With the American economy now booming along, he had adjusted his timetable but not his message; he had come to see that his ideas would have to accompany and temper American life, starting independent moral revolutions within individuals rather than directly shaping the course of public life. But this, he could reflect without rationalization, was in the very nature of the doctrine. "Wherever a man comes," he had written, "there comes revolution,"[19] and he was committed to walking this path. He could, therefore, accept that such outrageous pieces of public behavior as the annexation of Texas were to be resisted because they were immoral and yet were inevitable because they proceeded from irresistible feelings. More and more he received signs that individuals—Margaret Fuller, Henry Varnum Poor, Henry David Thoreau

—were taking his message and from such, eventually, America would take its most consequential shape.

While at home Emerson was a sage committed to cutting across the national current, abroad he was an American voice. In inviting him, the Mechanics' Institutes were inviting an American who would speak to their condition from the perspective of a more liberal society in which the dignity of the worker was more sacred than in England and the opportunity for his advance far less restricted.

Americans had always been edgy about the English view of them. They responded at times with abject humiliation and at other times with defiant aggressiveness to English criticism, revealing in either response a deep prerational attachment. England still stood as parent. What had the youthful nation to show as compensation for the rich cultural inheritance it had forsaken when it cut the family ties?

Travelers came to America from France and Germany and Russia to learn what this new society could tell them about the reorganization of their societies, a reorganization they felt was inevitable; the principal question was whether America could supply the vital clues to the forces of liberalization or whether reorganization, when it came, would result in reenforced autocracies. But travelers who came from England were free of such concerns. Their identity was solid; their future was not revolutionary but would be shaped by specific reforms in keeping with the national character. Their curiosity was directed at the manners rather than the ideals of the Americans because life in Britain had taught them that ideals were vapor, while personal conduct was the essential mark of what a people is. They did not listen to what Americans claimed for themselves, but they listened to their tone and found it dreadful.

Hence the raw sensitivity of Americans to judgments offered in a British accent. Such judgments seemed to claim validation from the very tone in which they were offered, and Americans could not respond adequately because, whatever principles they proclaimed, they had no certain tone as counterweight. Emerson had felt this inequality of force when as a young man he had visited England and had returned home to the realization that the British influence there was prejudicial, and that Americans seeking their own voice had to be on guard against it. "Genius," he concluded, "is the enemy of genius."[20] During that first visit to England he had been an avowed learner, grateful for the time and courtesies extended his unknown self by such as Wordsworth and Coleridge, for all the finger-wagging admonitions about America that they also extended without solicitation. Now, in 1847, he was to learn through listening to himself whether the American had developed a characteristic voice that in itself proclaimed the existence of a significant society. He had tried to prepare for the test. Even in the flush of his first recognition in America he had seen his own potential limitations when he had looked at a young American admirer and commented, "He does not see any body who calls him to account or who in all respects overtops him & so he has contented himself with easy exertions. . . . The Americans are too easily pleased."[21]

Emerson's mature reflections on his English journey, *English Traits,* were not published until 1856, a larger lapse between occasion and reflection than was usual with him. The book's pages are dominated by images of solidity, of the concrete, immovable "thereness" of the Englishman's face and body and lands and houses and monuments, a coherent density that is so weighty it thickens customs, religious practices, and social rituals into corporeality. In a manner that must today strike us as anachronistic, he attempts in one chapter to get at the English character through a consideration of the races that contribute to it, but even here the dominating concern is that of physical manifestation. He is not so much asserting the real existence of racial traits as attempting to account for the ponderous import of the people and their culture. So sure and steady is this presence that mind must yield to tradition among the English: "They have difficulty in bringing their reason to act, and on occasions use their memory first."[22] This is said as much in respectful awe as in criticism.

What Emerson arrives at as he probes this impressive presence is the factitiousness of English life. The term today has immediate pejorative connotations, and such are not, eventually, missing from Emerson's use. But in his first reach he is attempting to convey the long and man-made history of the English, the sense in which they carved their landscape from what it at first was not, blended their primitive races into a better mix that became the Englishman, and formed their society as a conscious product of political economy. "Artificial," another pejorative word, meant "by art," and in describing the artificiality of England Emerson was not condemning so much as he was marveling at the ability of these people to have moved against nature rather than in accord with it and to have converted brute races and a dreary island climate into the center of civilization as well as the most massive political force in the modern world. The result was a great society, and the question arose as to whether American success as well must come from such a conscious human opposition to the primitive. Was political economy the necessary shaper? Was nature the stone for carving rather than the correspondent to the questing soul?

Moved by the mellow decencies of the dinner hour, by the embodiment in London of social life at its best, by the existence in Oxford of a world in which fame could be had for study, he went also to Manchester to learn the lesson that it and all the industrial towns of England had to teach. What he saw was the degeneration of men, a cruelly actual reduction of them to the fragments he had personified in his Harvard address as walking monsters—a good finger, a neck, an elbow. He saw that England had come to its wealth and culture through the degradation of its workers, and that America would also soon, if it persisted in following the same industrial path. "The robust rural Saxon degenerates in the mills to the Leicester stockinger, to the imbecile Manchester spinner,—far on the way to spiders and needles." Strength, wit, and versatility were stolen by the division of labor that put in their place "a pin-polisher, a buckle-maker." The principles of political economy dictated that whole towns would have to be sacrificed "like ant-hills, when the fashion of shoe-strings supersedes buckles, when cotton takes the place of linen, or railways of turnpikes." The free trade he had managed consistently to admire in America and in world history as the conveyor of ideas as well as commodities, the relentlessly beneficial destroyer of the walls of prejudice as well as the walls of nations, he now saw also eventuated in the deceits compelled by a competitive market in which the lowest-priced goods were the goods bought in quantity. "England is aghast at the disclosure of her fraud in the adulteration of food, of drugs, and of almost every fabric in her mills and shops," he wrote, "finding that milk will not nourish, nor pepper bite the tongue, nor glue stick."

With this perception of the base of the splendid English edifice, Emerson's admiration of the factitiousness of the world's greatest culture, its magnificent, deliberate assertion in the face of and counter to nature, now took on a pejorative tone. "In true England," he concluded, "all is false and forged." The last word resounds its double meaning: forged because struck off from resisting materials and forged because fake.

Emerson looked at essentially the same conditions as Marx and Engels were observing in essentially the same regions, and his analysis is not innocent of their sharp sense of economic cause. And yet the counter he offers to such conditions is in value curiously detached from the observations that formed its occasion. "Society," he says, "is admonished of the mischief of the division of labor, and that the best political economy is care and culture of men."[23] Critic that he was of the ravages let loose in America as well as England by the doctrines of unrestricted capitalistic enterprise, he was, nevertheless, totally distrustful of collective action as the remedy. On the basis of his American experience, collective or class consciousness meant mob consciousness, and he could not but conceive of that as a meretricious extension of the manipulation of the American politicians and journalists who had created from men the fiction of a mob in order to gain power. His mind adhered to the necessity of remedying economic exploitation by confirming the laborer in his individuality rather than entrenching him more deeply in his nonentity through subjugating him to a collective will. History, he insists as he looks at history's greatest modern monument, England, must not be yielded to as real, or all is lost. Ideals may not, as actualities must, yield tone, yet ideals are the reality.

One afternoon in England, Emerson and his British friends, Carlyle among them, found themselves trapped indoors by rain. They had planned a continuation of their tour and in their frustration, conversation moved heavily, perhaps even a bit irritably. His friends began teasing Emerson, asking him "whether there were any Americans?—any with an American idea?" He recognized the question for the blunt but accurate challenge that it was. He could not respond by telling them of the theory of democracy, for, indeed, had that not come in good part from English thinkers? Nor of the Puritan notion of the sanctity of the soul and its unimpeded access to the divinity, for had that not also migrated to America from England? He could not cite American institutions—certainly there was an American practice but these men were teasing him to produce an American idea. Had there ever been, was there one?

"Thus challenged," Emerson recalled, "I bethought myself neither of caucuses nor congress, neither of presidents nor cabinet-ministers, nor of such as would make of America another Europe. I thought only of the simplest and purest minds; I said, 'Certainly yes;—but those who hold it are fanatics of a dream which I could hardly care to relate to your English ears, to which it might be ridiculous—and yet it is the only true.'"[24] Then, taking the plunge and, as it turned out, gaining little understanding, he attempted to explain it. In 1848, that year of failed revolutions, America's leading thinker, compelled to produce an original American idea, talked not of religious freedom, universal suffrage, or common literacy. He mentioned, rather, what he called the "dogma of no-government and non resistance."

This dogma is, centrally, that of the Garrisonian abolitionists. Derived by them from Christ's injunction to individuals not to resist evil, it was transformed by those who in Emerson's America were called nonresistants into an opposition to any pretension on the part of man to regulate his fellow man through legal coercion. Slavery, although the most flagrant, was not the only example of a widespread, blasphemous usurpation of the governing power that is God's alone. In one sense of the word these people were anarchists, although in their application of the term they were sincerely antianarchist, because the rule of Christ was for them the rule of order while that of human government was the rule of disorder.[25] In citing them Emerson was announcing that the original American idea is that it is the right, indeed the duty, of each person to resist any human authority—parent, institutionalized church, state, public opinion—that goes counter to his conscience. The only true majority, even in a democracy, is the majority of one man's sense of right.

In the year before Emerson left for England, his friend Thoreau, in whose care he was to leave his home, refused to pay his poll tax to Massachusetts, since the state, he felt, condoned slavery by remaining in union with slaveholding states and cooperating in the unjust Mexican War. When, as a result, he was imprisoned for a night, he shrugged the matter off with the comment that under a government that imprisons men unjustly, the only place for a just man is prison. He likened the state to a timid old woman in fear of losing her spoons.

Emerson agreed with Thoreau's principles, but he disagreed with the particular gesture of nonpayment of taxes. He was thus compelled to an explanation of why he would go on paying them:

> The State is a poor good beast, who means the best: it means friendly. A poor cow who does well by you,—do not grudge it its hay. It cannot eat bread as you can, let it have without grudge a little grass for its four stomachs. It will not stint to yield you milk from its teat. You who are a man walking cleanly on two feet will not pick a quarrel with a poor cow. Take this handful of clover & welcome. But if you go to hook me when I walk in the fields, then poor cow, I will cut your throat.[26]

The state figured in the European imagination as a leviathan, a labyrinth, a devouring machine, an impregnable fortress. These Americans saw it in images of a fearful old woman, a poor cow. Where puny man is contrasted with the might of authority in other cultures, Emerson's contrast is between an upright, cleanly creature and a dependent, lowing beast who should repay kindness but who, if she does not, can easily be dispatched. Nothing he imagined about America could exceed in stature and in power the simple, separate person. In European political philosophy individualism was synonymous with selfishness, social anarchy, and divisive, egocentric assertion. Its function at best was one of generating a transition to a higher level of social harmony than the level of class exploitation. So Giuseppe Mazzini, exiled in England, who went to hear Emerson lecture there because he knew him to be the friend of his own dear friend, Margaret Fuller, could only report to her, "His work, I think, is greatly needed in America, but in our own world we stand in need of one who will . . . appeal to collective influences and inspiring sources, more than to individual improvement."[27]

In America, however, individualism was the goal itself, Emerson felt, because the freedom for which America stood, the new chance offered by that continent, was freedom from the fiction of the herd, the chance again to attune one's instincts to what nature echoed.

The rain finally abated and Emerson and his friends went on their way to Winchester. The conversation became more sprightly, and passing through the gentle, molded English countryside, the companions began to talk about American landscape, forest, houses. Emerson was asked questions about them he did not find it easy to answer. He says, "There, I thought, in America, lies nature sleeping, overgrowing, almost conscious, too much by half for man in the picture, and so giving a certain *tristesse,* like the rank vegetation of swamps and forests seen at night, steeped in dews and rains, which it loves; and on it man seems not able to make much impression." This rankness, this resistance to man, was, in the bone, the source of the doctrine of nonresistance that he had elaborated as the American idea, and now, in the sunshine following rain, the cultivated beauty that was England and of which he felt himself quite too sensible— "Every one is on his good behavior and must be dressed for dinner at six"—overwhelmed him and he could not adequately explain the details of the rough, unfinished landscape whence he came nor why he loved it.

He thought of his homeland, "that great sloven continent," with yearning and yet with a deep inability to express to his dear friends why this should be, why his heart went out to the slovenliness, not in pity, as he contrasted it with the finished beauties through which they were passing, but in hope that it would never lose its unfactitiousness, would harbor it and visit its meaning on its native sons. "In high Alleghany pastures, in the sea-wide sky-skirted prairie, still sleeps and murmurs and hides the great mother, long since driven away from the trim hedge-rows and over-cultivated garden of England,"[28] he thought.

He thought; but he could not speak it to his friends. The common language no longer grew from common things.

Chapter Three

Right Naming: Emerson, Language, and Literature

In his earliest full pronouncement of his idealistic philosophy, *Nature* (1836), Emerson talked theoretically about the source of language. "Words," he said, "are signs of natural facts,"[1] and even terms that express intellectual or moral facts can be traced to some material appearance, so that, for instance, right comes from straight and wrong from twisted.

But, he continued, "It is not only words that are emblematic; it is things which are emblematic. Every natural fact is a symbol of some spiritual fact." A river reminds us of the flux of all things and the firmament suggests values such as justice, truth, and love. Because of the radical correspondence between visible things and human thoughts, he says, primitive people speak in figures, and he claims we notice that the "same symbols are found to make the original elements of all languages." That is why passages of the greatest eloquence, although in different languages, approach one another in power.

Still, we cannot rest here; the plenitude of nature is too great to be regarded as mere dictionary: "Whilst we use this grand cipher to expedite the affairs of our pot and kettle, we feel that we have not yet put it to its use." What we must finally perceive is that "the whole of nature is a metaphor of the human mind." Spirit manifests itself in material forms and the mind in touch with itself manifests the selfsame spirit, so that mind confronting nature is spirit confronting the terminus of the invisible world and reading in it the common idea in the mind of God.

Although it is difficult to ascertain Emerson's degree of awareness of the fact, there moves powerfully through his theory of language the magic of the Book of Genesis: "And out of the ground the LORD God formed every beast of the field, and every fowl of the air, and brought *them* unto Adam to see what he would call them: and whatsoever Adam called every living creature, that *was* the name thereof." Here a potent if ambiguous relationship is established between language and fact. On one hand, the ancient world asserts the power of a name because Adam in the act of naming the creatures summoned them into the field of thought and gave them the completeness they previously lacked. In order to exist fully they are dependent on man's language. For the ancients, he who knew the right name determined in the very naming what the named would be like, how it would have to behave. Guess my real name and you control me, says Rumpelstiltskin, and among many a primitive society the true name of a person is not widely known but is reserved for his intimates because of the loss of control he will suffer should his name fall into the wrong hands. Some vestige of this aboriginal belief surely stirs in modern society when names are withheld from those with whom we strike up casual conversations in public places, or when first-naming is regarded as a violation of personality unless expressly invited.

On the other hand, the very fact of primitive control asserted in naming argues that the name first given—the true name—is not fortuitous, that there is such a thing as the one right name, because the right name is what the named *is,* whereas a merely discretionary name serves only to signify a fact that may be mentioned but in the mentioning is not controlled. Adam could not have had dominion over the beasts if in looking at the leopard he had given the name "ant." The leopardness of the leopard dictated his right naming. Our present linguistic knowledge that assures us of the arbitrary nature of names is scientific information that runs counter to deep, irrational beliefs that motivated ancient man and still smolder in us. Emerson in his theoretical statement chose to reassert primitive correspondence because the new man on the American continent, if he was to realize his potential, had to arrive at this control of his environment through permitting it to exist in him as the vehicle of his thought.

When he was a young man studying for the ministry, Emerson noted, "The community of language with England, has doubtless deprived us of that original characteristic literary growth that has ever accompanied, I apprehend, the first bursting of a nation from the bud."[2] Then he was specifically concerned with the problem of why the pulpit language of his day, descended from that of the Puritans, no longer had vigor. But as he moved to wider concerns in his career, this inert observation stirred once more to life. The American language would always be English, yet it must be a different kind of English because freedom from political dependence could not by itself lead to cultural integrity. The great works of English literature, he feared, would continue to serve as models for the American writer despite their growth from different historical circumstances. As a result, the American's imitation would fall sterile from his pen. Americans must be made to perceive that within the common language they had to reclaim a different language, one that reflected their unparalleled exposure to the mighty mother, nature. He told his audiences, "I think we must regard the *land* as a commanding and increasing power . . . the sanative and Americanizing influence."[3] He saw the continental expansionism, which on political and moral grounds he had frequent occasion to deplore, as a necessary cultural counterforce to the applications of steam power, which were threatening to narrow the Atlantic to the size of a strait and thus deliver America once again into the bondage of the language as historically used. Thanks to the "nervous, rocky West," he felt, "we shall yet have an American genius."[4] Not necessarily a man from the West, but a man whose literary powers stemmed from the language that the wildness of the West made available.

The American language and aboriginal force had to draw close. Look about you in a stable or a menagerie. Perhaps you are no longer called upon to name these beasts; the names they possess may serve. But do you not suffer fellow feeling when you catch the moist and wandering gaze of a beast? "What! somewhat of me down there? Does he know it? Can he too, as I, go out of himself, see himself, perceive relations? We fear lest the poor brute should gain one dreadful glimpse of his condition, should learn in some moment the tough limitation of this fettering organization."[5] We fear for the brute because his nature binds him inescapably and it is therefore best that he not know it. But we would have to fear also for ourselves, that we are fallen from nature as the beast is not, did we not possess language. This product of our fall from nature is also the means whereby we can establish a higher relation to it.

If we cannot so use our language, then "Nature is the tyrannous circumstance, the thick skull, the sheathed snake, the ponderous rock-like jaw; necessitated activity; violent direction."[6] The escape from tyranny is by way of language, through relation and connection to right naming. We must face it, Emerson insists: Providence is wild and rough and so we have to exert a corresponding energy, rather than approach it with a debased vocabulary that dresses up the muscular actuality "in a clean shirt and white neckcloth of a student of divinity."[7]

The turn to an American language so conceived was the ultimate and crucial turn away from history. Nuance, subtlety, tension, richness, display, were features of the English language that had been acquired over centuries of social advance from the primitive and had been consolidated in the literary monuments that marked the advancement. What Emerson was proposing to burn as stubble was collective human experience, and the charred field could be expected to yield only the gauntest crops. Too frequently accused of inconsistency, was he not here being far too ruthlessly logical in his insistence that, since America was free from the determinations of European history, or, what was the same, could magnificently free itself by an act of perception, then America had no need of the artifices of historical language? He insisted that history could not be cited in contradiction of his stance:

> Our faith comes in moments; our vice is habitual. Yet there is depth in those brief moments which constrains us to ascribe more reality to them than to all other experiences. For this reason the argument which is always forthcoming to silence those who conceive extraordinary hopes of man, namely the appeal to experience, is for ever invalid and vain.[8]

And in his notebooks, where he brought the events of the day into balance with his thoughts, he constantly administered to himself such reminders as "We must never reason from history, but plant ourselves on the ideal."[9]

The literature that would come from such a view of the language of life was one that would overleap the middle distance of community. Since experience is in so subordinate a position to the facts of nature and their responding depths in man, the American writer, in Emerson's scheme, is not concerned with social man—his membership in institutions, his feeling for the past, his adoption of a code of manners. A traditional portrait shows the central figure, saint or merchant or prince, in a full costume that bespeaks the figure's ties to the society about him and the society that views him: robes, staff, or money-scales linking the figure with the ways of men even as his features individuate him. Then the eye travels from the figure, out the window or along a path, and before it reaches the sun, the peak, or the hovering cherub, it traverses a middle distance in which tiny men are plowing minute furrows, wee fishing boats cast slender nets, diminutive drovers guide miniature oxen. The middle distance binds the sizable figure before our eyes to the ultimate reality of star, pinnacle, or angel, and that middle distance is community, the ways of men, over which ultimate truth presides just as it presides over this one man or woman.

But Emerson has no such middle distance in view when he contemplates the possibility of a literature in America. Rather, there is the foreground of the human figure and the background of uncultivated nature, intended to harmonize and yet, because of the lack of mediating images binding one to the other, set also in stark opposition. For all his disagreements with the church, the liberal Emerson resounds a Puritanic theme: man is placed in the frame together only with his god, there to achieve balance or there to picture forth an awesome isolation. Foreground strong and background strong; no middle distance.

Although Emerson's conception of the literature that would befit his country was, in his mind, the application of the only true ideal philosophy to his nation, a working-down on actual conditions from above, it was, of course, at least equally the result of those conditions working upward on him. Historical shallows affected his dismissal of history; the powerful social content of English literature affected his dismissal of traditional language. At the time when Emerson was calling for a literature based on his perception of America's unique access to the uncultivated, a young American who wished to be a painter left for Europe. He explained that he went not just for training but for subjects:

> In American landscape the element of the picturesque is a serious deficiency. What is old is the wild and savage, the backwoods and the wild mountain, with no trace of human presence or association to give it sentiment; what is new is still in the crude and angular state in which the utilities are served, and the comfort of the man and his belongings most considered. Nothing is less paintable than a New England village; nothing is more monotonous than the woodland mountains of any of the ranges of eastern North America.[10]

But for Emerson the picturesque was to be feared as an element that would reduce the human accessibility to the divine by contenting the imagination with little things.

He recognized that a seeming bleakness might be the result. "We fancy that men are individuals," he told himself, "but every pumpkin in the field goes through every point of pumpkin history."[11] If he was to dismiss the middle distance, he realized, then rather than having a distinct individual in the foreground he might, instead, be left with each man as the type of all men, no more different from his fellows than one pumpkin is from other pumpkins. Viewed as he chose to view him, as an object of natural rather than social history, man threatened to be mere monotonous outline. What counter to such bleakness? In the writer's eyes, he said, "man is the faculty of reporting, & the universe is the possibility of being reported,"[12] but the very words in which the perception is phrased lift it to a chilling abstraction and promise, insofar as promise here exists, a literature of generalized, orphic remoteness.

And such, to be sure, emerged from Bronson Alcott, Ellery Channing, and many another haunter of the Concord lanes. Cold, detached, crusted utterances hailed down from a stratosphere thinned of any air that man could breathe. Hawthorne was right. The place was full of bores. And the bores were bored by Hawthorne. Ellery Channing, consumed with the need to capture sublimity in his poems, thought "he is the lucky man who can write in bulk, forty pages on a hiccough, ten pages on a man's sitting down in a chair; like Hawthorne."[13] So much for neighbor Hawthorne, so much for the novel, so much for the location of meaning in the corporeal lives that accompanied the spiritual lives that men led. Emerson liked Hawthorne and recognized his great gifts, seeing far more merit than did Channing. But he could not comprehend why Hawthorne was so concerned with technique: "Hawthorne invites his readers too much into his study, opens the process before them. As if the confectioner should say to his customers, Now let us make the cake."[14]

Since faith, for Emerson, came only in moments, both the act of literary creation and its product were dependent upon inspiration in its narrowest, most fleeting sense. One composed from the frenzy rather than from one's life, and even in the poem itself the moment of inspiration was distinguishable from flatter moments. His poems and essays are remarkable for the dynamic lines that leap forth, attaining a penetration far beyond that of their context. As a consequence, such lines, while they thrill, also diminish if not betray other lines. The drive seems always to be toward some pithy figure, some cryptic metaphor, some chanted phrase that will contain everything—a drive to utter all in the smallest, related, ultimately, to a hurtling toward silence.

The homologous relationship of man and nature was an idea; it was only rarely realized as an experience by Emerson. In going to Walden Pond Thoreau sought to avoid such a division and to convert idea into continuous experience. But Emerson did not write from such an immersion in experience; he offered ideas, flecked, when the inspiration came, with a felt experience.

The ideal power to which Emerson attached himself and to which he desired to attach his countrymen was one that he habitually imagined as a flux or an afflatus. There is little sense in him of a still point beyond this flow; to him, nature is a generalized locale rather than a specific sacred place. It is relatable to man at every point, but there is no sure umbilical to the gods that is imagined as anchored to a special place on earth. Just as he asserted that every moment was the potential moment of renewal and so was attracted to a variety of creation myths but did not reenact any given myth, so for him all of nature was charged with the divinity but no one piece of it was the birthplace, the seat of the temple, or the site for the erection of the city of heaven. For all his belief in the idea of God, Emerson's world is markedly drained of sacredness. America was a promised land only in that it had not been ravaged by history. It did not at any point send upward the shaft or erect the sacred pole that marked the human point of connection with the divine intent. Although Americans thought of "our world" as a potent cosmos and the world outside it, especially along the western frontier, as a chaos, the advance upon chaos was not an extension of the sacred cosmos but rather a reassertment of man upon the unspoiled in a series of restartings. Emerson's mythic imagination was, finally, profane: while it sought to check a commitment to the mere actualities of history and to control life through an assertion of the higher character available to man, it did not counter history with the inescapable substance of myth—an account of *the* beginning and a sacralization of *the* place.[15]

As a consequence, for Emerson the American artist preeminently had to yield to unsocialized feeling:

> Nothing great was ever achieved without enthusiasm. . . . Dreams and drunkenness, the use of opium and alcohol are the semblance and counterfeit of this oracular genius, and hence their dangerous attraction for men. For the like reason they ask the aid of wild passions, as in gaming and war, to ape in some manner these flames and generosities of the heart.[16]

The artist expresses aboriginal power and seeks the aboriginal in his audience. Burrowing beneath the superstructure of historically induced ideas and prejudices to the bedrock of our primitive organization, literature restores us to the simplest state of mind. But science and letters in the United States as yet only contribute to the "old chronology of selfishness and pride." They do not show the way into nature: "The idiot, the Indian, the child and unschooled farmer's boy stand nearer to the light by which nature is to be read, than the director or the antiquary."[17]

Democratic literature should be for all the people, for them as aborigines who derive their value from a common source rather than for them as a political mass. What succor does the study of the history of Rome or Paris or Constantinople have "for the Esquimaux seal-hunter, for the Kanaka in his canoe, the fisherman, the stevedore, the porter?"[18] The sources of a writer's inspiration must be the same as those that give law to the existence of such men. The writer in his naming is the lawgiver. That power is his only, and that is his commanding ground.

Such ideas were delivered by Emerson from the platforms of village halls. But they were not unaffected by the eyes that stared back at him—or winked closed. "Our American lives are somewhat poor & pallid . . . no fiery grain,"[19] he thinks after one series of audiences. That is a comment upon himself far more than upon them, and so, "Best swallow this pill of America which Fate brings you & sing a land unsung. Here stars, here birds, here trees." Shivering in a Wisconsin winter, he recognizes that the people as well as the climate present him with a new test, and when "the stout Illinoian, after a short trial, walks out of the hall," then "these are the new conditions to which I must conform." The lawgiver must meet the conditions that govern the lives of those to whom he would give law; "he is no master who cannot vary his forms and carry his own end triumphantly through the most difficult."[20]

Finally launched on the Mississippi in 1853, Emerson looks out for that "rocky, nervous West" of power and finds "dog-men, that have not shed their canine teeth." The huge mud trough of a river warps the men who must obey it, "chop down its woods, kill the alligator, eat the deer, shoot the wolf," so that every one has "mud up to his knees" and dinge on his shirt collar. But, he asks himself, what did he expect? "The people are all kings," he is happy to affirm, "and I notice an extraordinary firmness in the face of many a drover, an air of independence. . . ."[21] It is that independence he must meet and confirm in the sources of its power before the truckling and adulatory politicians and poetasters corrupt it. For all the miles between the Mississippi levee and the Massachusetts snowbank, between the ungrammatical drover and the literary lecturer, between torchlight carousing and lamplit conversation, he is empowered to cross them and to speak to the independent individual because he too is independent and understands the common identity. Harriet Martineau, as early as 1838, had told her countrymen in England that if one did not know Emerson one did not know the United States, because in him

> one leading quality is to be distinguished . . . modest independence. A more entire and modest independence I am not aware

> of ever having witnessed; though in America I saw two or three approaches to it. It is an independence equally of thought, of speech, of demeanour, of occupation, and of objects in life: yet without a trace of contempt in its temper, or of encroachment in its action.[22]

Although he did not regard himself as a great man, Emerson recognized the gap between his stature and the stature of the average man whom he addressed in lecture and in essay. In *Representative Men* (1850), he explained why great men—his illustrations were Plato, Swedenborg, Montaigne, Shakespeare, Napoleon, and Goethe—were great as representative of, rather than superior to, the common man. "We have never come at the truth and best benefit of any genius so long as we believe him an original force,"[23] he said. Rather, the originality resided in the vaster mind, shared also by the common man; the great man shows to the common man a greatness that can be his because it is an effect of the same cause operating in all men. Standing before his audiences, Emerson finally attempted to cross over to them through the implicit connection he and they shared with the vaster mind. And here again he was denying history in favor of the shaping power of the soul. If great men were regarded as causes, then society awaited them to take a further step. But if they were effects, as he affirmed, then they represented only what any man could do to control his life. Even Shakespeare was seen by Emerson more as penman than as original genius. He wrote the poems of our common lore.

In America, a new lore, attached more closely to nature, was in evidence, and so America was awaiting its poet, "for the experience of each new age requires a new confession." The thought is prior to the form, and the new thought in his age, Emerson insisted in a statement that is rightly seen as predictive of Walt Whitman's work, would yield a new form: "For it is not metres, but a metre-making argument that makes a poem,—a thought so passionate and alive that like the spirit of a plant or an animal it has an architecture of its own, and adorns nature with a new thing."[24]

Emerson's contemporary and acquaintance, Horatio Greenough, a sculptor who lived in Italy of professional necessity yet insisted he was but a "Yankee stonecutter," thought of the future of the spatial arts in America along lines that paralleled those of Emerson on literature. He deplored the classical facades behind which American institutions worked their modern ways, and insisted, "I contend for Greek principle, not Greek things."[25] The American energy was a tinkering energy, as a French visitor noted when he said that "there is not a schoolboy who has not composed a ballad, written a novel, or drawn up a republican or monarchical constitution . . . there is not a laborer who has not invented a machine or tool."[26] This same phenomenon Greenough saw as a surfacing of the American principle that should determine American art: "The men who have reduced locomotion to its simplest elements in the trotting wagon and the yacht America, are nearer to Athens at this moment than they who would bend the Greek temple to every use."[27] In contrasting American efficiency, commonly regarded as colorless, with Old World inefficiency, commonly regarded as picturesque, Greenough, like Emerson, was revealing what he believed should be the American artistic confession:

> If a flat sail goes nearer the wind, a bellying sail, though picturesque, must be given up. The slender harness, and tall gaunt wheels, are not only effective, they are beautiful for they respect the beauty of a horse, and do not uselessly task him. The English span is a good one, but they lug along more pretension than beauty; they are stopped in their way to claim respect for wealth and station; they are stopped for this, and, therefore, easily passed by those who care not to seem, but are.[28]

American experience was developing an American art, but American observers, shaped by the aesthetic theories of the past, were blind to these manifestations. In a striking metaphor of the priority of practice to theory in the arts, Greenough declared, "The nightshade 'never told her love' to the eye, 'twas in the writhing stomach of experiment that she talked the true, Catholic tongue, English to Englishmen, French to Frenchmen, and they who saw believed."[29]

It was in 1842 that Emerson announced that not meters but the meter-making argument made the poem and insisted that such meter-making would have an architecture of its own. It was in 1852 that Greenough published his manifesto:

> By beauty I mean the promise of function.
> By action I mean the presence of function.
> By character I mean the record of function.[30]

This, curiously, echoed the very principles that had given rise to Emerson's criticism of Greenough's heroic statuary many years before. Greenough could not have been aware of the criticism, confined as it was to Emerson's notebook, but he had come to share it in principle if not in specific application to himself. Greenough's heroic figures, together with such literary exercises as Byron's *Sardanapalus,* wrote Emerson, "are futile endeavors to revive a dead form & cannot succeed." When he looked about him for the signs of living form, Emerson, like Greenough, could not locate them as yet in what was conventionally regarded as art, but he saw their tentative manifestations. His equivalent of Greenough's yacht and sulky were "a speech in Congress, Channing's Work on Slavery, & the Volume of Revised Statutes."[31] There resided the vital function, awaiting its release into beautiful forms.

But it was waiting. "The Americans appear to me to be an eminently imaginative people," Harriet Martineau reported. Still,

> they do not put their imaginative power to use in literature and arts; and it does certainly appear perverse enough to observers from the Old World that they should be imitative in fictions (whether of the pen, pencil, stone, or marble), and imaginative in their science and philosophy, applying their good sense to details but being sparing of it in regard to principles.[32]

Emerson attributed this to the rapid wealth available in the recovery from the panic, which promoted an incessant expansion of population and mechanical arts, making America "the country of small adventures, of short plans, of daring risks" rather than of patience and great schemes. "Our books are tents not pyramids,"[33] he said. The same image occurred to James Russell Lowell: "We are a great bivouac as yet . . . and pitch tents instead of building houses."[34]

This did not, however, absolve Emerson from the feeling that he himself had failed somehow to render, rather than to talk about, the superiority of the common man. Had he not, after all, for whatever claims he wished to make on the simple individual's behalf, produced Napoleon and Goethe as his examples? His *Representative*

Men had not been shaped from American clay, and did not that fact, despite his ideal intent, constitute another failure of the American writer to express the culture that was there? Here were his Concord neighbors, farmers such as George and Edmund, whose superiority he had felt a hundred times; "yet I continue the parrot echoes of the names of literary notabilities & mediocrities, which, bring them (if they dared) into presence of these Concord & Plymouth Norsemen, would be as uncomfortable & ridiculous as mice before cats."[35]

He felt this keenly, yet he could never overcome his conviction that the function of his writing was to provide a platform that would afford a point of purchase on American life. It had to be built outside the field on which it was meant to operate, and so, in retrospect, he saw it lacking in the common touch. He could talk to the man with mud on his feet and dinge on his collar but could not speak as he did or render him as the focus of his writings. But the power of Emerson comes in good part from his sense of what he could not do, as well as what he could, and one day, sitting at his notebook, he described the democratic hero who would have to be his alter ego, arriving to complement his work. It is a remarkable passage:

> He whose sympathy goes lowest—dread him O Kings! I say to you, dread him. See you a man who can find pleasures everywhere, in a camp, in a barn, in a schoolhouse, in a stage coach, in a bar-room so that he needs no philosophy; but drops into heaven wherever he goes, because of the great range of his affinities . . . who is so alive to every presence that the approbation of no porter, groom, or child is quite indifferent to him and a man of merit is an object of so much love as to be a *fear* to him—see you such a man . . . then mark him well for the whole world converts itself into that man & through him as through a lens, the rays of the Universe shall converge, whithersoever he turns, on a point.[36]

The rhetoric of the passage is prophetic chant, Emerson warning the Old World to prepare a way for the man who will express the New World. It glimpses Thoreau tramping through the Maine woods, Ishmael undergoing rather than doing, yet doing all in that he is the sole teller of the tale, and Walt afoot with his vision.

But Emerson the poet was like Emerson the essayist, the occupier of a platform built above the world. He attempted to write from the rhapsodic moment only, at the point when he had been surprised out of propriety, and a remarkable portion of his verse is devoted to such symbols of passionate frenzy as Bacchus. It is a little sad to view the learned Yankee who encouraged separation and insulation communicating across that barrier in terms of what he considered to be shared instincts rather than in terms of human gestures and small kindnesses. "Give all to love," begins one poem. "Obey thy heart." And he goes on to counsel no refusal to that "brave master" love. Yet what he must extract from this necessity is the higher necessity within love of keeping free, because to bury identity in the new twoness that may seem to emerge from the separate onenesses of the lovers is to lose the very source of love itself, one's instincts and their attachment to the divine source. A total surrender to the loved one is finally a descent from self into nonentity. That lover best loves who can admit to the loved one that there is "a joy apart from thee," and who is able to relinquish the loved one when she, too, arrives at the perception. The modified love is not a failure but a higher stage:

> Heartily know,
> When half-gods go,
> The gods arrive.[37]

The poem's relinquishment is moving because of its passionate rendering of the value of what is relinquished. It is, however, a curious poem because the passion which is its motive is converted into thought; the volcano is capped by the peak of snow. And this is characteristic of Emerson and his sincerely rendered passion. It rounds upon itself into thought, as he well knew:

> Line in nature is not found;
> Unit and universe are round;
> In vain produced, all rays return;
> Evil will bless, and ice will burn.[38]

Such rounding left the individual, as poet or as subject, starkly alone with himself, hot words instantly turning to snowflakes as they left the mouth.

Deep down Emerson's theory of language is at work, and what that theory does is deprive the utterance of lyric capability. Rather, right naming is a solo chant, a putting things in their place beyond any auditor's ability to respond emotionally. In the poem that in tone and structure is least like his characteristic verses, Emerson celebrates the snowstorm, which works like a master artist, hanging wreaths on coop or kennel, investing the thornbush with a swanlike form, and building a tapering turret for the gate. This storm artist cares nothing for number and proportion, and in the sunlit morning following its efforts human art is left

> To mimic in slow structures, stone by stone,
> Built in an age, the mad wind's night-work,
> The frolic architecture of the snow.[39]

In the face of this, art itself becomes suspect when compared with the things of nature; the words will never achieve the perfection of the thing. Although he praised metaphor as that which would join man once again to the mother from whom he had been too long alienated, Emerson knew also that the power of the ancient world that existed uncorrupted, free of history, was a power beneath words, one that was perfect in its silence. The old men, he wrote in a poem, studied magic in the flowers:

> Preferring things to names, for these were men,
> Were unitarians of the united world,
> And, wheresoever their clear eye-beams fell,
> They caught the footsteps of the SAME. Our eyes
> Are armed, but we are strangers to the stars,
> And strangers to the mystic beast and bird,
> And strangers to the plant and to the mine.[40]

He was here attacking modern exploitative technology that regarded nature as mere unresisting economic opportunity. In destroying nature it was destroying humanity. Industrial men were "thieves and pirates of the universe," and the result of their piracy would be not a fattening on the plunder but so great an estrangement from the universe that mankind would "turn pale and starve." But the terms of his attack asserted the superiority of the thing to the name and suggested that the naming of the writer was also exploitative of nature and thus a parallel to the mining of the industrialist. In a perfect reattachment to the natural world, words would no longer be used.

Of course, America could not arrive at perfection, and Emerson well saw the consequent importance of an American language that would more properly express the saving relationship between the American and his environment than did the historical usages he had inherited from Europe. But Emerson's turn away from history and his constant assertion of the creative potential of each man each day was an attempt to offer myth as the true American reality—a New World, indeed, not because it was younger than the Old World but because it had jettisoned history and could constantly make itself anew; in that way it united with the oldest world of all. American posthistorical ahistoricity could approximate ancient prehistory.

Prehistory, however, was sacred and compelled its inhabitants to a ritual reenactment of the original moment. Emerson's posthistory was profane and suggested a perpetual restarting. In informing American restlessness he was, finally, yielding to it rather than stabilizing it.

In April 1853, Emerson wrote to Carlyle, telling him "America is incomplete." It has not stopped its restless movement and thus shows no sign of terminating in a hero or a bard. For America to have such great men, its society, like those of Europe, would have to sublimate itself into a genius. In England the writer was supported by a population of drudges whose acceptance of their debased condition fed his "porcelain veins" from their "brick arteries." But in America, clearly, he of porcelain veins would starve before his countrymen fed him. The democratic Americans leveled themselves up and in so doing leveled genius down in the national "riot of mediocrities."[41]

How, then, was a democracy to have its artists? The question was important but, as Emerson himself was demonstrating, the same culture that impeded the appearance of the artist was compelling works of art.

Chapter Four

Contributions and Offspring: Society, Politics, and the Identification of an American Literature

The first number of ***Putnam's Monthly Magazine*** appeared in January 1853. Unlike its closest rival, ***Harper's,*** it did not clip English journals (unprotected by copyright in America) for any portion of its content. "***Harper's Magazine,***" Henry James, Sr., said, "is a mere stale and dishonest hash, when it is not a stupid vehicle of Methodism."[1] ***Putnam's*** widely solicited work from American authors, normally paid them at the rate of three dollars a page (more for "important" writers), and gave poets from ten to twenty-five dollars a poem. In its first four years it attained a circulation of from twelve to twenty thousand copies per number, and it published work by Cooper, Longfellow, Lowell, Thoreau, and Melville. The collapse of the western bond market in 1857 and the subsequent financial panic marked the end of the initial run of the magazine.

Putnam's was one small index of the state of the authorial profession in America. Notably, this journal, which treated native authors more decently than had its predecessors (although it did print foreign authors and was concerned with journalistic matters well beyond belles lettres), nevertheless adhered to a policy of authorial anonymity. In part, of course, the policy helped the unknown author toward a hearing. Most of the eminent or popular contributors were recognizable by theme and style. The work of a lesser-known writer benefited from the company it kept and the general anonymity gave him the appearance at least of equal access to the audience. But the policy also revealed that the names of American authors did not in themselves exert a strong commercial appeal.

In a prospectus sent to the eminent men he hoped would contribute to his magazine, George Putnam emphasized that it was time there existed an organ of American thought. Emerson, predictably, responded with enthusiasm: "Nothing could be more agreeable to me than the establishment of an American magazine of truly elevated and independent tone, and if you shall really and perseveringly attempt that you shall be sure of my hearty co-operation and aid." Indeed, he went Putnam one better: "Perhaps my interest in such a project is even more serious than your own."[2] With his customary absorption in the idea before him, Emerson, to his credit, was able to conceive of an interest greater than that of risking capital. He had done his best for *The Dial,* the transcendental organ of the Concord bores, but he was especially exhilarated by a genuine commercial attempt to encourage the distinctively American, an attempt, moreover, that came out of New York rather than Boston and so promised to be harder-headed and more national.

A different response came from Richard Henry Dana, Jr., son of the longtime editor of America's only low-circulation and high-prestige intellectual journal, the dreary *North American Review,* author of a minor masterpiece, *Two Years Before the Mast,* scholar, lawyer, gentleman, and yet also maverick within Boston high society because of his adherence to the Free-Soil party. Well, there had always been such in Boston, most notably members of the Adams family, who were capable of allowing morality to deflect them from class loyalty.

Dana took alarm at the American note struck by Putnam and warned, "You are not going to put in a spade to help dig the ditch (which some in our city are so hard at work upon) between our literature and that of our Fatherland." The "some in our city" were the Irish immigrants with no reason to love England and the Democratic politicians who fed their resentments and in the process kept them opposed to Negro rights. Dana's advocacy of free soil was a sincere and admirable opposition to them, but he betrayed a social bias also in the image that came to his mind—ditchdiggers. He rejected any talk of a distinctively American culture because he suspected that it merely meant a vulgar exploitation of Anglophobia. The "best readers" would not stand for it, he warned Putnam, and "commonplace will beget commonplace." Be American if you will, he said, but you must also be, because literature itself is, "duly English."[3]

Although they were responding to the same prospectus, Emerson and Dana were not talking about exactly the same thing. Emerson's faith in America as separate and special was not political but philosophical. He wanted to make potential energy kinetic. But by 1852 Dana had reason to take the term "American," when used as a cultural designation, to mean anti-English—the sacrifice of civilized standards for base political advantage. He saw most of the talking-up of the literary patriots as the behavior of Yahoos flinging dung down upon their betters.

The difference, an important one, is further illustrated by the contrasting reactions of Dana and Emerson to Dickens's sharp and unexpectedly negative report on his 1841 visit to the United States, *American Notes*. America's popular press and its political demagogues seized upon the book as evidence of the continuing incurable arrogance of Great Britain and vilified Dickens. Better was expected of him. He had come to America, not as did the aristocratic traveler, with tweeds and gun-case, willing to shrug off quaint crudities in exchange for his chance to see live Indians and shoot a buffalo. He had come as America's favorite novelist, a reformer who saw the inequities in his own society and who had a specific schedule of social institutions to visit in America in order to learn about social progress. So why was he not impressed? This Englishman, of all Englishmen, it would seem, was qualified to see the virtues that lurked behind imperfect manners—besides, was he such a gentleman himself?—and to meet Americans on a common ground of concern for social justice.

The unspeakable Frances Trollope, who had published the most cutting commentary on America before Dickens, was more easily dismissed, although her remarks had rankled. The gulf she insisted upon between England and America was really only a gulf between Americans and people of her own stuffy sort:

> I have conversed in London and in Paris with foreigners of many nations, and often through the misty medium of an idiom imperfectly understood; but I remember no instance in which I found the same difficulty in conveying my statements, my impressions, and my opinions to those around me, as I did in America. . . . It is less necessary, I imagine, for the mutual understanding of persons conversing together, that the language should be the same, than that their ordinary mode of thinking, and habits of life, should, in some degree, assimilate; whereas, in point of fact, there is hardly a single point of sympathy between the Americans and us.[4]

But Dickens clearly came with more than one "point of sympathy." He had been warmly received, indeed adulated, and yet had published severe criticisms, especially on the manners of the Americans.

His strictures, however, were welcomed by those in America who believed that their culture would best realize itself only in fidelity to the English tradition in which it was rooted. Such were the Boston gentry, whose most refined gathering place was the dining table at George Ticknor's, and fresh from there Dana reported, "All think Dickens's book entertaining & clever."[5] Since Dickens's novels had reached a mass audience in America, how welcome was his reminder to the masses that they had a good way to go before their society reached an acceptable standard.

Emerson also believed that Dickens "is doubtless of much use to this country." But, he recognized, even Dickens had fallen into the common error of the British visitor, had been so affronted by bad manners that he had not penetrated to the national character. As a result, the message Americans could take from Dickens's reaction to them was not of significant intellectual or moral content, but came down to "the lesson which is pasted in the waterclosets of public houses,—*Do not spit, & please close the covers*."[6]

The Concord view was that America was an idea and American literature would have to be its expositor. To look at the life itself was to look in the wrong place. In significant respects, this preference of the abstract to the actual was a continuation into secular areas of the New England addiction to theological speculation. For more than a century of winters the Puritans and their descendants had fed on sermons and doctrinal polemics as a means of entertainment every bit as much as a spiritual necessity. The semiweekly preaching was not ritualistic—ministers who read from a prepared text, even, were disapproved—not a celebration of communal solidarity through submission to formulas that sank the personality in a larger communion with God. The altar had been replaced by the pulpit as the focus of interest, and from the pulpit flowed ideas and opinions to be wrestled with by each hearer in the days following. The process confirmed the hearer in the separateness of his soul and in the habit of honing his mother wit on pure theory.

In New England, Harriet Beecher Stowe said, devotion is doctrinal, not ritual. A young woman developing in the churches of Europe, if she had an intense religious sensibility, might receive beatific visions, might melt herself into an experience of Mary or Jesus; "but unfolding in the clear, keen, cold, New England clime, and nurtured in its abstract and positive theologies, her religious faculties took other forms."[7] She read and pondered treatises on the will and attempted to master the great thesis of Jonathan Edwards, that virtue was benevolence to being in general rather than merely behaving morally toward your friends and neighbors. The spirit that moved within such maidens, Stowe felt, was the same that made poets and artists elsewhere, "but the keen New England air crystallizes emotions into ideas."

Blaming the weather for this is not a mere fancy of Stowe's. The New England puritanic penchant for speculation had a profound symbolic relation to the climate. On a matter-of-fact level, the connection stems from the annual withdrawal of the New England farm family into the house as winter took its grip on the countryside and darkness came early. The room with the large fireplace for cooking and for warmth became the center of living, and in that room, while harnesses were mended and stockings were darned, books were read aloud, sermons were analyzed and debated, and talk on ideal as well as practical matters went forward.

When Longfellow, Lowell, Whittier, and Holmes became known, their publisher shrewdly marketed them as "fireside poets," that is, writers designed to be read in the family circle driven indoors for long, sedentary periods. But they were fireside poets in another sense also because they hymned the virtues of the hearth over those of the fields. In their verse, albeit it is sprinkled with conventional celebrations of spring and summer, one feels uneasiness with the untempered sun, the fecund fields, all things in nature that in the hot weather teemed and reproduced. The winter, which put a stop to the flaming signs of procreation, encouraged a sense of one's coming back into oneself and exerting greater self-control than was possible during the ragings of summer. Intellect regathered itself to assert its superiority to passion; ideas triumphed over experience; sexuality was bracketed as the merely natural phenomenon it was.

Whittier is typical. His greatest poem, *Snow-Bound,* is, of course, a celebration of the annual withdrawal from the passionate transient into the spiritual permanent. And elsewhere he repeatedly reveals a distrust of ravening nature. The woods give of their "sacramental mystery" not when in growth but during the "October holocaust" that destroys growth.[8] When he receives a basket of summer fruit during the cold season, the pleased poet tells the donor that the fruit must have come from a vine that Eve smuggled out of Eden so that

> the waste
> And fallen world hath yet its annual taste
> Of primal good, to prove of sin the cost
> And show by one gleaned ear the mighty harvest lost.[9]

The fruit, while welcome, is a reminder that he, New Englanders, all righteous persons, live in a fallen world. Those shameless summer days have passed, and, rightly, humanity must lead a life of winter rigors to be saved.

Taking a last walk in autumn, Whittier feels that all things in the bleak landscape are yearning, but they are not yearning toward the coming spring of bud and fruit; rather they

> Seem praying for the snows to come,
> And, for the summer blooms and greenness gone,
> With winter's sunset lights and dazzling morn atone.[10]

Excess, profligacy, passion, are the qualities that summer symbolizes, and winter, welcome winter, brings the necessary purification.

Moving powerfully beneath such an attitude, of course, is also the gathering sectional strife over slavery. The northerner is preparing himself to assert the superiority of his sparse landscape, dotted with glacial boulders and barely sustaining small farms, to the southern landscape of opulent breadth, and so to symbolize the morality of hired labor and the viciousness of slavery. But the shaping impetus is puritanic, harkening back to the days when outraged Bostonians replied to Cromwell's offer of the West Indies as a far more promising climate for them, their posterity, and their contribution to the homeland by asserting the moral rightness of the New England climate, thus forging a connection between spirit and cold as opposed to body and hot, ideal and control as opposed to actual and teeming, an attitude that marked the imaginations of their successors.

In the same decades in which the fireside poets emerged, the Connecticut painter George Durrie discovered that snow need not be dully represented by a streak of white, but that the drops as they clung to boughs and the crust as it came from the runners of sleighs had texture. The snow paintings he did and the many by those who followed him found an eager market through the agency of such firms as Currier & Ives. This spoke of deeper preferences than a love of winter, as did also the widespread interest in Arctic and Antarctic exploration, which, beginning with the Wilkes expedition of 1838, was reflected in the fiction of Cooper and of Poe and achieved its apotheosis in 1856 with the runaway success of that eminently readable book, Elisha Kent Kane's *Arctic Explorations*. American geographic curiosity was gratified enormously by accounts of icy barrens, sparsely populated wastes, frigid stretches on which moved no life but that of the perceiver. Here was an environment to match the soul's loftiest condition and to test the superiority of sheer righteousness.

The symbolic complement to winter cold was not, then, summer heat, but the fire on the hearth, the flame kept flickering by human effort rather than let loose by the uncontrollable sun. Poem after poem after poem centered on the gathering at the hearth, the smoke ascending from the chimney, the sizzle of the sap running under heat. Hearth contained the heart, which balanced the abstract meanings of the soul as embodied by the snow. As the bleak landscape argued moral superiority to imagined tropical cultures that yielded facilely to passion, so the homely objects decorating the hearth argued cultural superiority to the urban mansion with its objets d'art sprinkled throughout in detachment from a justifying connection with the human heart. Longfellow wrote:

> Each man's chimney is his Golden Mile-Stone;
> Is the central point from which he measures
> Every distance
> Through the gateways of the world around him. . . .
> We may build more splendid habitations,
> Fill our rooms with paintings and with sculptures,
> But we cannot
> Buy with gold the old associations.[11]

Culture, in the conventional sense, was to be distrusted as essentially alien to the central values of the American home, a moral realm that was self-contained and happily closed off from the merely aesthetic, as the house itself in winter was self-contained and closed off, purifying its inhabitants after the licentious assault of summer.

Even Melville, distinctly antisentimental in intent, offered his own acerbic celebration on the theme. His story "I and My Chimney" is marked throughout by a conscious exploitation of the phallicism inherent in a symbol that others employed less consciously. But even with this dimension in his story, Melville was also asserting the importance of the chimney as the central point of social cohesiveness. He chronicles the narrator's opposition to the fashionable scheme, concocted by his wife and daughters, that would replace the central chimney of their house with a series of fireplaces against the outer walls, where each inhabitant could warm himself or herself in privacy.

The extraordinary volume and appeal of winter poetry, snow pictures, and accounts of polar explorations, with their accompanying celebrations of the controlled fire on the hearth, form perhaps the best single metaphor of the condition of the popular culture with regard to what America meant. To be sure, this was essentially sectional, a New England or Northeastern idea, but it traveled well to quasi New Englands such as Cincinnati, and the responding voice from the South did not even vaguely approximate its force. The highest standard was abstract—America was an idea—and that abstraction was often fleshed out in the observation and celebration of man assailed by and joyfully responding to winter.

Within the metaphor there was tension, a pull between those who emphasized the purity of the American idea and consequently felt it was compromised by a too easy admiration for sentimental folkways, and those who emphasized the rightness of the folkways and consequently felt the literary task should be a trimming of the best that other cultures had to offer to the dimensions of the hearth. In the latter pursuit, Longfellow was preeminent. Following along the path blazed by Washington Irving, he tirelessly accumulated legends, sagas, ballads, and romances from the Old World and whittled them down to American domestic size, showing that the sentiment that informed the actions of a Spanish student or a Norse king were essentially the same as those that informed the life of a decent American. To such works he added retellings in verse of American legends, again emphasizing the continuity of sentimental moral decency within the land.

"Nationality is a good thing to a certain extent," says one Longfellow character who clearly speaks for the author. "But universality is better. All that is best in the great poets of all countries is not what is national in them, but what is universal. Their roots are in their native soil; but their branches wave in the unpatriotic air, that speaks the same language unto all men."[12]

Clearly, this attitude so watered down the strength of the American idea as he conceived it that Emerson remained opposed, fearing the homogenizing effect of such sentimental celebrations. The individual who must represent America could only be blurred by such cozy associations. Theodore Parker, Boston's popular radical minister, agreed with Emerson and minced no words on the subject. The mark of the American is an inclination toward ideas rather than facts, he insisted, and accordingly Americans have departed from the sensational philosophy of the empiricists in favor of transcendentalism (an observation that would be fully examined in *Moby-Dick*). Parker praised Americans for beginning with universal abstract ideas in their politics—that is how the Declaration of Independence and most state constitutions commenced—and in their religion, which was fed by doctrinal preaching, so that even after the theology withered, Calvinism brought forth metaphysical fruit.[13] American literature, to be true, must also work down upon life from the lofty. But what one encounters in the hymners of the hearth is the influence of the powerful merchant class confirming the exploited in their compromised condition: "All is the reflection of this most powerful class. The truths that are told for them and the lies."[14] The cunning lawyer, the tricksy harlot, the deceitful minister, and the writer were all consilient to the same deplorable end. "The organized Literary Power," said Parker, ". . . has no original ideas, but diffuses the opinion of the other powers [Trade, Politics, Church] whom it represents, whose Will it serves, and whose Kaleidoscope it is."[15] He preferred the voices of the Ishmaels and Esaus, yet to be recognized by Americans: "Others have read of wild beasts; here are men that have seen the wolf."[16]

W. J. Stillman provides an anecdote, disconnected from any such concerns in his mind and yet apt as a symbol of the disagreements among literary New Englanders about the nature of American literature. Stillman managed a wilderness camp in the Adirondacks where such as Lowell and Emerson went in the summer for an annual taste of uncultivated nature:

> I did my best to enrol Longfellow in the party, but, though he was for a moment hesitating, I think the fact that Emerson was going with a gun settled him in the determination to decline. "Is it true that Emerson is going to take a gun?" he asked me; and when I said that he had finally decided to do so, he ejaculated, "Then somebody will be shot!" and would talk no more of going.[17]

As their participation in Stillman's camp, in literary societies, or in eating clubs demonstrates, the New England writers who differed from one another over the nature of American literature were friendly acquaintances, often friends, and their disagreements were rarely severe. None of them, moreover, was solely dependent upon writing for his income: Emerson had modest investments; Lowell and Longfellow held academic posts and had married heiresses; Holmes was a doctor; and Whittier was a journalist. This does not argue that they were not committed, professional writers. It signifies that in the absence of a literary marketplace that could support the American writer in comfort, many a writer succeeded in the marketplace that did exist only after establishing an economic base outside it.

Writers with no other source of income had to undertake dreadful hackwork. Many of these professionals—Poe was an exception but, since he starved, a qualified one; and Hawthorne and Melville for a time attempted to be exceptions—succumbed readily to notions of what would please the public and produced vulgar, meretricious work that stood at or below the level of political reporting in the journals in which they appeared.

When these professionals alone were considered, then, American literature was better represented outside of belles lettres. There might be, after all, something to the notion that literature as the world had hitherto known it was an institution of privilege, dependent upon a leisure class of patrons who, in turn, rested upon the base of the exploited mass of men: porcelain veins fed by arteries of brick, as Emerson had phrased it. True democratic literature, then, might not be belles lettres at all, but the daily writings that grew from the activities of the republic: journalism, legal opinions, sermons, accounts of natural history. Literature, that is, would be the most vital things written by people engaged in the doings of the nation rather than in literary activity itself.

The aging expresident, James Madison, believed this. He told a visitor "that the utterance of the national mind in America would be through small literature, rather than large, enduring works. After the schools and pulpits of the Union are all supplied, there will remain an immense number of educated sons of men of small property, who will have things to say; and all who can write will."[18]

In elaborating this theme, Daniel Webster emphasized the practical. He said that Americans were not impressed by the sheer fact of learning because they had seen that learning can exist without being useful and that in itself it does not argue mental superiority. "The question after all, if it be a question," said Webster, "is, whether literature, ancient as well as modern, does not assist a good understanding, improve natural good taste, add polished armor to native strength, and render its possessor, not only more capable of deriving private happiness from contemplation and reflection, but more accomplished also for action in the affairs of life, and especially for public action."[19] In short, why should not literature, like everything else in the new democracy, earn its way through public service?

Diametrically opposed as he was to Webster in so many political matters, Charles Sumner nevertheless paralleled him in this area: "Literature and art may widen the sphere of its [a nation's] influence; they may adorn it; but they are in their nature but accessories. *The true grandeur of humanity is in moral elevation, sustained, enlight-*

ened, and decorated by the intellect of man."[20] Here, to be sure, we are in the presence of a far greater New Englandly passion for abstraction than was Webster's, but they had in common a concern for the public utility of literature in a democracy and its duty to serve moral rather than aesthetic ends.

James Russell Lowell was in basic agreement:

> They tell us that our land was made for song,
> With its huge rivers and sky-piercing peaks,
> Its sealike lakes and mighty cataracts,
> Its forests vast and hoar, and prairies wide,

but he has found that although American scenery is grander than English, this is not enough to stimulate an American literature. The English have a landscape rich in human associations and Americans do not, so that American poetry fails unless it builds on an idea that exists beyond the spectacle of sublime nature:

> Though we should speak as man spake never yet
> Of gleaming Hudson's broad magnificence,
> Or green Niagara's never-ending roar . . .
> Our country hath a gospel of her own
> To preach and practise before all the world,
> The freedom and divinity of man
> The glorious claims of human brotherhood.[21]

And so we are returned again to the all but sterile commitment of American literature to an abstraction.

The view that American literature was, materially, the writing produced by men in practical pursuit of the duties of the republic and, formally, the embodiment of great principles led to the conclusion that, although there might be letters in America, there would be no such thing as the profession of man of letters. In Boston where money had stabilized and accepted its obligations to culture, this conclusion was modified. The feeling was not so much that the wealthy man would identify and patronize literary ability as it was that members of the gentlemanly class would in their leisure make whatever literature was possible in the crude state of the nation. Those associated with the merchant class were English in thought, in habit, and in blood. They had little faith in republican polity and small confidence in the good sense and steadiness of the people.[22] In believing they would be the producers as well as the consumers of the best American literature, they easily fell into the stuffy notion that literature was not only for the well-bred but could be produced only by the well-bred. Dana, for example, disapproved of William Cullen Bryant, a notable writer but a rough, country-bred man: he "has good feelings, good principles & a beautiful mind, but I was never in company with him, & especially when he was the entertainer, that I have not been made to feel unpleasantly & to wish he had been taught the artificial, the insincere, if you choose, habits of a gentleman."[23]

Oliver Wendell Holmes, a valued member of the best class, was licensed to satirize it lightly because he embodied its principles so well. He twitted the humorless vulgarians who insisted upon an indissoluble connection between literature and moral righteousness in America—at one time alarming the dour Calvinist theologian Professor Calvin Stowe by cheerfully assuring him after a good dinner that he knew whole families in Boston who were unaffected by Adam's fall—and he chided his own associates with the reminder that their superiority was in the process of becoming biological as well as cultural.

> We are forming an aristocracy; and transitory as its individual life often is, it maintains itself tolerably, as a whole. Of course money is its corner-stone. But now observe this. Money kept for two or three generations transforms a race,—I don't mean merely in manners and hereditary culture, but in blood and bone. Money buys air and sunshine, in which children grow up more kindly of course, it buys country places to give them happy and healthy summers, good nursing, good doctoring, and the best cuts of beef and mutton. . . . As the young females of each successive season come on, the finest specimens among them, other things being equal, are apt to attract those who can afford the expensive luxury of beauty. The physical character of the next generation rises in consequence. It is plain that certain families have in this way acquired an elevated type of face and figure, and that in a small circle of city-connections one may sometimes find models of both sexes which one of the rural counties would find it hard to match from all its townships put together.[24]

Thomas Higginson, growing up in Cambridge in the 1840s, experienced a distinctly graded society in which the town boys were regarded as beneath the young gentlemen attending the college, and country boys enrolled at the college did chores at professors' houses and were treated as servants. "I can remember no conversation around me," he said, "looking toward the essential equality of the human race," although there was the amusing annual spectacle of the militia muster when, in the closest thing New England had to a saturnalia, the president of Harvard put on his major's uniform only to take orders from his manservant who was a colonel.[25]

When George Ticknor, Boston society's standard-bearer, said, "In a society where public opinion governs, unsound opinions must be rebuked,"[26] he meant the rebuke not merely to be the assertion of sound opinions but the social exclusion of those who were wrong in their beliefs.

Ticknor's contribution to the national letters was his *History of Spanish Literature* in three volumes, published in 1849 after some thirty years of preparation. It was based on extensive research conducted in Europe, during which period Ticknor had been welcomed to the dominant courts, salons, and coteries of Paris, London, Dresden, Berlin, and Madrid, so that his regency in Boston society was patterned on the going models. That he was an extraordinarily dull man seems to have helped because it underlined the fact that wealthy Americans were not necessarily pushy but could prose on and doze on with the best. That his contribution to the national letters, and it was considerable, should be on such an alien subject was entirely fitting. America must make its mark by attaching itself to high culture, and, confronted with a shallow history at home, the American, despite Emerson's odd ideas, had to conquer other histories. The fact that these were not his history only pointed up his superiority: Ticknor had mastered ancient Greek and German at Göttingen, French at Paris, Spanish at Madrid, Portuguese at Lisbon.

In Ticknor's footsteps, but climbing higher, had followed William Hickling Prescott with his *History of the Conquest of Mexico* (1843) and John Lothrop Motley with *The Rise of the Dutch Republic* (1856). They, too, were from good families, had resided abroad for long periods, corresponded internationally with the socially powerful, and could count on a rich, highly respectable, and politically powerful core of readers to serve as the first audience for their works. The men who saw Boston society as a club aloof from the excesses of republicanism and the gaucheries of such theorists as Emerson or such reformers as Parker used their money to purchase time—for travel, for research, for reflection, for refreshment, and for compilation of their massive, three-volume units. As popular as Prescott's and Motley's works proved, their royalties in their lifetimes could not have covered their expenses during the many years in which they prepared their histories. They did not regard Europe as the enemy—far from it; but to those who did visualize a literary war they were proving that Americans could and should take the battle to the enemy's ground and win their great victories there.

On January 10, 1850, Henry Hallam, author of important works on Europe in the Middle Ages, the constitutional history of England, and the literature of Europe, wrote Ticknor from his English home:

> America is fast taking a high position as a literary country; the next half-century will be abundantly productive of good authors in your Union. And it is yet to be observed that there is not, nor probably will be a distinct American school. The language is absolutely the same, all slight peculiarities being now effaced; and there seems nothing in the turn of sentiment or taste which a reader can recognize as not English. This is not only remarkable in such works as yours and Mr. Prescott's, but even, as it strikes me, in the lighter literature, as far as I see it, of poetry or belles-lettres.[27]

Nothing could have burst more sweetly against Ticknor's palate. And yet Hallam was writing at the outset of the 1850s and in his view of America there was no hint of the literary and linguistic differences that would in that decade result in the work of Thoreau, Whitman, Hawthorne, and Melville. Edwin Whipple, Boston's miniaturized answer to Macaulay, was proud of the reputation gained by his townsmen, but noted a bit nervously, "Their productions being . . . *contributions* to the national mind, rather than offsprings of it, are contemplative rather than lyrical, didactic rather than dramatic."[28]

What part of the culture would nourish the offspring rather than receive the contributions?

The answer came with full, rude vigor from the pit of political squabbling, from the cultural ditchdiggers scored by Dana. In October 1837, Jacksonianism, recovering from the panic and launching itself against the powers represented by the Bank of the United States, linked its opponents to pro-British snobbery in its appeal to its working-class constituency. The *Democratic Review* was launched, dedicated to "that high and holy DEMOCRATIC PRINCIPLE which was designed to be the fundamental element of the new social and political system created by the 'American experiment.' A democratic culture founded on the 'voluntary principle,' is one for the masses; our 'better educated classes' imbibe anti-democratic habits from English literature."[29]

The *Democratic Review* and similar journals, even of the opposing parties, began boosting America in a steady stream of predictable clichés, claiming that the country that possessed enormous spatial breadth and sublime political promise was the country destined to have the most sweeping and elevated literature. One did not have to possess Dana's exaggerated social sensibility to see through it all. Even the mild, congenial Longfellow felt it necessary to issue a caveat. His character, Mr. Hathaway Passing, is an editor who wishes to found a magazine that will circulate fifty thousand copies. It is to be called *The Niagara,* and Passing explains:

> We want a national literature commensurate with our mountains and rivers. . . . We want a national epic that shall correspond to the size of our country. . . . We want a national drama in which scope shall be given to our gigantic ideas, and to the unparalleled activity and progress of our people. . . . In a word, we want a national literature altogether shaggy and unshorn, that shall shake the earth, like a herd of buffaloes, thundering over the prairies.

The gentle New England poet whom he is soliciting begs to remind him that "with regard to England our literature is not an imitation, but . . . a continuation." He tells Passing that a national literature can truly arrive only after centuries of fertilization. "And as for having it so savage and wild as you want it, I have only to say that all literature as well as art, is the result of culture and intellectual refinement."[30] And, indeed, Longfellow's own great Indian poem, *Hiawatha,* came as the result of the study of the best sagas of the ancient world, not as some fancied grunt of American nativisim.

One result of the Passings being unconvinced by such arguments, or, rather, being confirmed in their belief that the opposition to crying up everything American was an unpatriotic capitulation to foreign ways, was a deluge of just about the worst kind of "national" literature imaginable. Bad in itself, it produced worse effects by debauching audiences and establishing bad taste as a necessary accompaniment to right political belief.

William Charles Macready, the great English tragedian, came to America on his first tour in 1843, not just to meet the popular demand for his acting but also to consider whether he would settle in the new nation. An admirer of Cromwell and the Pilgrim Fathers, he despised the "tyrant" Charles Stuart and was repelled by the idolatry of him in the Church of England, to which, he fervently said, he did not belong because he professed to be a Christian. But the country that he imagined he could adopt was too much for him:

> I quite abandon all idea of settling in this country. The press is made up, with few exceptions, of such unredeemed scoundrels, and the law is so inoperative, that "the spurns which patient merit from the unworthy take" in England are preferable to the state of semi-civilization here. I disagree with Dickens whilst I quite sympathize with his disgust at these wretches.[31]

Democracy, Macready had hoped, would foster the cultivation of taste and artistic power. But look at Forrest, America's leading actor, a man with "all the qualifications, the material out of which to build up a great artist . . . for all the world."[32] He has become an actor for the less intelligent because his countrymen have undiscriminatingly encouraged his slightest effort and thus imperceptibly transformed him into a performer who feeds their love of spread-eagle ranting and extravagance in all its forms. Such was also the case with the national literature promoted by the whoopings of the popular press.

And yet the mindless literary protectionism that resulted from chauvinistic editorial policy brought forth a small and excellent crop within its field of tares, one that would not have been so encouraged had not all things American been uncritically promoted. Hawthorne of Salem came from a family of importance in the annals of that mercantile city, but the Hawthornes had slid into poverty and Nathaniel learned that the American aristocracy had no room for good blood fed by little means. His literary aspirations could not find family subsidy, as did those of Ticknor and Prescott. As he worked at his craft in relative isolation, allegiance to the Democratic party did help him find some market for his tales among the jingoistic journals that were aggressively buying American (if also underpaying American). Conservative as was his party on issues such as slavery, he nevertheless associated himself with that radical wing of it known as Young America. The chief aim of this group was to extend the official support of the United States government to revolutionary forces in Europe, such as Kossuth's movement for a national Hungary. Young America believed that "Manifest Destiny" meant not only America's inevitable westward movement but also the inevitable spread of American-supported republics in Europe.

Melville, too, benefited from his allegiance to the Democratic party and from the uncritical promotion of American writers. When in 1850 he reviewed Hawthorne's *Mosses from an Old Manse,* he was quite willing to ring all the popular notes, albeit with a degree of acuteness derived from his own genius and sharpened by his recognition that in Hawthorne he did indeed have before him an American author of world standard. He seemed to adopt the outrageous hyperbole of the chauvinists when he likened Hawthorne to Shakespeare. But he also made it clear his comparison was not meant to imply a similarity in absolute stature but rather to point to their common perception of the darker truths of human nature, of what he called "the power of blackness." He thus satisfied the most exuberant of the nationalistic expectations of his popular audience and yet moved to correct the excesses of national taste deplored by Macready, because he was reminding his readers that Shakespeare's greatness resided not in the rant that the masses loved but in the expression of terrifying truth. The similarity was that Hawthorne, a very undramatic, very quiet authorial voice, nevertheless also breathed forth a profound sense of the human capacity for evil, a sense as hidden from the careless reader as was Shakespeare's sense from those in the pit who came to hiss humpbacked Richard.

Some may say, Melville recognized, "that if an illustration were needed a lesser light might have sufficed to elucidate this Hawthorne, this small man of yesterday."[33] But he would not oblige them, because Americans had to become accustomed to measuring themselves against true greatness rather than just shouting about it. So long as they kept the measure in mind, it was an absolute necessity that they promote their own as a first step in the development of their potential greatness: "let America first praise mediocrity even, in her own children, before she praises (for everywhere merit demands acknowledgment from every one) the best excellence in the children of any other land."[34]

Melville recognized the formula his audience expected—the relation of the grandeur of the land to the grandeur of the artist—in his peroration. But he had before him a writer of exquisite small pieces concerned with psychological and ethical matters, one who was nevertheless far superior to any who wrote of stampeding buffaloes and dreadful chasms in the Rockies. If Hawthorne had to be likened to the landscape, a meadow or a sheltering hill would have to do. Melville, however, wrote: "The smell of your beeches and hemlocks is upon him; your own broad prairies are in his soul; and if you travel away inland into his deep and noble nature, you will hear the far roar of his Niagara."[35]

It is an ingenious remark, at one and the same time applicable to Hawthorne, representative of Melville, within the popular expectation, and yet identifying within that scope the real source of power upon which American literature would draw in that decade. American literature would match American geography not by mirroring it in words or by trumpeting national slogans. Niagara, that is, would not be on the page but in the consciousness of the American writer. With depth and nobility there, the actual work of art would be American in its psychological concentration. Behind the popular roar for echoes of the mighty falls, as the deploring Dana did not perceive and as the chiding Longfellow could not conceive, it was possible for writers who were not, after all, Ticknor's or Hallam's idea of the American branch of that fine old firm, English Literature International, to find their voices.

Melville in his essay on Hawthorne neither defied the nationalistic fervor of the untutored democracy nor abased himself before it; he accepted its impulse as crucial and modified its outlet to accommodate and charge with force the unique literature he felt Americans were destined to write. His dual allegiance, to democratic America and to artistry, was one that his great contemporaries also felt. They were, at most points, their country's severest critics, but their criticisms grew from the roots of love and understanding. They were not contributing to the culture offerings garnered elsewhere. They were the culture's offspring.

Chapter Five

The Self Divided by Democracy: Edgar Allan Poe and the Already-Answered Question

Notoriously, Edgar Allan Poe was a man without a country. He had no allegiance to the America imagined by his fellow countrymen, and no definite location within any unit of his homeland. Born fortuitously in Boston, the child of a touring actress, he developed an opposition amounting to hatred toward all that he believed New England and its literati stood for, yet he unhesitatingly announced his first volume of poetry as by "a Bostonian." Raised by stepparents in Richmond, Virginia, he asserted sympathy with the southern code of gentlemanliness, but he was literally cast out of that society by his stepfather, and, ironically, at bottom recognized that his stepfather was not really of the southern gentry but was a merchant. His poems and tales are only rarely set in a recognizable part of America, bear no conscious relation to the habits of abstract speculation that marked much of its literature, bypass explicit moral themes, are unconcerned with social matters, and adhere to a "literary" diction that is confected.

Indeed, one encounters throughout Poe a deliberate effort to construct a fictive world that observes its own laws of verisimilitude and does not pretend to correspond to specific circumstances in the real world. The details that Poe assembles in a description of a person or place cannot be found in combination outside of his pages. Ligeia, for example, has tresses that set forth the "full force of the

Homeric epithet 'hyacinthine,' " a nose of a perfection to be seen only in "the graceful medallions of the Hebrews," a chin such as that the "god Apollo revealed but in a dream to Cleomenes," eyes that were "fuller even than the fullest of the gazelle eyes of the tribe of the valley of the Nourjahad," and a complete beauty that was of the "beings either above or apart from the earth, the beauty of the fabulous Houri of the Turk."[1] She is the result of her creator's looting of a range of discontinuous civilizations and eras, taking whatever liberties he wishes with the spoils, just as the characteristic Poe chamber with its tapestries, statuettes, censers, and crimson curtains clashing with one another is no room that ever existed outside of the imagination.

"Proprieties of place, and especially of time," Poe tells us, "are the bugbears which terrify mankind from the contemplation of the magnificent." The spirit "writhing in fire" seeks "wider visions," visions of the "land of real dreams."[2] Such a view of the disconnection between the products of the creative spirit and actual objects extends beyond man's social environment to the world of nature. What was for Emerson the correspondent of the soul is for Poe a landscape from which man is permanently alienated and, accordingly, one he must inhabit imaginatively through redesigning it rather than attempting to integrate with it as it exists.

"In the most enchanting of natural landscapes," Poe says, "there will always be found a defect or an excess—many excesses and defects. While the components may defy, individually, the highest skill of the artist, the arrangement of these parts will always be susceptible of improvement. In short, no position can be attained on the wide surface of the *natural* earth, from which an artistical eye, looking steadily, will not find matter of offence in what is termed the 'composition of the landscape.' "[3]

Even as man's capacity to imagine separates him from the harmony of nature—he accepts its outline but ceaselessly recombines its components—so the natural world exists in essential independence from man. It is "one vast animate and sentient whole," which is cognizant of man only as an animalcule that inches along its uppermost crust.[4] Although man regards the earth as mere material, an interchange is constantly in progress between shadow and water, rock and earth, wind and leaf; nature is a living, feeling system that excludes humanity.

It is, therefore, futile for the creative artist to attempt to achieve unity with nature through, for example, the use of metaphors that pretend to join thought with natural phenomena. The gap between him and the self-contained sentience of nature is unbridgeable. Rather than engage in a fruitless effort to re-create the paradise that can no longer exist, the artist must invent a human analogue to it from the fragments available to his imagination. He will thereby satisfy the thirst for beauty, which cannot be quenched by an imitation of an external world that ignores us. Because of man's radical alienation from nature, the attempt to achieve such imitations results in a far greater fiction than does the acceptance of the gap and the consequent invention of an analogue that serves the dreaming mind.

In "To Helen," his greatest short poem,[5] Poe draws his images from artificial objects and relies upon connotation to the almost exclusive disregard of denotation. Helen's beauty is like "Nicéan barks of yore." There is not, of course, any suggestion that she looks like a ship, nor can the reader's mind respond with a definite picture of a "Nicéan bark." Rather, the suggestiveness of Helen's beauty depends upon the sound and rhythm of such words and the activity ascribed to the invented object: it carried weary, wayworn wanderers home again. Beauty is like a release from care rather than like any thing in nature; ultimately, of course, like death rather than any thing in life.

In the second stanza Helen is given "hyacinth hair," an image based on a mythical event filtered through Homeric diction. Her face is "classic," her air is "Naiad," and the home to which she brings the poet, the complement to the "native shore" of the first stanza, is totally conceptual: "the glory that was Greece, / And the grandeur that was Rome." Insofar as these are places in a denotatively known world, they are two different places, separate temporally as well as spatially. The single home they form is one to which only the imagination can return.

Helen stands, in the final stanza, "statue-like," holding an artifact, an "agate lamp." Again she is likened to a thing of art produced by the self-reflective imagination without direct reference to the world of nature, or, for that matter, of life, since the images push toward the dead past and invoke the marmoreal chill of funerary carvings. The poem is cut off from the present of the reader.

Poe's chief subject matter is the closed world of the troubled mind, and its isolation is heightened by the perception that even a tranquil mind is essentially cut off from nature and thinks in images that come from human action and aspiration rather than from direct, natural observation. Mental anguish only compounds an already fearful situation, and the quality of intense disturbance Poe communicates stems finally not from the dreadful event—a descent into a maelstrom or the tortures of the Inquisition—but from the sense that such events are, after all, externalizations of the normal human condition of the isolated mind both producing and consuming the terms of its existence.

Society is scarcely depicted by Poe, and so obvious is the self-absorption of his narrators that other characters in their tales have no objective existence; they are agents in the dramas of hallucination. Accordingly, physical settings are also sealed from the wider world: tombs, shipholds, tunnels, basements, and dungeons. Rooms are shut off from their surroundings: doors locked, heavy curtains hung, artificial light employed for all the twenty-four hours.

Open physical space has no function in the work of Poe because, obviously, mental space, with which he is centrally concerned, is a caged area. But even after recognizing the coherence of this we must be struck by it. Poe wrote at a time of continental expansionism, when open space suggested the interchange of natural breadth and human potential. In closing down access to wide nature in the world of his fictions, Poe was taking a social stand, asserting that art, growing from the imagination, is confined to the pure products of the mind and has no commerce with the collective destiny of the people. Not only did he scorn the public arts, such as political speeches, as no art at all, but he almost compulsively identified the more conventional art of such as Longfellow as plagiaristic. To be sure, he meant that literally, and he ceaselessly and unconvincingly cited specific evidence. But underneath these petty and spiteful displays is a voracious demand for an originality that arises directly from psychic sources. The American artist, preeminently isolated both from an unimaginative society and from a literary tradition, should be preeminently concerned with his own inner depths.

Like Emerson, Poe feared the mob, but unlike Emerson he believed the mob was real, not a conceptual mistake that could be explained away. He regarded it as "the most oblivious and insupportable despotism that ever was heard of upon the face of the Earth."[6] The borrowed dignity it acquired from the natural breadth of America was for him an evasion of its truly terrible nature. For the orphaned and deracinated Poe, being an American meant being locked into the self, and being an American artist meant being thrown more completely upon pure, imaginative energy than were artists of other societies who had, at least, some group or class with refined standards to which they could relate and some landscape that reflected the ordering of the imagination. The America that locked out Poe, who wanted to attach himself to it through shared fantasies, appeared to him, as a consequence, to lock each man into his own nightmares as the essential expression of the American self. Abstractions about equality or progress, sops intended to sate the self's hunger, in fact drove it ever more deeply back upon its imagination.

As a professional writer, Poe affirmed the need to protect native literature and assert it in defiance of England,[7] but he ridiculed the belief that this literature could grow from theoretical connections such as those he associated with the school of Emerson, or from moral themes such as those he deplored in Hawthorne, whom he otherwise admired, or from chauvinistic celebrations such as those that filled the periodicals. America offered no condition for art other than that of isolation, and the American artistic response must be a seizing of that exclusion and the examination of the isolate soul as the true arena of the drama of the self.

Poetry depends for its existence, Poe says, on "an immortal instinct, deep within the spirit of man."[8] If this, in theory, appears to be a simple reassertion of the traditional belief in the universality of art, in Poe's practice the result was something different. That traditional belief rested ultimately on the assumption of the universality of morality—we recognize, as Aristotle put it, that some men are better, some worse, and some just the same as we are, and our emotional response to fictions is governed by our sense of the fictive characters' moral standing; we pity or fear for them accordingly. But Poe's universality had a source that in his day was peculiar to him. The psychic anguish he depicts is caused not by conflict within an accepted moral code but by recognitions (self-recognition on the part of the narrator, sympathetic recognition on the part of the reader) of division within the self. The wholeness that is shattered and thus results in horror is not that of the human community but the fragile integrity of the individual's psychic structure. Reference to this inner standard has, since the latter half of the nineteenth century, become a characteristic of modern art. From that period worldly circumstances have been increasingly perceived as delusive, and objective verities—nature, God, human goodness—discredited. The widespread failure of the revolutions of 1848 and the emergence in that year of *The Communist Manifesto,* which rejected human betterment in terms of a return to a golden standard and embraced the dynamic of historical change as the engine of inevitable social progress, signaled the end of the common belief that the world of art was rooted in the unchanging world of social thought. The failure of the idealistic imagination to realize itself in social organizations based on justice turned artistic activity inward as a self-validating form of engagement immune from the disasters of the body politic. As one scholar observed of the beliefs that emerged among writers after mid-century: "A self-conscious preoccupation with artistic problems encircles the examination of all that exists within the various states of human personality. To look at this preoccupation as self-indulgent immersion in a vacuum is to miss the agony of these writers. For them, art is the only realm left in which one can still assemble one's wits in order to make some coherent assessment of the state of values. Thus the efforts of writing correctly, of writing well, constitutes a victory of integrity over incoherence."[9]

While in Europe this development waited upon the failures of 1848, Poe, dead in 1849, was launched on this interior journey by the early 1830s. He had never recognized the American Revolution as anything but a failure. In so reacting to his America, he preceded the Europeans into the subjective world of modern art, even as his countrymen claimed to be preceding them into the democratic future. Higher civilization, he said, rests upon the "laws of *gradation*" that visibly pervade all things on earth.[10] If we respond to our world sensibly rather than speculatively, we feel that by nature men differ from one another and do so hierarchically, some being stronger, more beautiful, or more intelligent than others. The recognition of these distinctions and the building upon them are what is meant by civilization and are what elsewhere and earlier made art possible. To say, as Americans now do, that equality is the system of nature is to affirm a theory in the face of contradictory evidence. Democracy, the political result of a blind, abstract assertion, is a system nowhere observable in nature save, perhaps, in a village of prairie dogs.[11] It is a system that wars with sensibility and thus with art and the artist so that art is compelled to withdraw from the everyday actual.

Poe's political views are to be inferred from his writings on other matters; he never offered them explicitly at any length. The affinity between his implicit outlook and Edmund Burke's extended *apologia* for social conservatism, however, provides a striking context that illuminates the discontinuity between art and society experienced by Poe and helps explain his characteristic themes.[12]

Observing the tallow-chandlers and hair-dressers who came into political authority immediately after the French Revolution, Burke wrote: "Such descriptions of men ought not to suffer oppression from the state; but the state suffers oppression, if such as they, either individually or collectively, are permitted to rule."[13] Those who permit them to rule, he said, think they are combating prejudice but in reality they "are at war with nature." Opposed in the name of nature to the licentiousness of the mob, Burke was equally opposed to any theoretical form of authority exercised by the mob or over it in the name of reason. If the passions represented by the mob were aberrant, a flying-off from the true balance of nature, so were the exercises of detached reason. Rather, both passion and reason must be held by a human center, that of the untutored feelings, which men possess by virtue of their human nature first, but also by virtue of the social nature and their having been born into a social world already formed in response to the feelings of the many who have lived in it.

The enlightened rationalists who swept away such a meeting place of passion and reason said that these feelings were nothing more than prejudices. Rather than oppose the pejorative term, Burke embraced it and explained prejudice's value:

> In this enlightened age I am bold enough to confess that we are generally men of untaught feelings; that instead of casting away our old prejudices, we cherish them to a very considerable degree, and to take more shame to ourselves, we cherish them because they are prejudices; and the longer they have lasted, and the more generally they have prevailed the more we cherish them. . . . Many of our men of speculation, instead of exploding general prejudices, employ their sagacity to discover the latent wisdom which prevails in them. If they find what they

> seek, and they seldom fail, they think it more wise to continue the prejudice, with the reason involved, than to cast away the coat of prejudice, and to leave nothing but the naked reason; because prejudice, with its reason, has a motive to give action to that reason, and an affection which will give it permanence.[14]

Thomas Paine's response, made in the name of reason, democracy, and what he called nature, disposed of this binding center as in truth the irrational source of the power of unjust authority—the superstitious basis of the coercion of the multitude to submit to such manifestly unjust and unreasonable institutions as arbitrary government and a state religion. Believing that reason is adequate to all the tasks that Burke said required the support of untaught feelings, Paine supplied no middle term with which to replace prejudice. As a consequence, in the model of democracy that he offers there is no need for thought to borrow strength from feeling—when valid it immediately enlists the passions—and no room for the imagination. Paine consistently characterized Burke's *Reflections* as a performance, a piece of theater, a tragic invention designed to produce a weeping effect so as to turn the reader from an analysis of causes to an indulgence in unthinking sentiment.

Paine knew that he was vulnerable to the charge of denying the complex layer of human wants that simply could not be served by reason. Government, Burke had pointed out, is not made to meet the abstract perfection of human rights, but is "a contrivance of human wisdom to provide for human *wants*."[15] But Paine insisted that once reason is properly enthroned, it will be seen that most of these wants were artificially created, and they will therefore disappear. Although unmentioned, among such artificially created wants is one that earlier cultures had conceived to be natural, the craving to imagine other worlds. Implicit in Paine's theory is the notion that such craving stems from the bafflement of man's just social aspirations rather than from an intrinsic element in human nature and will disappear in a democracy.

Theories of modern literature as, on one hand, the writings produced for practical purposes by public men, or, on the other, the new, broad expression of man's "true" relation to the universe reflected the anti-imaginative potential of the democratic system.

Correspondingly, Poe's insistence upon the force of the imagination was a negative response to the democracy in which he found himself mislocated. Although artistically potent, his belief set him on a doomed course socially.

Burke's celebration of prejudice had a base in his society. He could cite the "spirit of a gentleman" and the "spirit of religion" because they were not mere notions but were manifest in groups or classes. But Poe had no social correlative in his America for the power of the imagination, despite his pathetically shabby attempts to represent himself personally as a gentleman.

Just as his society furnished Poe with no correlative for the imagination, so he could not locate in his fictions a center that would hold reason and passion in harmony. Disdainful as he consciously was of worldly circumstances, his deeper perception was of an America of either the passionate, ravenous mob, or the sagacious, superior, isolated individual. They had no ground on which to meet, such as that of the nobility, the priesthood, and the protected class of scholars in Burke's model, and so were constantly at war with one another. Burke had likened the newly liberated French proletarian to a madman escaped from the protecting restraint of a cell, but Poe's madmen have no such protections available to them: their liberty is a terror and their confinement is equally a terror. Runaway passion is madness but the countering reason is equally mad.

A Poe character is never more insane than at the moment he begins to reason with us. The emotions he feels as he descends into the maelstrom are no more terrifying than his ability, in the midst of them, to discourse on the Archimedean principles of flotation. The horror of his entombment in a rancid ship's hold is less than that we experience when, in the depths of his distress, he reads us a lesson on the scientific manner of lading a ship. Reason thus exercised is not the governor of excess, moving the narrator to a more balanced position, but an alternate form of mania, an indulgence in rationality for its own sake that is far less in keeping with the occasion than an irrational flow of fear, homicidal hate, or self-loathing would be. Poe's characters cannot achieve a reunification of personality any more than the aesthetic eye can rest content with the natural landscape. Original integrity is missing from the world; the Poe narrator has no self-concept that blends reason and passion, but submits to the insanity of one or the insanity of the other.

The most obvious displays of such division are the stories concerned with the theme of doubling. "William Wilson" centers on the subject of the ego's encounter with the alter ego, and the conflict between self and other self rages in "The Fall of the House of Usher" with a sibling as alter ego, "The Tell-Tale Heart" with a parental figure as alter ego, "The Cask of Amontillado" with a friend as alter ego, "Ligeia" with the lover as alter ego, and so on into other tales. Unable to overcome disunity through reunion, the divided self seeks the annihilation of one of its halves, knowing full well that means the annihilation of the other half, self-destruction. Poe conceives of no community binding the individual to others, but when he withdraws within the isolated self he does so only to discover there the ultimate fracture.

In death alone is a form of unity possible; there man returns to the sentient wholeness of nature from which living inevitably divided him. In the grave, Poe reports, the consciousness of being becomes progressively indistinct and is replaced by the consciousness of locality. As the idea of entity seeps out into the surrounding enclosure, the space that envelops the body becomes the body itself. A sixth sense then arises, "a mental pendulous pulsation" that is a "keen, perfect, self-existing sentience of duration."[16] So perfect is it that it can measure human time and judge the inaccuracy of ticking clocks. To be dead is to be incorporated literally into the natural system, translated into perfect place and perfect time. Such transformation is unavailable in life, although we yearn toward it. Hence narrators enclose themselves in muffled rooms and attempt to exchange their bodies for the space that surrounds them; hence they live by artificial light and eschew clocks in an attempt to become the regulating timekeepers of their world. They elect living deaths because only these provide an analogue for psychic wholeness.

The remarkable divisions that abound in the work of Poe all say unity is impossible this side of the grave, and yet Poe the aesthetician repeatedly asserts that the single, most important aspect of art is that it alone can approximate unity on this planet. The world of the mind, he says in "The Poetic Principle," is divided into Pure Intellect, Taste, and the Moral Sense. Poetry addresses itself to Taste and must have nothing to do with the first, with truth per se, nor with the last, with conscience. Such concerns lead to the heresy of the didactic, all too common in Boston, and to disunification. Unity stems from an exclusive concern with that part of the mind to which the work of art is addressed, and that part is precisely the internal area which in America has no public correlative—here taste is not institutionalized in a clerisy or a protected class of artists. This condition reinforces Poe's conviction that the imagination is keyed to the supernal and must be exercised in flight from the world; what he cannot locate in America he believes unavailable in the temporal universe. Central is the thirst for beauty, and this

> belongs to the immortality of Man. It is at once a consequence and an indication of his personal existence. It is the desire of the moth for the star. It is no mere appreciation of the Beauty before us, but a wild effort to reach the Beauty above. Inspired by an ecstatic prescience of the glories beyond the grave, we struggle to multiform combinations among the Things and Thoughts of Time to attain a portion of that Loveliness whose very elements, perhaps, appertain to eternity alone.[17]

The combinations of thoughts and things that constitute the subject of the unified work are by definition aimed at an imprecise ideal. But once the nature of the subject of the work of art is apprehended, then Poe, with an analytic ruthlessness characteristic of his narrators, moves from the necessary indefiniteness of ends to a calculating precision in the means. The contrast between the vagueness of the supernal and the mechanics of its achievement is so sharp as to make Poe the aesthetician yet another of Poe the author's madly self-divided narrators.

Since unity of effect depends upon unity of impression, "what we term a long poem is, in fact, merely a succession of brief ones." The best works of literary art will be limited in length to a single sitting of the reader. "Within this limit," Poe says, "the extent of a poem may be made to bear a mathematical relation to its merit—in other words to the degree of the true poetical effect which it is capable of inducing; for it is clear that the brevity must be in direct ratio to the intensity of the intended effect:—this, with one proviso—that a certain degree of duration is absolutely requisite for the production of any effect at all."[18]

Cool calculation in gauging the technique for the achievement of the ineffable takes over completely as Poe in "The Philosophy of Composition" represents himself as beginning his poem, even before he decides on its specific subject, by searching for a refrain that will provide variety within unity; settling on a single word as the best such device; choosing that word first for its sound rather than its sense; theorizing that the long *o* is the most sonorous vowel and the *r* the most producible consonant; and so, having hit upon "Nevermore" for those reasons, then proceeding to ask what a poem with such a refrain could actually be about. Such submission to near-algebraic formula in the construction of that most unscientific of all structures, the poem, is coherent as argued by Poe, and yet demoniacal in its studied separation of means and ends, its mad-scientist assertion that although beauty is above this world, all of it we can know will be achieved by the construction of a machine for its production in accordance with strict laws.

The laws lead Poe, after he has selected his refrain, to compose the climactic stanza first—actual writing beginning at the end, "where all works of art should begin" if unity of effect is to be achieved —and he flatly declares, "Had I been able, in the subsequent composition, to construct more vigorous stanzas, I should, without scruple, have purposely enfeebled them, so as not to interfere with the climacteric effect."[19] This makes perfect sense in view of what has gone before and yet strikes us as all wrong. Destroy one's best work for the sake of an a priori decision? But the machine has been set in motion and its needs must be obeyed. Poe, the alienated American in his identification of the true realm of poetry, is also Poe the representative American mechanic attempting to outdo his tinkering countrymen in the technical perfecting of his contraption.[20]

For the all-important end of unity Poe invents his climax first and then closes down any element that will not subordinate itself to it. His philosophy of composition parallels his tales in that it asserts a closed space as the field of mental operation. In a sense, all is bounded before anything starts. The poet's process is one of movement within severely prescribed limits, just as the narrator's process in the tales is one of psychological movement within a severely delimited area. Ultimate questions have been settled and the literary work is concerned with how the mind within the cage reacts to its confinement.

The most characteristic of Poe's structures, then, is that which results from the already-answered question, and the clearest model of this pervasive form is provided by the two-stanza poem "A Dream Within a Dream." The first stanza affirms, "That my days have been a dream." Hope has flown away and it matters little how or why it has done so, whether by night or day, in vision or in none. The final truth is, the stanza concludes, "*All* that we see or seem / Is but a dream within a dream."

The second stanza is:

> I stand amid the roar
> Of a surf-tormented shore,
> And I hold within my hand
> Grains of the golden sand—
> How few! yet how they creep
> Through my fingers to the deep,
> While I weep—while I weep!
> O God! can I not grasp
> Them with a tighter clasp?
> O God! can I not save
> *One* from the pitiless wave?
> Is *all* that we see or seem
> But a dream within a dream?[21]

Thus, after a metaphorical dramatization of the condition stated in the first stanza, the poem concludes with a series of questions, each of them already answered irrevocably. The final question, moreover, is a syntactic inversion of the concluding statement of the first stanza; we have already been told that all, indeed, is a dream within a dream. In choosing to move from answer to question Poe chooses to center on psychological rather than logical process. The effects he seeks are those of the mind, which, recognizing its confinement, reacts not by seeking a way out of the condition but by devising novel ways of keeping alive its horrified reaction to the condition. This is, from one point of view, a process of self-torture; from another, it is greed for the only delight—and that considerable—which mortality can offer, surrender to the feelings, since these are the only things that move in a dead scene.

"The Raven" has a similar structure. The lover-narrator chooses exclusive preoccupation with the absoluteness of the death of his mistress and employs the fortuitous appearance of the raven who can utter but one word to quicken his feelings of despair rather than to explore ways out of them. It would be unthinkable, for example, for him to ask how long his pain is going to last, because "Nevermore" is not the answer he seeks to that proposition. He does not believe in the reality of escape. He has settled into his agony, and what flies into his ken must be made to keep it sensitive rather than to anesthetize it or replace it.

The technique of "A Dream Within a Dream" is present in a range of Poe's works, although it is nowhere else quite so manifest as in that poem. Those other works commence with a claustrophiliac acceptance of a desperate situation as unalterable and then move to an exploration of its subjective effects rather than to a concern with events in themselves. The objective situation is not capable of change. "The Imp of the Perverse," for example, begins with what is in effect an essay on perversity, so that when the homicidal narrator closes his account of his career with a series of questions, we already know the answers from the essay. The process of the tale is the process of keeping the sensibility alive and responsive to pain in a closed situation that threatens to dull it through repetition.

Or a tale may begin with a question, but a question so framed as already to contain the answer: "True!—nervous—very, very dreadfully nervous I had been and am; but why *will* you say that I am mad?"[22] The tale then moves on to provide the evidence for the anticipated assertion that the speaker is deranged.

Graphicality in literature is essential, Poe maintained (even while raising the question of why there was not such a word as "graphicality"), and it stems from the subjectiveness of the narrative viewpoint that leads the writer "to paint a scene less by its features than its effects."[23] In bringing his focus to bear on the psychological reaction of the undergoer rather than on the moral effects of the situation or the intellectual perceptions the reader might derive, he led the way into modern literature, as Edmund Wilson has affirmed. Poe's maddened position as outsider in an indiscriminate, democratic society fitted him for a life of misery and a posthumous career as the first pioneer into a literary landscape that had to be explored by the artist in flight from a social world that had no place for the imagination. It was not so much, for Poe, a matter of art for art's sake as it was art for the sake of those psychic processes otherwise ignored, denied, or maimed by bourgeois democratic institutions.

Through the technique of the already-answered question,

through, that is, an acceptance of the inconsequentiality of worldly circumstances and a resulting concentration on subjective reaction, Poe organized not only tales of passion but tales of reason, the other half of the self divided by democracy. The valid claim that he is the father of the modern detective story is based essentially on two of his tales of "ratiocination," "The Murders in the Rue Morgue" and "The Mystery of Marie Rogêt." Unlike those writers, such as Dickens and Collins, who accepted a consequential public world and so wrote stories of crimes that are eventually solved through the progressive uncovering of evidence, Poe did not unwind his tales step by step, adding one fact after another until all was known. His detective does not go out into the world and learn something that leads him to another thing and that to yet another. Rather, Poe's detective arrives at his solution in the isolation of his mind and does so before the story proper has gotten under way. While the other characters and the reader are baffled, the detective already knows the answer, from the same evidence that had provided them only with questions. The detective tale in Poe's development centers on the process of reasoning in the brilliant, isolated mind rather than on a series of increasingly revelatory events. It eschews the mechanical suspense of what will happen next, objectively, for the more intense subjective experience of how a superior mind came to the answer that already existed. The world is a closed system and therefore has no unanswered questions, although many a person is incapable of seeing that such is the case and therefore mistakenly seeks answers outside rather than inside himself.

The detective tale, then, parallels the structure of "A Dream Within a Dream." The closed problem is stated and by the end of the statement is already solved. For purposes of suspense, however, the fact that it has been solved, rather than the solution itself, closes this first movement of the tale. Then, in order to show how he arrived at the solution, the detective organizes a drama that reenacts the situation so that we, a bit chagrined by it all, can perceive why the question was already answered. With the emphasis placed on the drama of reasoning rather than the drama of events, Poe must create a narrator other than the detective, because to be privy to the detective's mind would be to know all instantly. That narrator, the detective's companion—as amiable, well-meaning, and vulnerable to deception as are we—intensifies the focus upon mental process as he wonders at each leap of the detective's mind. His presence completes the modern detective story.

In originating the genre Poe made clear that its central appeal was not so much in the horror of violence, although he developed all the grotesquerie available in the violent situation, as in the capacity of the mind to reduce the horror to rules. To be sure, there is an unbalanced differential between the gruesome mangling of the corpses on the Rue Morgue and the rational chain of events that led to their mutilation, one that echoes Poe's habit elsewhere of detailing the conflicting processes of the self without providing a harmonization. But whereas he was very much concerned with murder —especially one or another symbolic form of self-murder—when describing the tortured psyche in other tales, he is far less concerned with violence in the detective tales; their emphasis is upon ratiocinative processes. The horror these tales finally yield is the horror of the realization that extreme brutality *is* explicable.

In 1838, Poe was in New York, in transition, as it turned out, from Richmond, where he had written his earlier stories while employed by the *Southern Literary Messenger,* to Philadelphia, where from 1839 to 1843 he was to write the greater part of his best fiction while employed by magazines there. During his unsettled New York months he was compelled to undertake hackwork of an even more debasing character than earlier, so desperate was his condition, and he decided to compose a novel. His own strictures against literary works that could not be read at one sitting had to be subordinated to his sense of the opportunity for profit offered by a successful novel. Since he aimed at the popular market, Poe constructed his novel as an account of a voyage of exploration, a theme that promised to appeal to the large number of Americans who were following such adventures as the Wilkes expedition with eagerness and who were reading accounts of voyaging such as that of Benjamin Morell and even consuming the reports of committees of the Navy Department. The result was *The Narrative of Arthur Gordon Pym.* It is the longest fiction Poe ever wrote although, in the event, after its first part failed to attract a profitable readership, Poe discontinued it, stopping rather than ending, so that it is classified as a novelette rather than a novel.

In *Pym,* Poe writes essentially about an interior journey, for all his reliance on such works as the narrative of Morell. It is tempting, and many have yielded to the temptation, to view the literary exploration accounts of American authors of the period—Dana's *Two Years,* Thoreau's ramblings about New England and Canada, Melville's South Seas narratives, Parkman's *Oregon Trail,* for example—as self-explorations, and certainly that dimension exists and is important. But all such works are clearly tied first to an objective theme, a journey that had actually been made or a plot set in the recognizable physical world. Information about unfamiliar places is offered because these places do exist, and if supplying the reader's curiosity about them is not the primary purpose of the work, it counts as a strong second. Poe, however, departed immediately from physical reality, and although throughout *Pym* he offers quasi-scientific disquisitions on seamanship or natural phenomena for the purpose of verisimilitude, the former are patently copied from sources and the latter are patently invented—he is, that is, fabricating not only the tale but the natural world in which it is set. The physical reality through which Pym, the narrator, moves is constantly one of his own making, one that ceases to exist the moment he stops imagining it.

The signals of the subjective nature of even the objective world appear at once. In pitch, stress, and duration, the name Arthur Gordon Pym echoes the name Edgar Allan Poe. Moreover, Pym's native place, whence he ventures forth upon his exploration, is Edgartown. His voyaging is the free associating of Poe, and among the patterns that repeatedly emerge are the familiar themes of doubling, central to Poe's perception of the self, and of a self-contained natural world that does not recognize man. In that world, for example, a penguin colony is seen to organize life with geometrical precision, while neighboring humans in the fantastic subpolar village of Klock-Klock (who, as the name implies, are in imperfect relation with true time) live in slovenly disarray.

Two other patterns that will continue throughout Poe's work also appear. The first is that of rebellion against authority, which is seen not as reason, since reason in Poe is also a rebel, but as the governing moral concern of any collective enterprise, be it society or a ship. Pym cannot receive parental approval for his plans to voyage and so must embark secretly, in defiance of a family that commands him to integrate himself further into social life rather than launch into the unknown. As he proceeds to the ship in the disguise of a veteran seaman, Pym encounters his grandfather, the fountain of the family's wealth and the source of his good expectations for a profitable future, and he takes advantage of his disguise not only to deny his own identity, thereby disowning his family even before it can disown him for disobedience, but also to insult the venerable asserter of common sense and commercial profit. In this renunciation of his society, Pym also repudiates any connection his going to sea may have with the hardheaded motives of his fellow New Englanders. His friend and double, Augustus, he tells us,

> most strongly enlisted my feelings in behalf of the life of a seaman, when he depicted his more terrible moments of suffering and despair. For the bright side of the painting I had a limited sympathy. My visions were of shipwreck and famine; of death or captivity among barbarian hordes. . . . Such visions or desires—for they amounted to desires—are common, I have since been assured, to the whole numerous race of the melancholy among men—at the time of which I speak I regarded them only as prophetic glimpses of a destiny which I felt myself in a measure bound to fulfil.[24]

To go to sea is to seek his destiny in accordance with his temperament, which has already prophesied the events that will occur in order to complete him. The voyage is in one way the dramatization of the already-answered question, a search for the sensations of what is.

Moreover, in the only sailing experience he reports previous to his prolonged voyage, Pym goes out between sleep and breakfast, at dream time, and that night is the cause of a mutiny on board the ship with which he collides. As that mutiny is predictive of his rebellion against his family, so the *Grampus,* on which he stows away, is hardly out of sight of land before a mutiny replaces the authority of the captain (who is the father of his double, Augustus) with the authority of the lustiest and least scrupulous member of the crew. The mutineers, however, immediately divide again into a dominating group that seeks to continue the voyage as one of profitable piracy and another that seeks to continue the voyage for the sheer pleasurable excitement of sailing about with no purpose whatsoever other than a vague idea of finally arriving at a South Seas island of sensual gratification. Pym allies himself to the latter group and mutinies against the former with success, he and three others surviving.

The double repudiation of worldly motives is reenacted yet again when Pym, rescued from the derelict *Grampus* by the *Jane Guy,* successfully works on the practical captain of that vessel, persuading him to postpone his commercial intentions for the larger goal of charting an unknown region. In the event, Pym's bottomless appetite for new sensations results in the death of all but his double and himself. His remorse at being the cause of such a disaster, however, is perfunctory: "While . . . I cannot but lament the most unfortunate and bloody events which immediately arose from my advice, I must still be allowed to feel some degree of gratification at having been instrumental, however remotely, in opening to the eye of science one of the most intensely exciting secrets which has ever engrossed its attention."[25] The double self is again revealed: mad reason justifies disaster in the name of science while also saying —and the sentence with psychological truth may well have ended there—"I must still be allowed to feel."

The pattern of overthrowing authority regardless of consequences for the sake of the appetite for new sensations is accompanied by a pattern of entombments and resurrections. Pym does not suffer the actual deaths suffered by others because he yields himself up willingly to a series of symbolic deaths from which he can arise in the ripeness of time. Pym, that is, has no will toward achievement or self-definition, no mark to make on his environment, and no material profit to take from it. He has no ego to be killed. His motive is a hunger for the sensations that the given world can yield him.

Pym's bed in the hold of the *Grampus* is a coffinlike box, which he proceeds to inhabit "with feelings of higher satisfaction, I am sure, than any monarch ever experienced upon entering a new palace." The mutiny above decks and the shifting of cargo in the hold combine to trap Pym in his coffin, the entire hold becoming a tomb. He is thereby spared the actual death visited upon others at the time, and when he manages finally to emerge from the tomb he aids his faction in its mutiny not so much by acting upon their opponents physically, as his companions do, as by dressing in the clothing of a dead man and impersonating the living corpse so as to terrify the beholders into inaction while his comrades act. In the final episodes, his double and he escape the mass murder of another group of companions through undergoing a premature burial.

Arthur Gordon Pym is a glutton for sensations. Accepting the natural world in which he lives and the character with which he was endowed from birth, he closes the valves of his will and seeks to fill the pool of his consciousness. His commercial fellows are overpowered or die as the result of Pym's cravings. He alone escapes to tell the tale because he alone undergoes experience for the sake of how it feels, not so much sacrificing his identity toward that end—in a sense, he scarcely can be said to have one—as making that end his identity. He shadows Edgar Allan Poe, but he is not Poe; the voyage is away from Edgartown. Whereas, like Poe, he repudiates the ethic of his society, unlike Poe he has no perception of a world beyond the one he inhabits. That is why he must exhaust his world by experiencing it to its polar extreme, and that is why all his deaths are false deaths—he cannot arrive at the truth beyond consciousness of being, so that burial is but another sensation and he is doomed to arise from the tomb time and again. Pym's *Narrative* can have no ending; if it is to cease, it must be stopped.

From the extensive exercise in the exploitation of sensations which is Pym's voyage, Poe learned the limitation of such material. Pym, the servant, stocked the warehouse, but Poe, the master, now recognized the need to convert such stock to a poetic end rather than to display it for its own sake. Pym delivered to his countrymen the message that Poe, struggling with poverty in the year following the great panic, had for it: America was starving itself in its insistence on doing rather than feeling; it was not proceeding from a true grasp of the nature of life and so beggared the senses for the sake of the fiction of the will. Poe himself, after discovering what became of Pym, said farewell to the restrictions of America and sought attachment to the supernal. After Pym offered America a counter to the will, his author moved on to dramatize the perception that the divine oneness was not, as Emerson would have it, a flux that informed action in this world but a fixed beauty that demanded its analogue of the imagination.

Chapter Six

Social Nightmares: George Lippard and the Urban Apocalypse

When George R. Graham bought *The Gentleman's Magazine* in 1841, among the assets he acquired were a list of 3,500 subscribers and an editor named Edgar Allan Poe. Combining his new purchase with his former magazine, *Atkinson's Casket,* he renamed the whole *Graham's Magazine,* and embarked on a successful enterprise, although he quarreled with Poe and dismissed him within a year. When, in Hawthorne's *House of the Seven Gables,* Holgrave seeks to impress Phoebe Pyncheon, he tells her, "My name has figured, I assure you, on the covers of Graham and Godey, making as respectable an appearance, for aught I could see, as any of the canonized bead-roll with which it was associated."[1] *Godey's Lady's Book,* like *Graham's,* was a Philadelphia magazine, one to which the drifting Poe also brought his editorial talents, and the eminent list to which Holgrave referred included the names of Longfellow, Lowell, Cooper, and one Nathaniel Hawthorne.

In Philadelphia magazines were booming, but although more than one local author appeared in them, the emerging great names of the national literature were not of that city. Philadelphia had been the residence of all the American intellectuals Jefferson had cited in refutation of the claims that genius did not flourish in America, and the home of the nation's two greatest pioneering magazinists, Joseph Dennie and Charles Brockden Brown. It was the site of the majority of America's first great presses (among them those of Franklin and Bradford and preeminently of Sauer, who cast the first type made in America), and the place of publication of the first American editions of Shakespeare, Milton, and Spenser. Philadelphia in the 1840s maintained its prominence in publishing, but its literary prominence, brilliant beyond that of Boston and New York at the close of the eighteenth century, had faded. The rich mixture of enlightenment social theory, scientific inquiry, Quaker tolerance, and German speculativeness had yielded to squabbles between Catholics and nativists, professional narrowness, conservative banking manners, and the violence of agitation that surrounded abolitionism and responsive anti-Negro measures.

Between 1820 and 1860 the population of the United States rose 226 percent and the proportion of Americans living in cities rose 79 percent.[2] Although at the close of the period only one in five lived in a place of more than 2,500 inhabitants, the American city was moving toward definition as it encountered those problems that were to become the explicit concerns of social writers and activists after the Civil War: the visible distress of the urban poor (in 1829 throughout the country 75,000 persons had been jailed for debt, over half for amounts of less than twenty dollars); the violent clash of ethnic and religious groups; and the moral bleakness of alienated labor. Third to Boston and New York in intellectual prominence by the 1850s, and second to New York in commercial importance, Philadelphia was the first city to show the stresses of American urban life. It was, by location, the great border city between South and North, with an interest in slaveholding as well as a Quaker tradition of abolitionism; its population was a mixture of established British stock, equally established German stock now uneasily aware of the shift of economic power from its center on the farms, and burgeoning immigrant stock, with the Irish in the fore. In the realm of politics Philadelphia, with its system of autonomous neighborhoods attached to a downtown core, heightened the conflicts that elsewhere were blurred by a central municipal government.

Symbolic of the urbane culture that was passing and the urban travails that were to come was the endless bickering among all possible heirs over the will of Stephen Girard, who died in December 1830. Girard had been a penniless immigrant from France, blind in one eye, homely in person ("repulsive" many called him). Married to a serving girl (who spent the last twenty-five years of her life in an insane asylum), he began his commercial life as a small shopkeeper and made money during the Revolution by bottling claret and cider for the soldiers. After the war, he enlarged his business, first by trading with the West Indies, then by building ships for the Calcutta and China trade. Notoriously solitary and calculating—"a man whose sympathies appear to have been steeled against the world"[3]—he yet was a fervent republican who wore old clothes in the French fashion, labored on his own farm, decorated his house with the busts of Rousseau and Voltaire, and named ships for them as well as for Montesquieu and Helvetius. When the charter of the Bank of the United States, in which he had invested, was not renewed, he purchased it and established the Girard Bank, and so assiduously did he monopolize all debts that he could refrain from discounting them in hard times and meanwhile lend the government money against the return of flush times.

At his death Girard's estate was valued at some $7 million, but true to his principles, he left a scant $20,000 to friends and relatives, making charitable contributions to municipal causes, but leaving nothing to the individual needy. His most sensational bequest was that of $2 million for the establishment of a college for poor, white, male orphans. The terms of the bequest breathed into nineteenth-century, sentimentally Christian, politically conservative Philadelphia the air of its period of eighteenth-century glory, radiant with the perfectibility of man and the boundless future open to the pragmatic. The students of the college, said Girard,

> shall be instructed in the various branches of a sound education, comprehending reading, writing, grammar, arithmetic, geography, navigation, surveying, practical mathematics, astronomy, natural, chemical, and experimental philosophy, the French and Spanish languages (I do not forbid but I do not recommend the Greek and Latin languages) . . . I would have them taught facts and things, rather than words or signs; and especially, I desire, that by every proper means a pure attachment to our Republican institutions, and to the sacred rights of conscience, as guaranteed by our happy constitutions, shall be formed and fostered in the minds of the scholars.[4]

As further assurance that the sacred rights of conscience would be protected, Girard forbade any ecclesiastic, minister, or missionary from any sect whatsoever from a post or duty at the college. As a consequence, the bequest had a long career in the courts, challenged by those who asserted its invalidity because it sought to establish an infidel institution.

In the streets of Philadelphia in the 1830s crowds reacted to the Quaker-sponsored abolitionist activities with riots, and in the panic year of 1837 the unemployed of the city were so incensed by the establishment of an abolitionist meeting hall that they responded by burning the Shelter for Colored Orphans.[5] With mobs threatening antislavery meetings, the Philadelphia judges held that the menaced institutions rather than the mobs were the offenders, since the existence of such buildings as a Negro church constituted provocation.

Even as freed Negroes represented a threat to the working class with its large Irish constituency, so the Irish represented a threat to the earlier settlers, who, in 1837, founded the Native American Association, which, by 1844, had become a political party that had codified among its principles that (1) foreigners, although they could hold property, could not vote or hold office and could not be naturalized until after twenty-one years of residence; (2) the Bible, being nonsectarian, should be used in the schools as a reader; and (3) only native Americans should be appointed to public positions. Street clashes between Catholics and Native Americans ensued and the grand jury looking into the disturbances found for the Native Americans, judging that the difficulties were caused by "the efforts of a portion of the community to exclude the Bible from the public schools."[6]

Urban anarchy was sufficiently advanced in Philadelphia by the late 1840s to leave its mark even on that hallowed Philadelphia institution, the volunteer fire companies, which had been famous among Franklin's schemes for civic betterment. Now, rather than socially minded burghers, the men who turned out to pull the water-engines to the scene of the blaze were the economically marginal young street loafers, who pinned their social identity to the engine company to which they belonged and filled the fences of the city with graffiti that proclaimed their allegiance. At the fire they were sometimes as actively engaged in brawling with the gangs of other engines as in pouring water on the flames. To sound the alarm was to invite the attendance of the Killers, Blood-Tubs, Rats, Bouncers, or Schuylkill Rangers.

Poe walked the streets of this city, recognizing it in fiction if he recognized it at all, with but one story, "The Man of the Crowd," which, however, with his characteristic avoidance of the immediate, he set in London. It centered on a diabolic figure who moved nervously through the city from dusk to dawn, seeking always to batten on a throng, from homeward-bound workers, to gin-mill denizens, to early market men. Desperate and drooping when out of a crowd, maniacally gleeful when in sight of one, this figure, with his emblems of dagger and diamond, was, said Poe, the type of all hidden crime. This rare contemplation of the city shifted Poe somewhat from his center in the psyche and led him to proclaim the inescapable evil of mere density of population.

To Philadelphia also, from the suburb of Germantown, came George Lippard, an author who was to be one of Poe's few unwavering friends, but who unlike him was moved by the confusions of Philadelphia life to embrace the socially immediate in his fiction. He wrote, among other things, *The Monks of Monk Hall,* the most popular novel in America prior to *Uncle Tom's Cabin,* and he was a consistently successful journalist. His stories, larded though they were with vivid, sexual scenes and depictions of violence and degradation, always had an energetic social intent and a vital ability to create legends. George Lippard, widely read in his day and forgotten by the reading public ever since, translated the drama of Philadelphia into the melodrama of his pages. His sure instinct for the plight of the downtrodden provided both theme and audience for his wandering episodic plots, fashioned chiefly on the model of Eugène Sue's *Mysteries of Paris*. He constantly surpassed his model, however, in his depiction of sexual exploitation and the coming social apocalypse, even as he constantly fell short of it in all the details of literary execution. The counter Sue offered to the injustices of Parisian life was an unremitting benevolence exercised by a wealthy German prince, who employed a band of cohorts (most of them criminals he had reformed) to gather intelligence and execute his virtuous designs. No such figure of authority, wealth, and established power was available to the American artist, and Lippard tirelessly sought to develop a native source for the melodramatic righting of social wrongs. From his baffled struggle there arose in his penny-dreadful plots of sensational sex and sensational violence a vision of social injustice as the historical result of a deliberate conspiracy of the powerful few, and the need, therefore, for the proletarian opposition to proceed also by conspiracy. A secret cabal kept the masses divided and powerless, according to his fictions. Such notions found a responsive audience among those who read two-penny pamphlets and who existed in far greater numbers than did subscribers to *Graham's*.

Born in 1822 into the rural, German-American community on Philadelphia's fringe, George Lippard was a devout and somewhat mystical boy who sought expression in organized religion.[7] He was sent to a Methodist academy on the Hudson and intended to go on to college and become a minister, but before he was fifteen his father died and the family lost its farm home. About this time Lippard also withdrew from his formal education. One can only guess at the reasons—money was not a sufficient cause—but judging from his later novels, it is probable he experienced more than one disillusioning discrepancy between profession and practice on the part of his religious mentors in the areas of both social action and sexual conduct. His novels feature popular ministers who lust (with some success) after their female parishioners, and he criticizes the decision of almost all denominations not to extend their reforms into political economics. One Lippard character encounters Martin Luther and tells him: "As long as men like thee preach to the Poor the falsehood of a bestial submission to the Rich—so long as Men, chosen of God to give voice to the Poor man's agony, prove false to their sacred trust—so long will the efforts of the Poor, to free themselves, resemble only the struggles of a blinded giant, who rushes from his cell, and, knife in hand, mangles everything in his path."[8] In such a passage Lippard reveals his explicit view of the Protestant church's mission, one that brought him into close alliance with Philadelphia's maverick Universalist preachers, and also his persisting implicit struggle against and attraction to proletarian violence, which he saw as not quite thinkable and yet amply justified.

In 1837, the young Lippard drifted into Philadelphia, a penniless youngster—in later years he represented himself at that stage as a homeless orphan, not a complete falsehood, since his father was dead and the homestead gone, but not quite accurate, since his mother and sisters were alive and maintaining a residence. His social instincts sent him to clerking and studying law in a firm of prominent, politically involved Democratic lawyers, and his duties quickly acquainted him with the proceedings in the criminal and debtor courts, while his firm's populist allegiances sharpened a proletarian consciousness already shaped by religious fervor and economic hardship. Four years later when he gave up the study of law, Lippard was so familiar with the underside of Philadelphia and so energetically engaged in recording it that he moved with ease into the position of reporter for the Philadelphia *Spirit of the Times,* one of the city's lurid, cheap newspapers. From that time until his death in 1854 at the age of thirty-two of the tuberculosis that killed his wife, his child, and all his siblings save one before him, Lippard was a financially successful writer and journalist. In 1848, he founded a weekly, *The Quaker City,* in part because he wanted his own platform for the celebration of the revolutions of that year, which he hailed as the critical turning point that would lead to the social regeneration of the world. Like his other ventures, the weekly was a success, selling well at five cents the copy or two dollars for an annual subscription. But in the wake of the failures of 1848, Lippard abandoned all but the most propagandistic writings—even ceasing to write novels, although they had always had a high quotient of social protest in them—and from 1849 turned his major efforts toward founding and promoting a secret society, the Brotherhood of the Union. As did his literary efforts, the Brotherhood found an immediate constituency and survived through the century in chapters from Pennsylvania to Texas. Modeled superficially upon the Masonic and Odd Fellows orders, to both of which Lippard belonged, the Brotherhood differed from them in the socio-economic aims that were its chief reason for being.

In his fictions Lippard had always advocated fighting the coercive powers of the capitalists with the association of workers, modeled on ideas in Fourier and Michelet and weakly manifested in some of the labor organizations of his day. But from the point at which he accepted the failure of the 1848 revolutions, he modified his idea of association to mean secret society. In describing the Brotherhood to prospective members, Lippard wrote that it was to be

> a combination of a certain number of men, bound to each other by a common vow, dignified and strengthened by ceremonial rites, and having for its object some great action, in politics, religion or morals. . . . Not now need we touch upon the constantly increasing degradation of the Workers of America. To remove this degradation or elevate the Worker to his true position, to give him the power of Capital to defend his rights against Capital, you must teach him the great mystery of Combination. . . . In the Secret Society the great purpose of the entire Order, is the Supreme Ruler. The hundred thousand minds of the Secret Society form one Great Mind, their hundred thousand separate dollars one great purse. It is a Secret Society which must bind the masses together; which must . . . pervade the Union with one great idea. . . . The idea is feasible. It is eminently practical.[9]

A sufficient number of workers found this appealing so that at the time of his death Lippard was in good hopes that the Brotherhood, to which he had exclusively devoted the past two years of his life, was on its way toward achieving the goals he had set it.

In the period 1844–54, which saw the publication of *The Scarlet Letter* and *Moby-Dick,* George Lippard was, in all probability, America's most widely read novelist. The qualification stems only from the unreliability of sales figures for the period, and the varying relationships between sales and readership; that is, one who sold widely in the cheapest formats, as did Lippard, may not have been read by many more readers than are represented by sales figures, whereas more respectable writers such as Cooper, whose books were more durably printed and bound, may have reached a wider audience, in the home and through circulation in rental libraries, than is indicated by the sales figures alone. It is certain, however, that in his day Lippard was a surefire seller. His first novel, *The Monks of Monk Hall* (titled *The Quaker City* in subsequent editions), ran initially in ten separate pamphlets, commencing their appearance in September 1844, and when the first two-thirds were bound together, 48,000 copies were sold within six months. When the whole appeared as a book in May 1845, 60,000 copies were sold within a year, and within five years it ran through twenty-seven editions, although, it must be noted, no edition was larger than 4,000 copies and some were possibly as small as 1,000. Still, the popularity of *The Quaker City* was phenomenal, and one small sign of it is the common acceptance of the appellation. Quaker City, meaning Philadelphia—as obvious as it may seem—was not used before Lippard. Although he never matched such sales again, Lippard always found a ready and profitable readership for his subsequent fictions.

These were roughly of two kinds: historical fictions and legends centering on the American Revolution or glorifying the Mexican War; and urban novels of sensational criminal doings, social conflicts, and sexual seductions along the lines of *The Quaker City.* The works in the former category today defy the patience of all but the most determined historians, although in them Lippard so tellingly mixed legend with fact that he became the originator of more than one cherished piece of American folklore; most notoriously he is the inventor and popularizer of the notion that the Liberty Bell rang out independence, and no subsequent debunking by historians has made a dent on its popular acceptance. In justice to the courage and magnanimity of Lippard, it should also be noted that his enthusiasm for the Mexican War stemmed from his Christian Socialism, which idealized the West as the potential site of America's imminent return to revolutionary principles, a place where labor could establish itself free of exploiting entrepreneurs. When he came to perceive that the West, although still unfenced, was, in fact, already controlled by the moneyed interests as certainly as was any eastern factory, and was, therefore, to be the continued scene of the degradation of American labor, Lippard not only retracted his approval of the Mexican War but accelerated his plan for a secret society of yeomen bound to the cause of radical, Christian labor. This, he now believed, was the only answer to the way in which populist fervor had been manipulated.

Lippard offered *The Quaker City* to the public in "the same sincerity" in which he wrote it, as, he said, "an illustration of the life, mystery and crime of Philadelphia."[10] If his subsequent career did not amply demonstrate that his social outrage and religious principles were, indeed, sincere, this prefatory claim, on the basis of the novel alone, might be suspected of making the usual perfunctory assertion of virtuous intent as a license for indulging in prurience. The germ of the work was supplied by a notorious Philadelphia criminal case—the trial of a young man of good family who had killed his close friend because the latter had seduced his sister. As Lippard elaborated the tale in monthly installments, this became but one in a series of barely connected episodes of social and sexual degradation. The episodes were held together by setting more than by plot: they all occurred in or were connected with Monk Hall, a mansion within a retired part of the city maintained as a club and house of assignation by prominent male citizens, the "Monks." In Monk Hall these judges, ministers, and merchants directly indulged those lusts that in more devious ways governed their public action also. They thus revealed that their night side was their true side and in so doing revealed the viciousness at the heart of the powerful class in America.

Despite its claptrap transporting of the fictional castles and monasteries that were the settings of European gothic fictions to a modern American city, Monk Hall finally asserts a solidity and meaning because it embodies a vision of the city. On the upper stories, connected by corridors, stairways, and landings, are the chambers of luxury—bedrooms, dining rooms, gaming and drinking rooms. On the ground and basement levels are the kitchens and the dungeons to which troublemakers—the occasional reformer and the stubborn virgin—are consigned to death. But in addition to the architectural connection of the upper to the lower and the explicit fee-paying connection of the Monks to the bawds and ruffians who serve them within the hall, there is also a series of instant communications—secret panels that admit the pander directly to the bedchamber and trapdoors that dispatch the victim directly into the hands of the murderer. In Lippard's handling, the conventional castle of gothic horrors becomes a metaphor of the city, in which the wealthiest and most respectable have direct communication with the most vicious, who serve them in exploitation of the majority in the middle. The crew of criminal servants are, in effect, embodiments of the dominating vices of their masters, so that at certain crises the monstrous underling calls the tune for judge, minister, or merchant. To notice this is not to attribute a studied symbolic intent to the author of this carelessly written, rambling, yet arresting patchwork of a novel, but to recognize that his strength and interest resided in a social conscience that structured the dreadful doings into a dramatic vision of the city as American Apocalypse.

Within the larger and essentially unsystematic apocalyptic vision of each novel, Lippard at one point or another forced to the surface a specific apocalyptic vision. In *The Quaker City* it is a dream had by Devil-Bug, doorman and chief assassin at Monk Hall, who sees a Philadelphia of the future in which Independence Hall is in ruins and the shrouded dead walk the streets unremarked by the living. It is the day of the coronation of America's first king. At the tail of the procession the king leads toward his throne march the slaves of the city:

> Chains upon each wrist and want upon each brow. Here they were, the slaves of the cotton Lord and the factory Prince; above their heads a loom of iron rising like a gibbet in the air, and by their sides the grim overseer. Hurrah, hurrah! This is a liberal mob; it encourages manufactures. The monopolist forever, they yelled, his enterprise gives labour to the poor, hurrah, hurrah! The slaves lifted up their eyes at the sound of that tumultuous hurrah, and muttered to each other, of glad green fields, and a farmer's life, and then they clanked their chains together, and gazed at the ruins of Independence Hall.[11]

Before the king can be crowned, clouds gather and upon them appears the inscription "Wo Unto Sodom," after which the city is destroyed by thunder, steam, and terrestrial convulsion.

The socialism at the base here is the familiar golden-age scheme of a society that will advance to true happiness when it returns to a standard that had once been in force. There is no sense of the dynamic of history, which Marx was soon to expound. Lippard's eternal social verities are drawn from the teachings of Jesus, whom he saw and represented as a laborer who came to lead his fellow laborers, and these verities are made flesh by Tom Paine, George Washington, and Thomas Jefferson, who founded an ideal America. Forces of evil have undone their work, the city being the crowning achievement of that undoing, and Lippard, in his vividly animated fictional protests, finally offers a future that is a retrogression to the lost golden moment of the past—"glad green fields, and a farmer's life."

"History . . . correctly interpreted," Lippard wrote, "is the perpetual Revelation of Almighty God."[12] America as the city of God informed his legends of the Revolution, and his treatment of conditions in his own day was a dramatization of the battle between the agents of God's revealed will and the forces of darkness that in His secret will He permitted to have sway. In a late novel the spokesman for the dark forces says that in America the European despot will be replaced by the money changer, and that the lords of the land in the developing West will soon own the lives and souls of the millions who work on the land. "The very *presence* of the African race," this devilish voice predicts in 1851, "is sure to give birth at first to Disunion, and then to a war of races—a war of annihilation between the white and the black." In America all the injustices of European history will be recapitulated on a grander scale: "Progress is a lie. Mankind were born to be the prey of a few oppressors—born to work, suffer, and die. The instruments of degradation may change their names, but they are always the same."[13]

Lippard's counter to this prediction equally accepts the essentially mythic nature of the human condition, its status as a perpetual manifestation of a struggle between the evil, powerful few and the virtuous, powerless many, and claims that it is possible to regenerate through enacting the combined vision of Jesus and Washington, seen frequently by him as the religious and social faces of the same verity.

Wisps of the class struggle float through Emerson, Thoreau, and Hawthorne and are present more explicitly in Melville and Whitman. On the whole, however, it does not form an important conscious part of their outlook. The principal social conflict they make manifest is that between the imaginative questioning thinker and his self-assured, materialistic countrymen. Broadly put, the conflict is between the faded power of the old landed and professional families as represented by their actual descendants (Emerson, Hawthorne, Melville) and their yeoman allies (Thoreau, Whitman) and the new power of the prospering middle class. They do not dramatize an outrage at economic exploitation because they do not see American society as so fixed as to have cut off the possibility of American society's reflecting the true nature of man. In protean America the ablest writers were attracted by the question of just what that nature was. They left the class struggle to those such as Lippard who were at bottom men of simple, even touching, faith in the unquestionable goodness of humanity and who were therefore unaffected by questions of man's identity and his relation to nature, the deity, and the determining past. For such, a mixture of admirable Christian socialism and patriotic Revolutionary hagiography was the model of what was and could be again.

Lippard encountered opposition to his fictions because of their lurid content rather than their social protest. "The insipid French novels," said Alonzo Potter, Episcopal bishop of Pennsylvania, "with which our country is deluged are the seeds of robbery, arson, piracy and assassination."[14] What, cheerfully responds Lippard, does he mean by robbery—the act of a wretch who steals for bread? Or does he mean

> the act committed by a Church which *takes* the land of unborn generations—holds it by trick, by subterfuge, by every form of fraud—keeps it and enjoys its revenues, until the *taken* land becomes the eighth or ninth part of the greatest City in America, and is valued at forty million of dollars?[15]

The reference is to the Episcopal Trinity Church in New York.

When he responds to the charge of sexual viciousness, Lippard with malicious delight contrasts the virtues of Sue and of Sand, whom he confidently declares the bishop never read, with the demoralizing effect of *The Trial of Bishop Onderdonk,* a published report of the ecclesiastical proceedings against the Episcopal bishop of New York on allegations that he made improper sexual advances to females in his flock, a book that was not recommended reading for the young or the modest.

As for assassination, against the crime of the crazed murderer set this:

> A Church of God owns and rents in the City of New York, whole blocks or squares of houses which are devoted to Prostitution. The innocent working girls of Philadelphia, Lowell and Boston—aye and of New York too—have been lured from their homes and plunged into these very Brothels which are owned by this Colossal Church. How many *souls* have been assassinated in those hells of pollution . . . by THE CHURCH![16]

Beneath such sparring can be detected the connection Lippard felt between sexual behavior and the social system. The respectable society that cried out against his sensational scenes of seduction was one that enshrined the family and emphasized female chastity; women were thought not to have spontaneous sexual appetites, so that sexual desire, when it appeared in them, must have been calculatingly aroused by men. Lippard did not reject this physiology of female sexuality, but he despised the social goals it was made to serve. The sacredness of the family was a luxury enjoyed by those who had no material wants, and the ideal of the chastity of even the married woman was maintained by her husband's exploiting laboring girls.

Without Lippard's outrage, but with a shrewder sense of the invalidity of the "scientific" view of woman's sexuality, his witty contemporary in journalism Fanny Fern could make sly fun of it in imagery that, apparently, went unpenetrated by the many proper people who found her wholesome reading. A respectable woman speaking about her snug and prosperous husband says, "He does every thing—mercantile and matrimonial—by rule, square, and compass. When the proper time arrives, it 'comes off,' and it don't a fraction of a second before." She further reports that "I can double Cape Horn while he is saying, 'My dear.' "[17] Just what the lady is referring to is deliberately left vague by Fern; perhaps she is talking about the way they go over the household accounts. Fern, in the main, confined herself to glancing, covert attacks on her society's views of female sexuality, accepting their status as conventions needed to nourish middle-class America.

Lippard, with far less insight into woman's sexual nature, accepts the ideal of female chastity and the belief that women feel no spontaneous sexual desire, and precisely because he does so he writes his tinted scenes of seduction. He is outraged at the tacit exclusion of the powerless women of the poor from the enjoyment of their "natural" modesty. For him, seduction was a metaphor of economic exploitation.

> Soft murmurs, like voices heard in a pleasant dream, fell gently over her ears, the languor came deeper and more mellow over her limbs; her bosom rose no longer quick and gaspingly, but in long pulsations, that urged the full globes in all their virgin beauty, softly and slowly into view. Like billows they rose above the folds of the night robe, while the flush grew

> warmer on her cheek, and her parted lips deepened into a rich vermillion tint.[18]

This of a maiden lured into a luxurious Monk Hall bedroom —daring writing, what with the hallowed single bosom of conventional fiction rhythmically turning into the unmentionable plural as *o* and *l* are stressed in word after word to the heated point of "flush," after which *ee* and short *i* dominate. But what are this virgin and others like her doing in their night clothes in Monk Hall? They are powerless:

> Seduce a *rich* maiden? Wrong the daughter of a *good* family? Oh, this is horrible; it is a crime only paralleled in enormity by the blasphemy of God's name. But a poor girl, a *servant,* a domestic? Oh, no! These are fair game for the gentleman of a fashionable society; upon the wrongs of such as these, the fine lady looks with a light laugh and a supercilious smile.[19]

The exception who proves the rule is the maddeningly attractive Dora Livingstone, who, as the wife of a wealthy man, possesses resources in addition to her beauty and yet is discovered lying naked in the arms of her lover at Monk Hall. Do women, then, have lust after all? No, she explains. She is there because she believes her lover to be an English nobleman. She herself is the granddaughter of a carpenter and proud of it:

> Give me the honest Mechanic at the bench, if we must have a nobility, for your true republican nobleman: not the dishonest Bank-Director at the desk! But if you pass the Mechanic aside—whose honest vote sustains the republic—if you pass him aside when you form your Aristocracy, then, I say, give us the Titles and the Trappings of an English nobility! Let us at once have a Throne and a Court, a King and Courtiers.[20]

And so Dora is driven to lewdness by the failure of the American republic to make good on its democratic origins. In a corrupt time she embraces the Old World aristocrat rather than the imitation of him represented by her banker husband because she cannot have, since her country does not supply, nature's real aristocrat, the honored craftsman.

His political beliefs gave Lippard strength to respond when such as Bishop Potter deplored his work, but he was edgy when faced with the accusation that, regardless of his subject matter, he wrote in a wretched, subliterary style. Although his friend Poe was not one of those who made the explicit charge, he clearly stood as a model of all that Lippard was not as a writer and seemed to suggest that literature and explicit social commitment did not mix. In framing a reply to such notions, Lippard allied himself with the tradition of Protestant radicalism that saw the high value placed on learned subject matter and elegance of style as a strategy whereby the powerful kept the oppressed immured in silence. Leveller protesters against Cromwellian authority in England and Quaker and Anabaptist protesters against the New England orthodoxy had sounded this strain, equating literary style with concealment and lack of finish with honesty. They believed there was such a thing as nonstyle in which realities reported themselves directly in words, and to this Lippard also added the suggestion—later to be improved by naturalistic romancers such as Frank Norris—that literary polish was, in effect, an effeminate cover-up for lack of authorial virility.

In his contribution to the tradition that writers with a social conscience had too urgent a vocation to be able to indulge in "literary" matters, Lippard said:

> A strong man may make a bad style popular: the reader does not look at the dress, but at the form which that dress serves to clothe. A weak man may write ever so euphoniously; style, grammar, and words all correct, and of the smoothest sound; and yet he can never become a popular writer. The pretty dress of his words cannot conceal his emptiness.

Accordingly, he was unhesitating in identifying what should be the source of the great national literature, which seemed so far to be evading the culture:

> We need unity among our authors; the age pulsates with a great Idea, and that Idea is the right of Labor to its fruits, coupled with the re-organization of the social system. Let our authors write of this, speak of it, and then we shall have something like a National Literature.[21]

Holgrave, in *The House of the Seven Gables,* was to have a similar perception at one point in his development. But he was open also to the pleasures of American life. Ultimately attached to a rural and suburban society that gave a more tranquil perspective than did Lippard's apocalyptic Philadelphia, he saw his way to the slow historical redressing of the social injustices he noted.

Finally Lippard came to the conclusion that fiction was not the best vehicle for his social purposes, and he founded his Brotherhood. In stressing secrecy, ritual, and other assorted pieces of mumbo jumbo (the gothic now retranslated into reality), he was, on the face of it, moving away from a faith in the ability of the popular will to make itself felt in America—away from a belief in the effectiveness of political processes as a means to reform—and was insisting that, since corruption proceeded by secrecy, no opposition other than a counterconspiracy could hope to succeed.

Images of conspiracy had abounded in his novels. The Monks themselves were conspirators of a kind, but not systematically so. Their secrecy was primarily that of the hypocrite, although in *The Quaker City* Lippard seems groping for further connections, for ways of suggesting that what goes on in Monk Hall directly affects the way in which the masses of Philadelphia are manipulated. In his succeeding novels, images of the hidden cabal that determines the public actuality multiply. Forthright as he was in defense of the political rights of Roman Catholics, Lippard nevertheless was fascinated by the Society of Jesus as an organization with a definite concealed program for the conquest of America. He suggested that the honest Irish laborers were being used as pawns by Jesuits who were the agents provocateurs behind the Know-Nothing party. An agent from Rome explains:

> Hundreds of thousands of foreigners of our faith arrive in this city [New York] every year. Be it our task to plan an eternal barrier between these men and those who are American citizens by birth. To prevent them from mingling with the American people, from learning the traditions of American history, which gives the dogma of Democracy its strongest hold upon the heart, to *isolate* them, in the midst of the American nation. In a word, the first step is, to array . . . an envenomed *Native American* party.[22]

Besides keeping their own followers malleable, with this policy, the Jesuits will arouse public sympathy for Roman Catholics. It will be a means toward the ultimate goal, Roman Catholic control of the West and a linkage with the Roman Catholic hegemony in Latin America.

American capital also proceeds through hidden, consistent plotting. In an amazing scene that foreshadows twentieth-century visions of universal espionage, Lippard takes us into the seven secret vaults of the Van Huyden Estate, the nation's largest capitalistic enterprise, which is run by so complex a network of managers and agents that no one can be certain who is at the center and what the ultimate purpose of the enormous profit-making is. Each of the first six of the vaulted rooms is devoted to the records of one of the six major areas of investment with which the estate is concerned. The seventh, however, serves a larger, mistier, and more menacing purpose:

> Those shelves contain *briefs* of the personal history of prominent persons, and of persons utterly obscure: records of remarkable facts, in the history of particular families: brief but interesting portraitures of incidents, societies, governments and men; the contents of those shelves, sir, is knowledge, and knowledge that would be a fearful Power. . . . you stand in the Secret Police Department of the Van Huyden estate.[23]

In the novel proper Lippard does not know what to do with this particular insight that secret intelligence is power; it does not function effectively in the plot. But even though indigestible, it forced its way into the novel as a result of Lippard's imagining the nature of control in his society and is predictive of a world that was to be.

Although he was unique in the breadth of his insistence that social evil was the result of conspiracy and had to be met by conspiracy, Lippard was rooted in the widespread if frequently inarticulate folklore of paranoia in his society. Writing to his daughter Catherine from Philadelphia in 1830, for example, Lyman Beecher opens his plan to move to Cincinnati: "The moral destiny of our nation, and all our institutions and hopes, and the world's hopes, turn on the character of the West, and the competition now is for that of preoccupancy in the education of the rising generation in which

Catholics and infidels have got the start of us. . . . If we gain the West, all is safe; if we lose it, all is lost."[24]

Moreover, when Bishop Potter laid robbery, arson, piracy, and assassination at the door of the French novel, he meant the French novel as a symbol of the ideas of the French Revolution, which were, he believed, but one manifestation of the secret designs of a cabal older than the Revolution, one designed to overthrow revealed religion in favor of natural religion and to replace established governments with anarchy and the family with free love. His remarks were attached to the complex of muddled fears that slumbered in the popular mind after the specific historical bases for them had been rationally discredited.

These vague but powerful prejudices battened on the mythology of the Bavarian Order of the Illuminati, an actual order founded in Bavaria in 1776. It was a child of the Aufklärung and was devoted to the attaining of human progress through training men to perfect their reason and self-knowledge so as to dominate their own savagery and influence their fellow men to like action.[25] It was a local and insignificant society until 1780, when, under the leadership of Baron Adolf Franz Friedrich Knigge, it allied itself with Freemasonry and enjoyed a brief vogue, enrolling some 2,000 members, among them Herder, Goethe, and Pestalozzi. In 1784, however, the Duke of Bavaria moved to suppress the order and by 1788 it was dead.

The order was only one of hundreds of examples of Enlightenment idealism—Ben Franklin, too, founded a secret society for moral improvement—and was of trifling consequence as a living organism. However, it went on to lead an amazing life as a ghost. Conservative churchmen, politicians, and propagandists, incensed at the new ideas flooding forth to challenge pieties they regarded as inviolable, sought some explanation for them that was simpler and more striking than that of social evolution. The seed was planted by the arch-conservative *Wiener Zeitschrift,* which noted that Mirabeau was in Berlin in 1786–87 and after his return to France retained communication with German friends. On this basis, the journal proceeded to affirm that while in Germany he had joined the Order of the Illuminati, and that back in France he had enlisted others in the designs of the society, with the result that they had arranged the French Revolution on command from the order.

This patently ridiculous legend stimulated two separate but equally threatened conservative authors at the close of the century, the Scot John Robison and the Frenchman Abbé Barruel. Each wrote a book "proving" that the evils of contemporary society were directly traceable to the Illuminati, who still survived as a potent international conspiracy against church, state, and family. Detailed refutations of the unfounded claims were abundant, chief among them the inability of the accusers to point to any existing cell of the Illuminati, but the notion slumbered on. In America, the reactionary Massachusetts minister Jedediah Morse, faced with a slackening of clerical and Federalist authority in his world, attributed it to the covert activities of the order, which, he said, approved of self-murder, condemned patriotism and the rights of private property, and aimed to control the schools, literary societies, newspapers, and the postal service through insinuating its members into positions of distinction (hence, it may be remarked in passing, the Illuminati's twentieth-century reappearance as the real brains behind international communism). By 1800 Morse was laughed into silence, and privately admitted he had gone too far, but Timothy Dwight took up the theme in Connecticut and William Cobbett in Pennsylvania. Even Alexander Hamilton believed a league had been formed between the apostles of irreligion and anarchy, the officials of the French government, and the Democratic Societies of America, which opposed Federalist policy. "Its activity has indeed been suspended," he said, thereby obviating the need for him to point to its concrete presence, "but the elements remain, concocting for new eruptions as occasion shall permit."[26] The success of Jefferson's party again laughed the legend out of countenance, but the ghost keeps walking and has been seen by some in contemporary America.

Just as Bishop Potter was irresponsibly willing to invoke the dormant legend, so Lippard, frustrated by the survival of social injustice in Europe and its unchecked progress in America, accepted it also. From the many conspiracies he had dramatized in his novels he planned a counterconspiracy, the Brotherhood of the Union, which claimed the Order of the Illuminati in its pedigree: "The secret orders of the present day are but the broken details of a Great Order of Brotherhood, which at one time extended its mysterious Circle over the entire Globe. . . . Our Order, alone, has preserved its purity through the long night of ages."[27] Furthermore, he proudly accepted the idea that the Illuminati had played a causal role in the French Revolution.

The nightmares of Edgar Allan Poe are those of a psyche feeding on itself in isolation from the delusions of the apparent world. Ultimate explanation must be imagined and ultimate control exercised in a literature of precise effect. There, if style is adequate, reside the unity and balance we cannot hope to expect of our world.

His friend George Lippard rushed to embrace the actual as the real, and, brushing aside literary canons as obstacles between writing and its social potency, attempted to affect his society in his novels. Instead of Poe's marble-white and icy maidens, he offered warm and panting women in the throes of aroused desire; instead of Poe's enclosed spaces that numbed the will and widened the perception, he offered a city of conflicts that demanded strenuous action. Yet Lippard, too, ended in nightmare: reality as the product of conspiracy and the city as its apocalyptic consummation.

For both the writer as detached patrician and the writer as committed socialist, America was a chaos, a dream within a dream, a piece of theater manipulated by hidden producers. Poe was an artist whose life and works have exerted a lasting influence on modern letters; Lippard was a piece-worker whose writing only occasionally rises above that of the mere hack, but whose social vision did provide the first telling images of modern political paranoia. His nightmares are a cultural complement to those of Poe. Together they reveal the underside of America's proclaimed concept of itself, and embody the society's psychological terrors and political fears.

Chapter Seven

The Great Conservative: Hawthorne and America

Social woes are relative. Visiting America during the years 1834–36, the English writer and reformer Harriet Martineau was surprised at the fears for the future expressed by some of her American acquaintances: fear of the poor, of the unruly politics of the land-hungry Westerners, of the rising number of immigrant laborers. The inequities that furnished the scenery for Lippard's apocalyptic dream seemed slight to her when she compared them with the economic oppression she knew to exist in England. The sheer abundance of natural resources obviated the conditions of class warfare: "It is shorter and easier to obtain property by enterprise and labour in the United States," she noted, "than by pulling down the wealthy."[1] Like Emerson, she believed that the poor were not fixedly so but only the poor of the rich, and as Emerson was later to do when comparing their two countries, she felt that the raggedness of America, so frequently the topic of adverse comment by her countrymen, was actually the sign of a happy condition: "Nature is there the empress, not the handmaid. Art is her inexperienced page, and no longer the Prospero."[2] In her enthusiasm for an atmosphere free of the moral insolence in which she felt the English worker dwelled she went so far as to develop a positive relish for the conceited claims American braggarts shouted down the bell of her ear trumpet. They were a refreshing change from mock modesty and moral cowardice; besides, they were a necessary makeweight against the more dangerous American tendency to idolatrize popular opinion.

Martineau was especially taken with Salem, a town that struck her as the very model of what was right with America. There, she said, was a community of 14,000 with "more wealth in proportion to its population than perhaps any town in the world."[3] The Salemites know the Russian and Scandinavian coasts, speak of the Azores as they would of a nearby village, tell stories of Mozambique and Madagascar, and display ivory in their sitting rooms, shells from Ceylon in their cabinets, and Chinese copies of English prints in their portfolios. They double Cape Horn "and land, some fair morning, at Salem, and walk home as if they had done nothing very remarkable."[4]

All this was perhaps more exotic than typical, but she believed the socio-economic base was characteristic of what could be hoped for in general from the American experiment:

> What a state of society it is when a dozen artisans of one town—Salem—are seen rearing each a comfortable one-story (or, as the Americans would say, two-story) house, in the place with which they have grown up! when a man who began with laying bricks criticises, and sometimes corrects his lawyer's composition; when a poor errand-boy becomes the proprietor of a flourishing store, before he is thirty; pays off the capital advanced by his friends at the rate of 2,000 dollars per month; and bids fair to be one of the most substantial citizens of the place![5]

In that Salem lived Nathaniel Hawthorne, not in a two-story artisan's house but in a gabled structure of relative antiquity, as befitted the direct descendant of a family that had figured in the town's annals ever since the first Hawthorne (or Hathorne) had assisted at its founding in the seventeenth century. The family fortune, however, had declined steadily through the following century, and Nathaniel's widowed mother—his father, a ship's captain, died of fever in Dutch Guiana when his son was four—was dependent upon the assistance of her own family to support her two daughters, her son, and herself. The past glory of the Hawthornes did not serve her in republican America as it might have done in a more aristocratic land. "Amid the fluctuating waves of our social life," Hawthorne wrote in *The House of the Seven Gables,* "somebody is always at the drowning-point." Although the tragedy is familiar through repetition in America, it is, nevertheless, "felt as deeply, perhaps, as when an hereditary noble sinks below his order. More deeply; since with us, rank is the grosser substance of wealth and a splendid establishment, and has no spiritual existence after the death of these, but dies hopelessly along with them."[6]

In losing their wealth the Hawthornes had lost their place. American society in general accorded no respect to rank without money, and Salem's aristocracy in particular was relentless. Its members had an old reputation for inhospitality, one that had become a legend among the more genial members of the Boston aristocracy. Salem was noted for the East Indian trade, as opposed to the China trade more commonly associated with Boston, and Richard Henry Dana of Boston said, "The Boston people used maliciously to abbreviate East India merchants, into 'Stingy Merchants.'" He speculated that Salem's notorious social chill arose from "that small class of the earlier merchants who gave Salem its commercial importance, who were notoriously mean & eager men, disregardful of courtesies, & who set an example & fixed a habit wh. it is not easy to break through."[7]

Certainly, Nathaniel Hawthorne spared himself the effort to break through. Living at home after his graduation from Bowdoin College, where his financial support had come, in good part, from his maternal Maine relatives, he apprenticed himself to his books, the demands of the magazine publishers, and his own imagination, and for twelve years sat and wrote in what he later (and somewhat melodramatically) termed his "dismal chamber." When, in 1837, he gathered some of his pieces, previously printed anonymously or pseudonymously in the magazines, and published them as a book, *Twice-Told Tales,* he regarded this publication of his name together with a body of his work as an attempt finally to open an intercourse with the world. In the following year he had his say about his native town in "The Sister Years," a piece distributed in pamphlet form by the newsboys of Salem at the close of 1838 to remind their subscribers that the season of gifts had arrived. In the narrative, the departing 1838 greets her sister, the arriving 1839, and briefs her on the condition of Salem. The big event was the arrival of the railroad, which now might be looked to as the means that will finally carry off the immense accumulation of musty prejudices that bedevil the town. No place is in greater need of a freer circulation of society than is Salem, because, says 1838, "the moral influence of wealth, and the sway of an aristocratic class . . . from an era far beyond my memory, has held firmer dominion here than in any other New England town."[8]

And, indeed, Hawthorne's move outward was accompanied by a greater general social circulation. In another part of town lived the Peabodys, a substantial and respectable doctor's family, with, however, an attachment to the glory that should have been theirs through the fact that Mrs. Peabody had been a Palmer.[9] The three Peabody girls romanticized over their elegant origins, but they grew also into an awareness of the dynamic changes that were coming to pass in their society. Elizabeth set out to right the world's wrongs, and along her path was tutored in Greek by Emerson. She served as unpaid secretary to the great Unitarian minister William Ellery Channing, preparing from his notes fifty sermons for print; also took the notes that led to two of Bronson Alcott's books; assisted in the publication of the Transcendentalists' journal, *The Dial;* and busied herself about every worthy cause from the rights of Indians and women through abolitionism to the virtues of homeopathic medicine, which she vended in the bookstore she opened in Boston, together with the most complete list of modern French and German books available in America. The liberal minister, James Freeman Clarke, said of her "that she was always engaged in supplying some want that had first to be created."[10] But many of those wants were finally felt by her society, so that long after the Civil War the busy, unworldly woman with her broad face framed with white curls was recognized as she bustled about her errands on the streets of Boston. She had become a symbol of that city's passion for moral earnestness and was fondly called "the Grandmother of Boston." Her most notorious portrait is the Miss Birdseye of Henry James's *The Bostonians*. Thomas Wentworth Higginson offered a kinder but somewhat similar picture:

> I best associate her with my last interview a little before her death, when I chanced to pick her out of a snowdrift into which

> she had sunk overwhelmed during a furious snowsquall, while crossing a street in Boston. I did not know her until she had scrambled up with much assistance, and recognizing me at once, fastened on my offered arm, saying breathlessly, "I am so glad to see you. I have been wishing to talk to you about Sarah Winnemucca. Now Sarah Winnemucca"—and she went on discoursing as peacefully about a maligned Indian protégée as if she were strolling in some sequestered moonlit lane, on a summer evening.[11]

This Elizabeth Peabody was one of the banes of the existence of her brother-in-law, Nathaniel Hawthorne. His civility was worn thin by her on many an occasion. Consistently she failed to register the impression that his indifference if not downright hostility to each of her first five schemes for social improvement meant that he was also not to be interested in the next five or ten of them as they occurred to her. At one point the Hawthornes, then abroad, had to insist that Aunt Elizabeth desist from keeping their children posted on the plight of the slaves and the progress of abolitionism, since it was not a suitable topic, in their opinion, for children in general and certainly not for Hawthorne children in particular. And yet it was also this Elizabeth Peabody who had hunted up the reclusive Hawthornes in the days before Nathaniel had opened his intercourse with the world; she had heard that one of them was the author of the anonymous magazine pieces she admired. It was she who was able to report definitively that Nathaniel, not Louisa, Hawthorne had written them.

Mary Peabody, too, yielded to the winds of change and abandoned her moonings over the lost glory of the Palmers for a career as a philanthropist and colleague of her husband, Horace Mann, educational reformer and Free-Soil congressman. But Sophia Peabody, the third sister, felt that her claim to distinction through birth suited her, and if it did not count for something in America, it should. She underwent no call to do battle with social injustice, and when she fell deeply in love with Nathaniel Hawthorne, who responded with equal fervor, he thanked God that she had remained aloof from public forays and, even more wonderfully, from writing. With a deeper intellect than other women, he wrote her, thou hast "never prostituted thyself to the public."[12]

Hawthorne's engagement to Sophia lasted five years—they married in 1842—during which period he explored ways in which he could shoulder the financial responsibilities of marriage and yet remain a writer. His most notable explorations were political. At Bowdoin he had formed close friendships with two classmates who were already committed to rising in the world through politics. Horatio Bridge of Maine and Franklin Pierce of New Hampshire were both Democrats, and Hawthorne willingly followed them into a college society associated with that party. He was taking the first step toward what proved to be a lifetime political allegiance. It was not, apparently, a difficult decision for the lad from Salem. Whig politics was the religion of his native seaport and from its busy advocates the Hawthornes had received no comfort. The shy and socially conservative scion of the faded Hawthorne lineage easily joined himself to the party that was, as Emerson said, the representative of the people against property. As a very young boy he had lived for a year in a township in Maine established by his maternal grandfather, and that, he claimed, was the happiest period of his life. "I lived in Maine," he recalled, "like a bird of the air, so perfect was the freedom I enjoyed."[13] When he was back in Maine as a collegian, he readily responded to the Democratic talk of his Northern New England friends; they spoke for a happier world than that of the "Stingy Merchants." Thanks to his political adherence and the nascent success of his friends he was able to procure employment at the Boston Customs House for two years during his engagement, and then after his marriage to receive the post of Surveyor of the Salem Customs House. He refused to relinquish the belief that he was not actually a political animal but a writer deserving of public support so long as he gave a day's labor for a day's wages. He was, therefore, outraged that a change of political power resulted in his loss of the surveyorship. Politics might have been the road to subsistence, but his occupancy of the position, he had hoped, was in recognition of the needs of the literary class in his undefined nation.

Nonetheless, his commitment to the Democratic party was not merely expediential. It grew from his negative views of the acquisitive money-makers of Massachusetts, to be sure, but also from a positive assent to democratic principles, which, even if they were at times demagogic, did arise finally from the untutored passions of the people rather than from calculation, and so were to be trusted against the calculators.

Hawthorne's first experience as a customs measurer in 1839–40 involved such drudgery that it was nearly fatal to his creative life. Consequently, he was attracted to the Brook Farm experiment. He distrusted reformers because they very often seemed to him only the reversed image of what they opposed, and equally apart from the bonds of common human affection. But the Brook Farm community appeared to offer a writer some chance of earning his keep through a working schedule that took into account the fact that he was a writer. An actual subsistence from writing alone, especially the writing of fiction, did not appear to be within easy reach of an American. Washington Irving had achieved it, but he had also drifted into depending on patronage, both by the wealthy and by the government. James Fenimore Cooper had achieved it as a handsome dividend on what he had taken up as a leisure-class activity. Hawthorne had attempted to follow Irving's way but was unable, after one book and countless periodical pieces, to rely upon his craft for his income. Perhaps in fluid America the answer did reside in the socialist sharing of the labors of the head and hand; what capitalism demanded of the hand left nothing over for the head.

In April 1841 Hawthorne invested $1500 in Brook Farm and moved there, hoping it would furnish at least the minimum income and accommodation he and his intended bride would need. But he withdrew before the end of the year with his earlier prejudices against reform reinforced. Still, the experience had sharpened his appetite for society. He had moved among people who moved among ideas and he found that refreshing if, finally, insufficient. Although he thought of himself as having emerged from his dismal chamber, he had formed himself as an artist in that chamber. He was inside; the world was outside. His relation to it was one of a man looking through the window and down upon life, both morally and spatially. The attractive show of life in the streets carried no resonance, and meaning had to be supplied by the speculating mind behind the shutters if the daily show was to be expressive. Melville was a mingler and his moral conjectures grew from the range of characters he encountered in his mingling. But Hawthorne was reclusive, apart even in a crowd, and he produced the categories that the people he encountered were called upon to exemplify.

By the time Hawthorne moved out into the world as a gauger of casks or a tender of animals, his chamber manner was already habitual. Insofar as he was of the world he was not himself but another object for his observation; and when in his later writings he came to reflect on these periods of employment, he did so by treating the Hawthorne on the wharf and the Hawthorne on the farm as Dopplegängers. The real Hawthorne, Hawthorne the writer, was separate from that worldly double.

In recalling his happiness as a boy in Maine, Hawthorne had added, "But it was there I first got my cursed habit of solitude."[14] Freedom and solitude were compatible conditions in a nation with a vast, unsettled landscape. Cooper's Leatherstocking supplied a symbol of it, Thoreau's Walden experience a philosophy for it. But Hawthorne felt an unresolved opposition between the two, even as he experienced each as a necessary part of the other. Freedom was a self-realization that depended upon separation, but solitude was a curse that could lock freedom out of its share in our common humanity. The resolution of the opposition was at the core of his character and his art.

Hawthorne the man accepted the curse of solitude because it was the basis of his self-discovery and had become the condition of his realization as an artist. But Hawthorne the artist compensated in his writing for the coldness of his social detachment by consistently punishing those characters—even artists—who held themselves aloof as he did. Hardly a man of the people in his own conduct, he was in his fictions a vigorous defender of the mob. In his writings set in seventeenth-century New England, for example, he distrusted the populace only insofar as it tended to convert its distance from England into a detachment from the common traits of humanity, which at times of aberration it saw as belonging to the Old World rather than as universal. He used the mob as the standard of emotional health in his fictions. Unlike Emerson and Poe, he embraced it because its very undifferentiation meant truth to human feeling rather than adherence to mere ideas. It was the heart writ large even as public authority was the head.

Hawthorne's strategy for preserving his solitude misled acquaintances and even friends into believing him more available than he was. His son Julian said of him:

> Now Hawthorne, both by nature and by training, was of a disposition to throw himself imaginatively into the shoes (as the phrase is) of whatever person happened to be his companion. For the time being, he would seem to take their point of view and to speak their language; it was the result partly of a cold intellectual insight, which led him half consciously to reflect what he so clearly perceived. Thus, if he chatted with a group of rude sea-captains in the smoking-room of Mrs. Blodgett's boarding-house, or joined a knot of boon companions in a Boston bar-room, or talked metaphysics with Herman Melville in the hills of Berkshire, he would aim to appear in each instance a man like as they were; he would have the air of being interested in their standards. Of course, this was only apparent; the real man stood aloof and observant, and only showed himself as he was, in case of his prerogative being invaded, or his actual liberty of thought and action being in any way infringed upon. But the consequences may sometimes have been that people were misled as to his absolute attitude. Seeing his congenial aspect towards their little round of habits and beliefs, they would leap to the conclusion that he was no more and no less than one of themselves; whereas they formed but a tiny arc in the great circle of his comprehension. This does not seem quite fair; there is a cold touch in it; it has a look of amusing one's self at others' expense or profiting by their follies.[15]

The portrait is of a man ungiving socially whose affabilities shield his privacy. Unlike Melville, he has no direct road from his heart to his utterance; he finds it easier to assume the ebullience of his companion than to respond to it by showing himself. It is also the portrait of an artist whose imagination requires material to shape but will not shape itself to the material. It feeds like a bird, pecking at the food until it is fit for the crop, not like a snake adjusting itself to the dimensions of what it ingests.

Residing abroad from 1853 to 1860 and agonized by each successive piece of news from home about the excesses on both sides that were precipitating his homeland toward a civil war, Hawthorne wrote to William Ticknor in Boston, "You seem to be in such a confounded mess there, that it quite sickens me to think of coming back. I find it impossible to read American newspapers (of whatever political party) without being ashamed of my country."[16] At another time he wrote that he would prefer to be in America only if he could be "deprived of my political rights, and left to my individual freedom";[17] and at yet another time he opined that there would be no reason to return to so distressing a country were it not for his children, who were, after all, American. His nostalgia for his homeland was not stirred when he met with British arrogance or with continental squalor. He could even reflect that "an individual country is by no means essential to one's comfort."[18] Yet with such an attitude, he was moved to national feeling when he encountered a crowd. In Florence in 1858 he told his notebook, "For my part, in this foreign country, I have no objection to policemen or any other minister of authority; though I remember in America, I had an innate antipathy to constables, and always sided with the mob against law."[19] Reflecting further on the Italian crowd, he concluded:

> After all, and much contrary to my expectations, an American crowd has incomparably more life than any other; and meeting on any casual occasion, it will talk, laugh, roar, and be diversified with a thousand characteristic incidents and gleams and shadows, that you see nothing of here. The people seems to have no part even in its own gatherings. It comes together merely as a mass of spectators, and must not so much as amuse itself by any activity of the mind.[20]

As news from America worsened, Hawthorne's ire was addressed to the political leaders, not to the rioting mobs. He thought of Jackson, who had won his youthful adherence, and admired him afresh for his instinctive ability to do rather than think, to embody the best characteristics of a democratic people rather than preach to them. He absolved the mob from blame and placed it on the political leaders with their talk:

> It is only tradition and old custom, founded on an obsolete state of things, that assigns any value to parliamentary oratory. The world has done with it, except as an intellectual pastime. The speeches have no effect until they are converted into newspaper paragraphs; and they had better be composed as such, in the first place, and oratory reserved for churches, courts of law, and public dinner-tables.[21]

In so thinking Hawthorne reveals a finer democratic sensibility and a shrewder grasp of American political reality than can be found among the majority of his contemporaries. Others mourned the passing of Clay, Calhoun, and Webster, and saw the civil crisis as stemming in great part from the fact that no longer were there eloquent voices in the Senate. Hawthorne, however, trenchantly saw that the commonplace association of the art of oratory with the spirit of democracy was outdated in a republic in which decisions were made in an assembly remote from the regions that were affected. Print was now the crucial medium. This perception, in turn, stemmed from his belief that the essence of democracy was the feelings and prejudices of the people, which did not need guidance or refinement from leaders but required heartfelt embodiment in public life.

In hackwork that was not completely uncongenial, Hawthorne in 1841 had told the story of the American Revolution for children. In his setting, Grandfather recounts historical tales to a group of children, and when one of them protests his dislike of the brawlings of the Boston mob, he replies:

> The people, to a man, were full of great and noble sentiment. True, there may be much fault to find with their mode of expressing this sentiment; but they knew no better—the necessity was upon them to act out their feelings, in the best manner they could. We must forgive what was wrong in their actions, and look into their hearts and minds for the honorable motives that impelled them.[22]

The view thus simplified for children informed Hawthorne's most complex fictions.

In *The Scarlet Letter,* Hester Prynne challenges her semidemocratic community's assumptions about liberty and authority by asserting that nothing that is natural is wrong. She tells the father of the child who has published her adultery to the world that although she has accepted the civil punishment she has received since she did break public law, she does not believe they broke a higher law, that contained in the heart. "What we did," she affirms, "had a consecration of its own."[23] Hester's career in the novel tests the public consequences of spontaneous sexual love. In a new land fighting free of the artificialities of centuries-old customs, were government and religion to be modified by a new brotherhood while social relations—and specifically sexual relations—were left in their former, unexamined condition? Need freedom of conscience be confined to matters of belief or could it now be let loose into the regions of behavior?

At the outset of the novel Hester is fleetingly likened to Anne Hutchinson, who, historically, had advocated a doctrine to which Hester gives mythic embodiment. In the fervor of her commitment to the liberating power of the Holy Spirit, Hutchinson affirmed that the community of saints no longer required objective moral laws. It was, she maintained, kept from realizing the potentialities available in its new, free environment if its members were still required to abide by strictures meant for those in the bonds of the old dispensation. Her doctrine would have been less alarming if enunciated in the Old World, where a traditional society acted as a brake upon the power of a new perception to effect radical change. But in a land defining social relations anew, the conservative structure of feeling derived from an older system could more readily be cast aside in favor of one that reflected the liberated inner self. Was love, accordingly, despite its anarchic potential, to be public policy as democracy and community became one? The historical answer received by Hutchinson was that such could not be, and she was exiled.

Hester, in the nineteenth century, raises the matter again. The liberating power she now affirms is not grace but nature, its source not the Holy Spirit but the spontaneous heart; its potential is the same: a radical redefinition of community life. And again society answers in the negative, but in Hawthorne's telling, her political defeat—as opposed to the moral conclusion she reaches—is a defeat not of the heart but of the head. Hester translated the heart's truth into an intellectual doctrine. The solitude into which she was thrust initially as a punishment for her crime she willingly converted into isolation, which she maintained long after her community relented and attempted to resume association with her. She defended that isolation as the condition within which she could convert her experience into theory, and in so doing, from Hawthorne's viewpoint, she removed her experience from its proper sphere of influence.

"When an uninstructed multitude attempts to see with its eyes," Hawthorne explains, "it is exceedingly apt to be deceived. When, however, it forms its judgment, as it usually does, on the intuitions of its great and warm heart, the conclusions thus attained are often so profound and unerring, as to possess the character of truths supernaturally revealed."[24] The eyes of the multitude rested upon the scarlet letter fixed by authority, and in judging Hester by such evidence rather than by its feeling toward her, the multitude temporarily strayed from its true nature. Hester, however, scarcely awaited this reaction before she herself cast loose from the dictates of her heart by developing a countertheory in emulation of the punitive authorities who had judged her. Eventually even the authorities came round to the fellow feeling for Hester that the populace more rapidly recovered, delayed in their recognition by their "iron framework of reasoning."[25] But as tardy as they are in recognizing Hester's humanity, they are not so tardy as is Hester herself. She insists upon her isolation even after they begin to relent, and will not surrender her commitment to her new, desexed, intellectual self.

The mob is absolved by Hawthorne because it is, for whatever errors it strays into, a collectivity based on shared feeling: "The public is despotic in its temper; it is capable of denying common justice, when too strenuously demanded as a right; but quite as frequently it awards more than justice, when the appeal is made as despots love to have it made, entirely to its generosity."[26] Hester chooses not to make such an appeal, not even to accept affection proffered despite her aloofness, and although Hawthorne permits the reader to find her admirable in the courage of her lone stand, as, indeed, he does himself find her admirable, he is, nevertheless, ruthlessly democratic in his insistence that she will not prevail, because change must come from one who shares in the heart of the people.

Hester Prynne is Hawthorne's greatest creation—a splendid, free individual who courageously allows into her field of comprehension all the complexities that life presents to her. She makes mistakes, but she registers the lessons as she deals with a daughter who binds her to the future, a lover who cannot relinquish the trepidations he acquired from the past, and a malevolent husband whose thoughts are only for the present and who teaches her more about the dynamics of psychological process than she is for a long while willing to admit. These dealings, moreover, are conducted as she also negotiates her way within a society marked by the strong feelings of the populace and the iron reasoning of authority.

Like Hawthorne, Hester conceives of a freedom beyond political rights and like him she finds that the freedom is attached to cursed solitude. But she is, of course, a symbol, not a reflection of her creator, and so she moves in a world in which the issue of freedom and solitude cannot be softened, from time to time, by the relieving trivialities of daily life. Neither can it be distanced by projection into an artistic creation that, in its theme, redeems the guilt of its creator's reclusiveness. What Hester embodies fully, many a protagonist in Hawthorne's stories allegorized: an ambition for self-realization commencing in the heart but in its isolated ardor passing over the common feelings of humanity. Finally its aspiration becomes cerebralized and leaves the abandoned heart to turn to stone.

The need to adhere to the common heart of humanity was, for Hawthorne, the basic condition for the creation of an American literature. His fictions took their key from this common democratic denominator and reinforced its conservative instinct to retain a pattern of life beneath the flux of political theories and material changes. Those who spoke of the lack of history in America—as almost all theorists of the national culture did—had their eyes fixed on the future, which they wished to shape without restraints, rather than on the folk who had been shaped by the history of two centuries. But those who would write the fictions of America must turn to that shaping past.

In *The House of the Seven Gables,* Clifford Pyncheon has been brought to premature senility by the persecution visited upon his character, which even in happier days was none too stable. As a result, his memory has been annihilated. "He had only the visionary and impalpable Now," says Hawthorne, "which, if you once look closely at it, is nothing."[27] In almost every way, Clifford differs from the virile, resourceful, cheerful, intelligent young Holgrave with his varied experiences in every line of work, manual and mental, to which a clever Yankee lad might turn. But Holgrave is a social radical and as such is not, after all, so different from Clifford; although he has not forgotten the shaping past, he has at least discounted its power. He believes in a golden age to be realized in his lifetime, one in which all rotten institutions will be swept away and everything begun anew. Hawthorne admires his spirit, "that sense of inward prophecy,—which a young man had better never have been born than not to have, and a mature man had better die at once than utterly to relinquish," but says that Holgrave has his timetable wrong: "His error lay in supposing that this age, more than any past or future one, is destined to see the tattered garments of Antiquity exchanged for a new suit, instead of gradually renewing itself by patchwork; in applying his own little life-span as the measure of interminable achievement; and, more than all, in fancying that it mattered anything to the great end in view whether he himself should contend for or against it."[28] Here is historic determinism that goes beyond determinism to approach fatalism in its statement of the inconsequentiality of any given individual to the great process constantly working its way.

Since Holgrave is a flexible and likable chap, he falls in love, and with his heart thus engaged beyond himself Holgrave joins the slower, inevitable historical forces and leaves sudden reform to those more foolish than he. But even in his earlier career, Holgrave, at bottom, had the right view of the American past, although he was not entirely conscious of it. He had said:

> The truth is, that, once in every half-century, at longest, a family should be merged into the great, obscure mass of humanity, and forget about its ancestors. Human blood, in order to keep its freshness, should run in hidden streams, as the water of an aqueduct is conveyed in subterranean pipes.[29]

This, of course, is what eventually happened to the Hawthornes. But while Holgrave applauds the merging with obscurity as a means of economic redress, Hawthorne sees it as morally crucial because it is a return to the heart, to the structure of feeling beneath ideology, which is democracy's source of conservation. In illustration of this truth, Holgrave drew on his creative imagination and wrote a story in which the proud, rich, and aristocratic Pyncheons were brought under the controlling power of the proletarian Maules. The source of the Maule power in his story was a visionary faculty, which, in turn, Holgrave exerted in creating the story about it, and which, of course, Hawthorne is exerting in creating the novel in which

Holgrave tells the story. The legend within history gives the meaning that history itself, chronicling mutability, fails to register. It goes to the heart of the matter, showing a community the true source of its identity and constancy through time.

"If mankind were all intellect," Hawthorne noted, "they would be continually changing so that one age would be entirely unlike another."[30] The artist in America, where society too quickly accepted the notion that it was adrift from all traditions, had a duty to ensure that each age recognized its resemblance to an earlier one. As an American in England, Hawthorne was eagerly sought out by the liberals there who had sponsored Emerson's lectures, and who actually had read Thoreau, followed Margaret Fuller's career, and subscribed to *The Dial.* But whatever gratification he felt at this recognition of his countrymen was strongly overbalanced by his belief that radical literary taste did not sit well with the British character. In England, he thought, "the illiberals, the conservatives, the men who despise and hate new things and new thoughts are the best worth knowing."[31] They do not trifle with progress but wholeheartedly fit themselves to the inherited present and let the future alone. As a result, the British have a literature because they have a society recognizably itself from decade to decade; social history and legend merge. The American way promises only a literature of essayistic abstraction, albeit occasionally informed by genius, as in Thoreau. In opposing himself politically to reform, siding even with the likes of Franklin Pierce and James Buchanan against nationalized roadways or against abolitionism, Hawthorne was ultimately making an aesthetic statement. He was asserting art's need to grow from a layer of life deeper than the opinions of society. As a citizen he opposed centralization in government or in national habits, a process that would inevitably detach public action from private lives. As an artist he sought to identify and deepen that layer in his fictions.

"The great conservative," Hawthorne said, "is the heart which remains the same in all ages."[32] The larger part of his best work revealed this steady redemptive pulsation beating beneath the erratic flutterings of ideas. In *The Scarlet Letter, The House of the Seven Gables, The Blithedale Romance,* and a goodly number of stories, he measured social history against the slower chronicles of communal feeling. In that way he demonstrated his belief that the American, for all his idealism, mobility, and worship of change, was shaped by traditional feelings rather than progressive ideas. Hester Prynne came to accept that belief; Holgrave wryly subsided into it; and Zenobia and Hollingsworth were destroyed by their inability to appreciate it.

The many Hawthorne characters whose heads lose contact with their hearts—some temporarily, some permanently and fatally—symbolize the split that constantly threatens nineteenth-century American society: that between human nature, frail, sinful, conservative, and loving, and the type of social theory they seize, in their regional and ethnic diversity, as the expression of their common identity, potent, perfectible, progressive, and competitive. Hawthorne recognized the implicit didacticism in his writings about the American past. Of oral legends—some of which, paradoxically, he invented to enrich the context of his fables, others of which he made the core of his stories—he said, "Such . . . get to be true, in a certain sense, and indeed in that sense they may be called true throughout, for the very nucleus, the fiction in them, seems to have come out of the heart of man in a way that cannot be imitated by malice aforethought."[33]

Living in Europe in the gloomy years when each boat brought worsening news of political dissension from home, news of what was for him the insane triumph of the head over the heart, he mourned the coma if not the death of America's true self. Socially he turned waspish, preferring the company of solid, beef-eating merchants to that of men of ideas. And his democratic appreciation of the continental escapees from political persecution who sought his consular office in Liverpool, believing, as they did, that the United States was the home of any oppressed for freedom's sake, was checked and overcome by his dread of what further nonsensical, political turbulence they would create in vexed America: "Nothing is so absolutely abominable as the sense of freedom and equality, pertaining to an American, grafted on the mind of a native of any other country in the world. I HATE a naturalized citizen; nobody has a right to our ideas, unless born to them."[34]

At bottom his belief was not so much in democracy, or the democratic idea, as it was in what he conceived to be the way of life of the American people, which gave such ideals the validity they possessed. An alien could not connect with the essential America simply because he believed in liberty. But the events which were forcing the separation of the states signified to Hawthorne that this essential America, about which and to which he wrote, was disappearing. He had been a regional writer in his settings, but New England was for him a powerful vehicle for America at large. In defense of Pierce's recognition of the South's constitutional right to slavery he spoke of him in terms that could be applied to himself, as a man who loved "that great and sacred reality," his whole native country, "better than the mistiness of a philanthropic theory."[35] The country was its people's various established ways, their local differences insuring integrity. Andrew Jackson had rightly vetoed the Maysville Road Bill because its efect might have been "to place the capital of our federative Union in a position resembling that of imperial Rome, where each once independent state was a subject province, and all the highways of the world were said to meet in her forum."[36] Such a system was dangerous to liberty. Now, in asserting a theory of human rights that had to be universally observed, the North was destroying America in the name of an abstraction. The union being insisted upon was, in effect, leading to disunion in subordinating lived differences to an idea.

In Italy in 1858, Hawthorne noted, "I wonder that we Americans love our country at all, having no limits and no oneness; and when you try to make it a matter of heart, everything falls away except one's native State." He was attempting to convince himself that Massachusetts was all of America that he would require on his return home, but he recognized also the fragility of such a belief: "Yet, unquestionably, we do stand by our national flag as stoutly as any people in the world, and I myself have felt the heart throb at sight of it as sensibly as other men."[37] The capacity of one's native state to fill the longings of one's heart was, after all, dependent upon that state's relationship to a greater whole; as complete as that state might be in some ways, to remove it from the federation was to maim, "to tear it . . . bleeding and quivering."

The death of the Union coincided with the death of Hawthorne's art, and his life ended as the war ended. There is causality in the relationship. Writing in 1844 about the devotion of John Adams and other New Englanders to their region during the American Revolution, Hawthorne said, "Their love of country was hardly yet so diluted as to extend over the whole thirteen colonies, which were rather looked upon as allies than as comprising one nation. In truth, the patriotism of a citizen of the United States is a sentiment by itself, of a peculiar nature, and requiring a life-time, or at least the custom of many years to naturalize it among the possessions of the heart."[38] But he had in his life achieved that naturalization and in his art worked to bring others to it: he was an American author and he wrote of the condition of his country when he created characters who struggled to tune their lives to their society's sometimes sluggish but eventually truthful feelings and to avoid the efforts of the impatient head to cast off the vestments of the conservative heart.

"We never were one people, and never really had a country since the Constitution was formed,"[39] Hawthorne wrote as he was attempting to accommodate himself to life in America after the war had begun. But the Massachusetts that was now part of the North was not the Massachusetts he had developed his art in. His love of region could be indulged only when he allowed its humanizing power to others, enemies as well as friends. In a passage in his *Atlantic* essay on the war, which the editors consented to print only after they had added a footnote saying that they found its tone reprehensible and its tendency impolitic, he said of the southerner, "If a man loves his own State . . . and is content to be ruined with her, let us shoot him, if we can, but allow him an honorable burial in the soil he fights for."[40]

In that same article, Hawthorne observed, "The more historical associations we can link with our localities, the richer will be the daily life that feeds upon the past, and the more valuable the things that have been long established: so that our children will be less prodigal than their fathers in sacrificing good institutions to passionate impulses and impracticable theories."[41] Insofar as this is a description of one of the chief intents of his earlier writing it is also an admission, from the depths of his gloom at prevailing head-madness, that he had failed. Insofar as it is a program for his future writing, then to whom could such writing possibly be addressed? He tried to convince himself that "the sentiment of physical love for the soil which renders an Englishman, for example, . . . intensely sensitive to the dignity and well being of his little island"[42] could be duplicated by love of one's state. But Hawthorne's state was swept up in a great war caused in part by the fervid philanthropy peculiar to its religious history; if his love for it was to take the form of developing historical associations that showed the state to be quite wrong in its passionate commitment, then he was no longer writing for an audience but was immured in a chamber more dismal than that from which he had emerged many years before.

As the war progressed Hawthorne worked unsuccessfully on various fragments of novels, most of them, touchingly, haunted by the legend of an elixir of youth, even as he felt what resilience remained to him slipping away. Another persistent idea that refused to find its proper vehicle was that of a tale of the American Revolution. The sections he did write clearly reflect the effect of the Civil War on him, for all their Revolutionary setting. Septimius Felton, studious, furtive, melancholic observer of the American Revolution, feels the distress experienced by Nathaniel Hawthorne:

> This war, in which the country was so earnestly and enthusiastically engaged, had perhaps an influence on Septimius's state of mind, for it put everybody into an exaggerated and unnatural state, united enthusiasms of all sorts, heightened everybody either into its own heroism or into the peculiar madness to which one person was inclined; and Septimius walked so much the more wildly on his lonely course, because the people were going enthusiastically on another. In times of revolution and public disturbance all absurdities are more unrestrained; the measure of calm sense, the habits, the orderly decency, are partially lost. More people become insane, I should suppose; offences against public morality, female license, are more numerous; suicides, murder, all ungovernable outbreaks of men's thoughts embodying themselves in wild acts, take place more frequently and with less horror to the lookers-on.[43]

This being so, who would sit and write a novel, and for whom?

To Septimius there seemed to be "a stream rushing past him, by which, even if he plunged into the midst of it, he could not be wet. He felt himself strangely ajar with the human race, and would have given much either to be in full accord with it, or separated from it forever."[44] Hawthorne was too old, too much the conservative Democrat, to come into such accord. The eternal separation could be his only through death, and it came, prematurely, in 1864. By that time solitude and freedom were no longer the different aspects of a single, complex condition demanding creative resolution. They had become, rather, simply different words for the same bleak isolation from his country and his art.

Chapter Eight

Sexual Insight and Social Criticism: Hawthorne's Use of Romance

Our Old Home (1863) is a volume of the impressions Hawthorne formed during his residence in England (1853–57). The sketches are based on copious journal entries originally "intended for the side-scenes, and backgrounds, and exterior adornment of a work of fiction," one which, after many an abortive attempt, he admitted he was never going to achieve. Although he blamed the war for the breakdown of his intent, his phrasing of the reasons for his failure is familiar, very much in keeping with the prefatory remarks in each of his four novels:

> The Present, the Immediate, the Actual, has proved too potent for me. It takes away not only my scanty faculty, but even my desire for imaginative composition, and leaves me sadly content to scatter a thousand peaceful fantasies upon the hurricane that is sweeping us all along with it, possibly into a Limbo where our nation and its polity may be as literally the fragments of a shattered dream as my unwritten Romance.[1]

The actual which he claimed had finally gotten the better of him was an old and valuable antagonist. In his introductory essay to *The Scarlet Letter,* thirteen years earlier, he had defined the genre in which he wrote as neither the novel nor the fairy tale. The former, he said, was concerned with the actual, everyday world, but its very materiality resisted if not repelled him. Although he suspected that the wiser effort would have been to diffuse his thought and imagination through its opacity so as to achieve expression of "the true and indestructible value that lay hidden in the petty and wearisome incidents, and ordinary characters with which I was now conversant,"[2] he chose rather to retreat into another age, that of New England's seventeenth century. He claimed that the reality of the flitting hour provided material for a better book than he could write, but insisted that his "brain wanted the insight" and his "hand the cunning to transcribe it."

Although he did turn to a remote period, however, that setting was not a fairyland in which his imagination could have free rein. It was, rather, a region halfway between the actual and the imaginary, which permitted him to soften the obduracy of the former with the play of the latter while anchoring that play in a recognizable if distanced reality. He likened the romance to a familiar room at night, lit by the shine of the moon and the rays of the fire on the hearth. The shadows cast by such a flickering light blurred the hardness of outline of what was so well known by daylight, suggesting it might be another thing, investing it with a spiritual quality. That well-known chamber in clear daylight was the novel; the moonlight playing on ether was the fairy tale; the familiar shaded into unfamiliarity was the romance—his medium.

A year later in introducing *The House of the Seven Gables,* Hawthorne reaffirmed that his genre, romance, differed from both novel and pure fantasy. The writer who calls his work a novel, he said,

> is presumed to aim at a very minute fidelity, not merely to the possible, but to the probable and ordinary course of man's experience. The former [romance]—while, as a work of art, it must rigidly subject itself to laws, and while it sins unpardonably so far as it may swerve aside from the truth of the human heart—has fairly to present that truth under circumstances, to a great extent, of the writer's own choosing or creation. If he think fit, also, he may manage his atmospherical medium as to bring out or mellow the lights, and deepen and enrich the shadows of the picture. He will be wise, no doubt, to make a very moderate use of the privileges here stated, and especially,

> to mingle the Marvelous rather as a slight, delicate, and evanescent flavor, than as any portion of the actual substance of the dish offered to the public. He can hardly be said, however, to commit a literary crime, even if he disregard this caution.[3]

This second novel was set in the everyday present, but a present so haunted by the past that Hawthorne assumed license to dissolve nineteenth-century scenes to a degree of transparency sufficient to permit the characters and gestures of the two preceding centuries to show through the scrim of the present.

And in the following year, 1852, Hawthorne culminated a remarkably productive period by publishing his third novel, *The Blithedale Romance,* set recognizably in the Brook Farm at which he had toiled, although with certain liberties taken so as to make that community, called Blithedale in the fiction, a more bewitched area than its model. Hawthorne feared, nevertheless, that he had here strayed too far into the actual, thereby compelling his characters to resemble living mortals, so that "the paint and pasteboard of their composition" showed through rather shabbily. A remote atmosphere, he insisted, "is what the American romancer needs."[4] This is by now a familiar Hawthorne remark, save that here he has come to place special emphasis not on the genre but on its peculiar demands when practiced by an American.

Hawthorne had moved from a novel set in the remote past to one set in the present but dominated by images of the past, and then to one set in the present but in a locale isolated both physically and ideologically from the larger society. His final novel, published seven years later, *The Marble Faun* (1860), again took place in the present, but again Hawthorne pointed out in his prefatory remarks that he had developed a setting sufficiently exotic to license his characteristic effects. He then went on to a stronger complaint about America's inaccessibility to romance than he had yet made, one intensified, no doubt, by contemplating his return from the luxuries of an expatriate's spectatordom to the weight of a citizen's responsibilities in a time of impending war:

> Italy, as the site of his Romance, was chiefly valuable to him as affording a sort of poetic or fairy precinct, where actualities would not be terribly insisted upon, as they are and must needs

> be, in America. No author, without a trial, can conceive of the difficulty of writing a Romance about a country where there is no shadow, no antiquity, no mystery, no picturesque and gloomy wrong, nor anything but a common-place prosperity, in broad and simple daylight, as is happily the case with my dear native land. It will be very long, I trust, before romance-writers may find congenial and easily handled themes either in the annals of our stalwart Republic, or in any characteristic and probable event of our individual lives. Romance and poetry, like ivy, lichens, and wall-flowers, need Ruin to make them grow.[5]

The concluding sentences are familiar: Cooper had earlier made similar complaint, and James was to qualify it and then intensify it. But once we note this, we may well ask whether Hawthorne is here accurate as a characterizer of his own achievement. He certainly did not go back to Puritan Massachusetts Bay in *The Scarlet Letter* in order to have the freedom to be picturesque. If he was more "poetic" in that setting than he would have been in the present, he was so in the old sense of being a legend-maker rather than in the more sentimental nineteenth-century sense of fancifully embroidering an otherwise colorless reality. And although the house of the seven gables was an antique structure on its way to being a ruin, nevertheless it clearly was not selected as the site of ivy, lichens, and wall-flowers, and all they connoted in Hawthorne's 1860 remarks; its venerability deepened its menace rather than enhanced its charm.

In his remarks about romance in *The Marble Faun,* then, Hawthorne seems to be shifting his focus and reverting to a conception of romance more in keeping with the term as used, say, by Walter Scott, than by his younger, profoundly creative self. Scott referred to his fictions both as novels and as romances, the latter being for him descriptive of the kind of novel he wrote.[6] He did not, as did Hawthorne, think explicitly of the generic consequences of his chosen form, although in practice he amply illustrated them. His romances were related to the medieval romances he had read as a boy, tales of the doings of heroes who were often superhuman in circumstances that were affected by the supernatural. But such fictions, he felt, contained so many specious miracles that the mind was quickly sated; and in his search for lore he came to prefer histories, memoirs, and voyages—accounts that were, in great measure, true. Romance, when Scott came to write it, was a mingling of the two: a fiction of heroic (often chivalric) but not superhuman deeds occurring in a well-defined historical setting, the remoteness of which permitted the marvelous, but the specificity of which obstructed the miraculous. His center in the remote was not so much for him, as it was for Hawthorne, a license to dissolve materiality as it was an occasion to indulge in the vivification of his antiquarian knowledge, to get into the past for its own sake. Although his readers are led into his romances by the adventures depicted, they are soon involved equally, if not to a greater extent, in the sheer delight of learning through his dramas about the material culture and the manners of an earlier period, which, although past, has nevertheless left its inchoate rubble on the landscape and its obscure figures in the speech. Through Scott's romances these familiar but mute ruins reassemble into wholeness and speak.

This kind of romance, to be sure, was not available to the American writer because his landscape was not so marked. But neither was it the sort that Hawthorne had attempted in his first three novels. Only at the end, when everyday actuality meant not a prosperous bustle on the street but the death of the conservative, democratic heart at the hands of ideologues, did he seek—unsuccessfully—to visit such romance on the American landscape.

The license Hawthorne had sought for his earlier fictions was not so much freedom to indulge in descriptions of a world past as freedom to penetrate to what he regarded as the expressive features of the world present to him. By the time he embarked upon long fictions, the romance as practiced by Radcliffe or by Scott was no longer dominant. Moreover, its American uses, so to speak, had been fairly well canvassed by Charles Brockden Brown, William Gilmore Simms, Cooper, and others. Beginning in the 1830s the novel of immediate social experience, as executed by Dickens and Thackeray, was at the fore, and Hawthorne's creation of the genre he called romance was far more a response to this interest than it was a return to the earlier form. In his prefatory remarks to *The House of the Seven Gables* he had said that while his kind of romance "sins unpardonably so far as it may swerve aside from the truth of the human heart," nevertheless it has a right "to present that truth under circumstances, to a great extent, of the writer's own choosing or creation."

The human heart, in his view, was very much shaped by social reality, even though in massed and undifferentiated American society it did not manifest its individual complexity to anywhere near the extent it was enabled to do in a more traditional, subtly articulated class society. In the English novels of social experience there were some hypocrites, characters who pretended to be what they knew they were not, but such were patent to the reader. In general, the outward behavior of the creations of Dickens or of Thackeray was consistent with the private characters they possessed; the intricacy of the larger society in which they moved permitted a range of actions of sufficient breadth and subtlety to match their inner complexity. The individual in America, however, inherited little of class status or ideological allegiance with his birth. Where he terminated the crowd began; his subtler aspirations could not be dramatized through his social gestures. This did not mean to Hawthorne that the American was correspondingly uncomplicated. Rather, it indicated to him that if he dealt with everyday reality as it appeared in the observable actions of his fellow citizens he would not be able to convey their inner condition. He had discovered himself in solitude. There was in America a split between private and public (between what Whitman was to call one's self and en-masse), and he sought a setting more subtle than that offered by public American scenes in order to dramatize the moral reality of the American character. He claimed the liberty, therefore, to invent the circumstances of his creation, but at the center of the circumstances was an inescapable given—he called it the truth of the heart—which determined the nature of the circumstances. This blend, the romance, came into being not to exploit the picturesqueness of the remote but as a means of reaching what was terrifically present yet unavailable to existing fictional conventions—the psyche.

In *Our Old Home,* Hawthorne said, "It has often seemed to me that Englishmen of station and respectability, unless of a peculiarly philanthropic turn, have neither any faith in the feminine purity of the lower orders of their countrywomen, nor the slightest value for it, allowing its possible existence."[7] He was brooding upon his frequent observations of the almost automatic gratification of sexual desire available to the upper-class Englishman in a society in which his mere station gave him power over women of a lower social order. He believed that this operated to the moral detriment of the men, "who forget that the humblest woman has a right and a duty to hold herself in the same sanctity as the highest." Although he has evident sympathy for the women thus exploited, the center of his concern is not their debasement but the moral degradation of their exploiters, since the latter, as the voluntary agents in the transaction, can alone be brought to judgment. Yet he is struck by the fact that his English acquaintances, when the matter is remarked by an ingenuous American, register contempt for the morally critical attitude, believing it the expression of a purity that is too finely strained, if not, in fact, the product of a special squeamishness.

Characteristically, Hawthorne, when faced with this response, did not intensify his condemnation of the English but asked whether the American situation, in which such automatic sexual exploitation was impossible because of the very structure of that society, was, in the final analysis, in a healthier condition. He reflected:

> Making a higher pretension, or, at all events, more carefully hiding what may be amiss, we are either better than they, or necessarily, a great deal worse. It impressed me that their open avowal and recognition of immoralities served to throw the disease to the surface, where it might more effectually be dealt with, and leave a sacred interior not utterly prophaned, instead of turning its poison back among the inner vitalities of the character at the imminent risk of corrupting them all.[8]

Thus clearly does Hawthorne recognize that simple, open American society does not so much reflect a purity of character as block powerful inclinations from expression, so that they turn in upon themselves to fester. The American scene and the American psyche are not in phase, and the unhealthiness of this condition can be more detrimental than the frank if coarse and exploitative release afforded by English society.

The principal area of the private self in America that is compelled to remain locked into secrecy is, most obviously, sexual desire. There is good reason to conjecture that Hawthorne's simultaneous discovery as a boy of exhilaration (freedom) and a curse (solitude) stems from his first experience of masturbation, although to note this is in no way to undervalue the larger social perceptions he built upon these conceptual terms. His fictions, especially the shorter ones, abound in images and gestures that can be linked to masturbation —veils, mirrors, and hideaways more voluptuous than any public place. Wakefield, in the story of that name, keeps secreting himself from his wife; he loses, Hawthorne says, his reciprocal influence. Hooper, in "The Minister's Black Veil," insists his veil is symbolic of the fact that all men on this earth hide their hearts from one another and endeavor to shrink from the eyes of God; yet it is notable that the veil as he employs it serves to block the flow of human sympathy inward toward him while permitting him to release what he wishes. Although "even the lawless wind" respects his secret and does not blow the veil aside, from beneath it "there rolled a cloud into the sunshine."[9] But whatever part masturbation played in Hawthorne's first recognitions and subsequent dramatizations of the self that is hidden from public view, his dramatization of the division was the dramatization of a complicated truth about his society, not an extended rationalization of a secret sexual act.

The events that form the plot of *The Scarlet Letter* stem from an act of fornication that took place before the novel opened but is a matter of continuing public interest because the identity of the child's father is not revealed by the female even when she is punished. When the act is symbolically repeated in the forest, it is repeated in a setting that emphasizes its asocial, if not antisocial, nature. The theme of the novel is the exploration of Hester's perception that nothing natural is wrong, and, of course, the efficient cause of her contention was sexual desire. But in her questionings Hester goes beyond an attack on society's sexual mores to raise doubts about the larger matter of the entire way in which society is constituted with respect to the relative power of men and powerlessness of women. Her theorizings must be kept secret not so much because they are sexually daring as because they are socially revolutionary.

One may well entertain the conjecture, then, that in Hawthorne sexual attitudes are frequently symbolic of other aspects of the secret self at odds with society: the ambitious self that refuses to socialize its aspirations; the demonic self that seeks power or knowledge beyond what is safely admissible; the promethean self that dares to contemplate improvements upon the creation. Such a conjecture reverses the more familiar critical procedure whereby objects and gestures presumably representing publicly admissible meanings can be seen to be sexual symbols, and suggests that sexually initiated ideas in Hawthorne attain fictive embodiment and resonance as they make sex itself symbolic of other concerns. Hester's self-discovery through her realization of her sexual nature, for example, does not attain its greatest meaning when one recognizes the images in the novel that symbolize sex—after all, one such image is planted large in the title—but rather when one recognizes that her sexual self is a synecdoche for her fuller private self: she seeks to surpass Chillingworth in the power of psychological dominance and to surpass Dimmesdale in the power of spiritual and intellectual leadership. *A* for Adultery at the outset of the novel becomes at the end, Hawthorne tells us, *A* for Angel, but through the body of the work Hester repeatedly indicates that its most desirable meaning for her would be *A* for Authority.

Coverdale, in *The Blithedale Romance,* affords another strong example of the manner in which Hawthorne moves from sexual insight to social criticism. He is skeptical about whether the ideas of the socialist community are workable, but joins it nevertheless, since it offers greater promise of a public life organized in accordance with his private needs than does everyday Boston. In commercial America, Coverdale, a minor poet, is well on his way to triviality; his sexual passivity marks him as an observer rather than an actor in the passions of life. Competitive capitalism is powered by the energy that flows from the polarization of the sexes: the sharp differentiation between the attributes society calls masculine and those it calls feminine. But Coverdale senses that the division is artificial, not natural, because he possesses a great deal of what is termed feminine and yet feels himself complete. According to his society's values, however, he is a failure as a man.

Although Hawthorne deliberately makes Coverdale unattractive if not pusillanimous in his ditherings on the margins of others' lives, he nevertheless develops his character from attributes he knew were found in himself. Insofar as the portrait is negative, Hawthorne is engaged in the creative therapy of purgation. He, too, contained a great deal of what was conventionally denoted as feminine. "Talking with him," said Dr. Oliver Wendell Holmes, "was almost like love-making, and his shy, beautiful soul had to be wooed from its bashful pudency like an unschooled maiden."[10] In *A Fable for Critics,* James Russell Lowell wrote:

> When Nature was shaping him, clay was not granted
> For making so full-sized a man as she wanted,
> So, to fill out her model, a little she spared
> From some finer-grained stuff for a woman prepared.[11]

Margaret Fuller was sure that the anonymous author of "The Gentle Boy" was a woman, since it was marked "by so much grace and delicacy of feeling."[12] Other attributes commonly considered unmasculine were noted in Hawthorne by his wife: "The sacred veil of his eyelids he scarcely lifted to himself—such an unviolated sanctity was his nature, I his inmost wife, never conceived nor knew."[13] Thoreau found him always "simple and childlike,"[14] and an acquaintance noted that despite his analyses of mortality in his writings he had a severe inability in his social life to assimilate the fact of death: after Longfellow's wife died, Hawthorne remarked, "I shall be afraid to meet him again,"[15] and when his intimacy with Franklin Pierce made it inescapable that he attend the funeral of Pierce's wife, he admitted "he could not generally look at such things."[16]

At bottom, however, such attributes were no more feminine by nature than they were masculine, and beneath the manifest ideals of Blithedale—about which, indeed, Coverdale is doubtful—is the unspoken attraction of a society in which each individual may reveal openly the blend in him or her of masculine and feminine, so that social cohesion is truly that of a brotherhood or a sisterhood.

In his first weeks in the community Coverdale fancies he is on his way to experiencing just such a new world: the bearlike, virile Hollingsworth is maternal in his attendance upon him; the fleshy, sensual Zenobia is masculinely incisive and comradely; the unformed Priscilla, whose shaping comes from the group, assumes the role of little sister or boy companion as the needs of the moment dictate. When the communal dream collapses, it does so not because socialism in that situation proves economically unfeasible but because the members cannot, after all, shed the sex roles they acquired in conventional society. Hollingsworth reverts to aggressive male dominance (to so extreme a degree that when he breaks down at the end, he reverses and becomes a feeble child in need of constant care); Zenobia, for all her splendid self-assurance, dissolves into the most banal stereotype of nineteenth-century femininity, the abandoned maiden who kills herself from lovesickness; and Priscilla is compelled to pass immediately from nubile bisexuality to the role of mother without the natural accompaniment of childbearing. Thrust back into Boston actuality, Coverdale alone retains the blend of attributes that impelled him towards Blithedale, but now—and the now is the point of view from which he narrates the tale—in the failure of these attributes to find a suitable social outlet, he is confirmed in the petty oddities of behavior of an old-maid bachelor, the only role American society has for his kind.

The license Hawthorne claimed for romance was clearly not a route of escape from the concerns of his society but a means of exploring them. Class exploitation did not strike him, as it did Lippard, as an essential feature of American society—and it is notable that Lippard, for all his schemes of direct social reform, also dimly perceived in his novels that sexuality in America was a social indicator; accordingly, his final vision of socialism was one of brotherhood. What Lippard glimpsed at times but never clearly expressed Hawthorne made his theme: America lacked a way to give public outlet to the complexities of private character. But if Hawthorne saw discrepancies between the demands of the psyche and the arrangements of social life, he did not believe that because the latter were artificial, the former were natural. To be sure, a number of his characters, most notably Hester, entertained such propositions (Dr. Rappacini holds them in inverted form), but Hawthorne the artist did not believe in the existence of a true self that stood apart from the determinations of history. He believed the psyche was structured by the external world, not by an unmoved first cause such as nature or the deity. He did not deny that at some assumed original moment such a force may have shaped man—that there was a supernatural or prehistoric natural that gave rise to our historic condition—but once history commenced, time was irreversible.

One of his most explicit statements on the matter came in a piece first published in 1843:

> We, who are born into the world's artificial system, can never adequately know how little in our present state and circumstances is natural, and how much is merely the interpolation of the perverted mind and heart of man. Art has become a second and stronger Nature; she is a step-mother, whose crafty tenderness has taught us to despise the bountiful and wholesome ministrations of our true parent. It is only through the medium of the imagination that we can loosen those iron fetters, which we call truth and reality and make ourselves even partially sensible of what prisoners we are.[17]

At the close of the passage he offers a characterization of his art: in dramatizing the tension between the private self and its public show he is returning us to a sense of our prelapsarian selves, but only a sense. If we recognize what is nature and what is artifice we can move more freely because more consciously. But unlike Emerson, Hawthorne is too confirmed in his impression of the power of history to suggest that we can return to the natural. We cannot strike off the fetters; at best we can but loosen them and thereby gain a greater range.

The perversion of mind and heart that differentiates man's present from his original condition may be seen as the result of the fall, but that fall is not identical with the Adamic curse as elaborated by the Puritans, who provided Hawthorne with so many of his settings. They believed the fall of Adam was the inheritance of all men and redemption came only from the gratuitous operation of the Holy Spirit. Hawthorne took the curse to be the replacement of nature by human contrivance, a view, in general, that is compatible with both the orthodox view of the apple of knowledge and the liberal view (such as that of the Transcendentalists) of man's primal alienation from nature. His fictions amply demonstrate, however, that on this base he built the ideas that damnation is not inherited but chosen, and that it is redeemable through human agency. Most men, in electing worldly success, commit themselves to artifice, the head, rather than to nature, the heart, and in so doing curse themselves. But Hawthorne did not believe that a return to nature through immersion in the divine flux was possible, nor that the heart itself was unaffected by external reality. He saw history as inescapable, and therefore he saw the necessity of striking a balance between head and heart; the dominance of the head is to be avoided, but it must, in our historical condition, play a part, since the impure heart requires guidance. If one falls, however, redemption is available through the surrender of the ego to the love of another, in recognition of one's existence as a particle in the common heart of humanity. Phoebe Pyncheon is an example of a person who has escaped the curse through finding a balance that favors the heart, and Roderick Elliston (of "Egotism; or The Bosom-Serpent") of one cursed who is then redeemed by love.

Since the psyche is historically determined, Hawthorne's dramas set in the past or in distant lands present characters whose consciousness as well as their manners and ideas are different from those of the world of his readers. His seventeenth-century Puritans, for example, are coarser yet more zestful (as well as zealous) in their perceptions than their descendants. Hester was born too early to succeed not because her society was unprepared intellectually for her theories but because the development of human character on which they depended had yet to come into being. Moreover, when Hawthorne presents contemporary, ethereal women, such as Phoebe or Hilda, he does so with a sense that something has been lost as well as gained in the change from an earlier type. He contrasts them with more passionate women, such as Zenobia and Miriam, who, although doomed to be misfits in their society, do point up the relative vapidity of the woman idealized by the century. In an intemperate comment not at all intended to apply to such contrasts as that between Miriam and Hilda, but one that still has the relevance of apt caricature, Hawthorne told his notebook that the choice between an English woman and an American was the choice between "a greasy animal and an anxious skeleton."[18] With so highly developed a sense of social relativity, Hawthorne, although he attempted far fewer historical works than Scott or Cooper, nevertheless surpassed them in one aspect of that genre: he created the people of the past not just with different manners and costumes but with different sensibilities.

The historical period Hawthorne employed most frequently was that of the first generations of Puritan settlement in New England. With its firm belief in the primacy of the invisible over the visible world, Puritan society read the visible as symbolic of the hidden; the actual as a manifestation of the spiritual. It was, therefore, a setting in which Hawthorne could with probability make a physical scene symbolic of concealed concerns and embellish such a drama with the conjectures of oral legend. Although not a Puritan in the sense of believing in predestinarian doctrine and some form of congregational ecclesiastical polity, he was nevertheless attracted to Puritanism for reasons beyond its potential for symbolizing his fictional concerns. Hawthorne disagreed with liberal religions of the day such as Unitarianism and Universalism, which pretended to be true reflections of man's private condition, as well as with the more fundamental revivalism of the day, which opposed such liberalism but nonetheless offered absolution from sin at the will of the sinner. To Hawthorne, the human condition was dark and vexed, gravitating toward a brotherhood of guilt. If the guilt itself was escapable, brotherhood with the guilty was not. Even the escapees were human, therefore frail and marked for unhappiness. A young couple in "The May-Pole of Merry Mount" leave the mythic world of pagan sexuality to enter history when their love leads them to want to become husband and wife. Committed to the heart they are free of guilt, but in joining history they cannot be free of grief: "From the moment that they truly loved, they had subjected themselves to earth's doom of care, and sorrow, and troubled joy."[19]

At the center of the isolation of the private self from public structure in America—perhaps, indeed, its principal cause—was the Puritans' insistence on the direct exposure of the soul to the deity without mediating institutions or rituals. Hawthorne acquired an equally powerful distrust of persons or organizations that would presume to meddle with the sanctity of a soul, and his darkest villains are always those who probe the psyches of others. Toward the end of his career, after he had experienced European life at length and come to appreciate the comforting power of institutions that shielded the naked individual from the awful cosmos, he became critical of the psychological consequences of the American system, even as he was dismayed at its current political situation. In *The Marble Faun,* for example, he says of a young man praying at the shrine of his saint, "If this youth had been a Protestant, he would have kept all the torture pent up in his heart, and let it burn there till it seared him into indifference."[20] He permitted his Puritanic virgin, Hilda, to avail herself of the comforts of the confessional, although even then he was uneasy about the hold over her sacred purity that was thereby offered another human being, though he was a priest, and her final movement into Kenyon's arms is a movement away from this threat, among other things.

Nor did the institution of the family function for Hawthorne as a supportive qualification of the loneliness of the soul. Romantic novels in general, to be sure, found little use for the complete family. Orphans or children of unknown parentage occur in them with a frequency greater than in life; one-parent families seem to outnumber two-parent families; and siblings are not prominent (in passing it can be noted that Poe was an orphan, and Emerson, Hawthorne, and Lippard fatherless from an early age). To some extent the incompleteness of the fictional family is the element that spins the plot, its imbalance starting the flow into the wider world, as if a complete family would be intact against adventure.

But after noting this about the novels of the period in general, one is still struck by the severe isolation from immediate family of all of Hawthorne's central characters. The meaning that emerges seems loosely to be that the existence of America itself is the result of the breakup of a family—the British empire with monarch as parent—and of families—the immigrants having left parents, siblings, and even mates at home in the old country. As a consequence, although there are families in America as elsewhere, the unit has lost its function as a symbol of conservative continuity. Even in Hawthorne's novel expressly devoted to family, *The House of the Seven Gables,* the family consists of an odd arrangement: that is, an elderly brother and sister separated for so long that upon their reunion the brother finds the sister personally repulsive in spite of his affection for her; their first cousin, whom they hate; and a more distant cousin whom they come to know only in their last years. As uneasy as is the sibling relationship here, it is harmonious when compared with the only other one considered at length by Hawthorne, that of Zenobia and Priscilla, in *The Blithedale Romance,* also separated for the greater part of their lives. Although social historians may point out that the family unit, especially in the infertile agricultural regions of New England, was breaking down in the period as young men sought economic improvement in the West and young women began a slower drift to employment in the town or in the factories, still the absence of close kin in Hawthorne's novels is remarkable. His settings, after all, are towns and cities, not the high seas or the wilderness, which are probable locations for detached characters, so that Cooper seems perverse when he insists upon having fathers drag their daughters onto ships and into forests. Clearly, for Hawthorne the absence of family as a shaping force was symbolic of the condition of the individual seeking identity in protean America, rather than directly reflective of social actualities.

Puritanism again must be assigned some responsibility for this outlook. Although Puritan culture established the family as the basic unit of civil society, it also denatured it by seeing divine grace as a divider of families and redistributor of their members into spiritual groups more vital than the biological family, and at the same time by abstracting the meaning of family so that, for example, magistrates were to be regarded as fathers or grown servants as children.

But democratic idealism contributes to this symbolic condition in Hawthorne with at least equal force. In the beautifully realized story "My Kinsman, Major Molineux," young Robin leaves his family in rural Massachusetts to pursue a livelihood in Boston. That family is complete—he has two living parents, a brother, and two sisters—and seems a very part of the natural order. Robin's memory of those at home is an image of their being outdoors beneath a benevolent tree lit by the setting sun. Such a family has not turned him out to find his fortune as he may, but has, in keeping with its organic quality, arranged for the older brother to inherit the modest family acres and for Robin to be consigned to a kinsman, Major Molineux, who will promote his career and watch over him.

But unknowingly, Robin arrives in Boston in the period of accelerating anti-Tory violence that preceded the American Revolution and on the very night when his influential loyalist kinsman is to be tarred and feathered by the democratic mob. With his discovery of the major's degradation Robin has the obvious option of returning home, but he himself had become an accomplice of the rabble when, without reflection, he had burst into laughter at the spectacle of his kinsman's humiliation. That laughter, although cruel, was also liberating, signaling Robin's severance from family dependency and indicating the possibility of his achieving an independent identity. At the close he permits a benevolent democratic stranger to persuade him to remain in unknown Boston and to attempt to prosper solely on the basis of the talents he may possess. The dim ferry crossing that had brought him to the city that evening finally resonates as an irreversible transition between two worlds, but unlike the crossing of classical myth, it is a movement from a world now passing to one arriving—from monarchy to democracy, from patriarchy to independence. Something natural has been lost in the transition—Boston's man-made structures contrast grimly with the woods of home. But American history commences for Hawthorne with the departure from nature, and quite contrary to the Emersonian philosophy, he treats the sky, forest, and river as impersonal carriers of messages projected by the beholder, not those sent down from a higher reality. As such, nature does not speak to historical man of absolute truths. It is not the area of unsanctified lawlessness that Hester's townspeople believed it to be, but neither is it a trustworthy sanctioner of human impulse. In treating nature this way, Hawthorne also departed from the outlook of such as Radcliffe and Cooper, who orchestrated their natural scenery in accordance with theories of the sublime, the beautiful, and the picturesque so as to insist upon its moral value. The isolated American in Hawthorne could no more find an objective reflection of his complex inner life in the wilderness that surrounded him than he could in the simple institutions of his society. His fate was to make history and his doom would come if, in the making, he forgot to conserve the values of the heart that formed his only inheritance from prehistory and supplied his only anchor against meaningless mutability.

At the end of his life Hawthorne feared that the age of meaningless mutability had arrived. But his great fictions were created in a period when the geographic and social mobility of adolescent America was simultaneously destroying prejudice and threatening chaos. His art was devoted to the embodiment of what had to be retained privately and made expressible publicly if his democracy was to prove itself successful, not as a political entity nor an economic enterprise, but as a historically created environment for the cherishing of humanity in its frailty as well as its vigor.

Chapter Nine

The Superiority of Their Women: Margaret Fuller's Worlds

Margaret Fuller was a great humbug, Hawthorne felt. She "stuck herself full of borrowed qualities, which she chose to provide herself with, but which had no root in her." What was rooted in her, he insisted, was her female nature, "a rude old potency" that she could not remake. He was quick to believe the worst gossip that he heard about her when he visited Rome after her death because it confirmed his view of the inescapability of one's sexual nature. Fuller, he accepted, had had Ossoli's child out of wedlock, but "I like her the better for it; because she proved herself a very woman after all, and fell as the weakest of her sisters might."[1]

The insistence upon indelible sexual attributes, the visible relief felt when this formidable woman behaved, after all, like a woman, and the eagerness with which she was categorized as "fallen," as if extraordinary intellectual gifts could belong only to a sinful woman, are not, at a glance, consistent with the view exposed in Hawthorne's great fiction. There the difference between the sexes had been dramatized so as to reveal the artificiality of nineteenth-century society's emphasis upon separate sets of attributes that belonged exclusively to each sex. But even in those tales Hawthorne had emphasized that social enactment of a just perception of the relation between the sexes depended upon the slow processes of social change. The trailblazers would have to be women who accepted social convention and were content to advance the cause by inches. Those who attempted to vault forward at a bound, such as Hester,

Zenobia, and Miriam, had, through their previous sexual behavior, already located themselves outside the conventions. They were, therefore, to be understood but not to be followed because their feminist theories were suspect compensations for their outcast state rather than disinterested ideas. Hawthorne could not conceive of a reformer (male or female, witness Holgrave) who was not rationalizing his or her own social misconduct or sublimating libidinal drives. He was, therefore, bothered by Margaret Fuller's seemingly chaste sexual conduct and relieved to learn, at last, that it was only apparent and he could, after all, consign her to the same category as that of his fallen heroines.

Hawthorne's attitude cannot but appear mean today, although it is far from foolish. His attachment to the conservative heart led him in an age of abundant fuzzy social theorizing to look for the motive in the structure of feelings rather than in the ideas themselves. Although he did injustice to those such as Fuller who possessed a vigorous independence of mind, he also glimpsed the rudiments of Freudian psychology and the yet-to-be formulated Marxist theories of social change. Faced with the feminist Zenobia in *The Blithedale Romance,* Coverdale quickly infers: "Zenobia has lived, and loved! There is no folded petal, no latent dew-drop, in this perfectly developed rose!"[2] If this shows his shabby personality in addition to telling us a truth about Zenobia, it is because Hawthorne has designed the effect. Unlike his lesser contemporaries, he was quite willing to criticize the audacious woman while at the same time revealing that she was driven to her audacity because the men in her society were sexually fearful.

When Fuller's *Woman in the Nineteenth Century* appeared in 1845, Sophia Hawthorne wrote her mother that she felt not the slightest interest in the woman's movement. Marriage was the woman's sphere, and no man who knew a noble woman treated her as an inferior. The ill treatment of women was the result of women's behaving ignobly. Mrs. Peabody disagreed with her daughter, although she did not agree with Fuller, and she insisted that Christian behavior was the only standard: "He has the physical power, as well as conventional, to treat her like a plaything or a slave, and will exercise that power till his own soul is elevated to that standard set up by Him who spake as never man spoke."[3] Both Mrs. Peabody and Margaret Fuller conceptualized woman's role after accepting man's role as it then was, but Fuller centered on the nature of woman and her capacity to make a direct contribution to the national life through realizing that nature. She did not treat such a contribution as supplementary or complementary to a more important male enterprise.

Daniel Webster told a gathering of women, "It is by the promulgation of sound morals in the community, and more especially by the training and instruction of the young, that woman performs her part toward the preservation of a free government."[4] And how different, after all was Fuller's friend Emerson when he addressed the Woman's Rights Convention in Boston in 1855?

> Man is the will and Woman the sentiment. In this ship of humanity, Will is the rudder, and Sentiment the sail. . . . When women engage in any art or trade, it is usually as a resource, not as a primary object. The life of the affections is primary to them, so that there is universally no employment or career which they will not with their own applause and that of society quit for a suitable marriage. And they give entirely to their affections, set their whole fortune on the die, lose themselves eagerly in the glory of their husbands and children.[5]

He went on to say that civilization is nothing but the power of good women decorating life with manners, proprieties, order, and grace. He supported woman's right to property and to the vote, revealing in passing that he had probably read Melville when he said that he would like to hear woman's voice on the questions of "whether men shall be holden in bondage, or shall be roasted alive and eaten, as in Typee."

Fuller was by no means the only woman to take exception in print to the political and social attitudes represented by so differing a pair of orators as Webster and Emerson, although her counter was the most explicit and by far the most sharply focused. Others recognized the fictitiousness of woman's natural dependency but did so in passing and with a shrug. After hearing Emerson lecture, Lydia Maria Child wrote in 1843, "*Men* were exhorted to *be,* rather than to *seem,* that they might fulfill the sacred mission for which their souls were embodied; that they might, in God's freedom, grow up into the full stature of spiritual manhood; but *women* were urged to simplicity and truthfulness, that they might become more pleasing."[6]

An English critic said there were two Fanny Ferns, one to be read in the closet, and the other to be read aloud in the evening.[7] The closet Fanny Fern was presumably supported financially by her fireside sister, and their successful creator did not insist that her audience accept any more truths than it liked. She always surrounded her truth-telling with conventional sentiment, but it was there at the core. In *Ruth Hall,* a novel greatly admired by Hawthorne, the youthful heroine is thus described:

> Ruth had always shrunk from female friendship. It might be that her boarding-school experience had something to do in effecting this wholesale disgust of the commodity. Be that as it may, she had never found any woman who had not misunderstood and misinterpreted her. For the common female employments and recreations she had an unqualified disgust.[8]

Margaret Fuller, trapped in girlhood circumstances that made her arrogant in her possession of superior qualities and miserable in the isolation she felt as a consequence, was not unlike Ruth Hall. She dwelt at such length on her superiority and yet her powerlessness that she came half to believe, as Emerson reported, "that she was not her parents' child, but an European princess confided to their care."[9] When the changeling went to Europe to claim her true, intellectual inheritance, rumor reached Boston that the poet Mickiewicz wanted a divorce in order to marry her and that Mazzini had actually proposed to her. Emerson could credit neither these stories about plain Margaret, nor the one about the young nobleman Ossoli wooing her against all denial, but Elizabeth Hoar, his close Concord friend, set him straight: "It is not at all wonderful. Any one of these fine girls of sixteen she had known here, would have married her, if she had been a man. For she understood them."[10]

Fuller seems to have possessed the blend of intellectual incisiveness and shared sympathy that women in her society vainly sought in men. When it was manifested it could deeply disturb both women and men because, if not explained away, it undermined the terms on which they had organized their lives. When the feminine in Hawthorne was noted, it was meant as a compliment to his creative expansiveness, although, to be sure, he could himself never get rid of an uneasiness at being an observer rather than a virile doer. But when the masculine in Fuller was noted, it was meant to account for her freakishness. "Let it not be said," Fuller insisted, "wherever there is energy or creative genius, 'She has a masculine mind.' "[11] But it was said. The social function of her masculinity was limited to private lives, whereas Hawthorne's femininity made possible his public career. Horace Greeley, in whose household Fuller lived when she worked on the staff of his *Tribune,* observed of her:

> Women who had known her but a day revealed to her the most jealously guarded secrets of their lives, seeking her sympathy and counsel thereon, and were themselves annoyed at having done so when the magnetism of her presence was withdrawn. I judge that she was the repository of more confidences than any contemporary; and I am sure no one had ever reason to regret the imprudent precipitancy of their trust. Nor were these revelations made by those only of her own plane of life, but chambermaids and seamstresses unburdened their souls to her, seeking and receiving her counsel.[12]

The condition of American women as seen from abroad rather than from their own viewpoint was recognized as not only admirable but perhaps the finest result of democracy. Americans were, as Tocqueville observed, both a religious and a commercial people and so were doubly disposed to take marriage seriously. Religion regarded the regularity of a woman's life as the best sign of her morals, and commerce regarded it as the best security for the prosperity of her household. Within marriage woman had such an influential sphere that she enjoyed a strength of character unknown elsewhere. Tocqueville said:

> It would seem in Europe, where man so easily submits to the despotic sway of women, that they are nevertheless deprived of some of the greatest attributes of the human species and considered as seductive but imperfect beings, and (what may well provoke astonishment) women ultimately look upon themselves in the same light and almost consider it as a privilege that they are entitled to show themselves futile, feeble, and timid. The women of America claim no such privileges.[13]

So viewed, the price paid in the American system for the moral and intellectual strength of its wives was a denial or at least a marked lack of recognition of the passional in relations between the sexes. It was a price, Tocqueville felt, well worth paying for the strength of character it brought out in its women. But the society that was formed in such a fashion, it must be noted, was one that further reduced the fare with which it fed its novelists. To the litany of no ruins, no distinct social classes, no picturesque costumes, would have to be added no stirring love affairs. *The Scarlet Letter* stands alone in the period as a novel centered on the love of a man and woman for one another, and it is removed from the nineteenth century in setting, while its theme is scrupulously abstracted from personality into the sphere of general human morality.

Later in the 1830s another French traveler, Michael Chevalier, also became fascinated with the American way of marriage when he compared it with that of his homeland:

> We buy a woman with our fortunes as we sell ourselves to her for her dowry. The American chooses her, or rather offers himself to her, for her beauty, her intelligence, or her amiable qualities and asks no other portion. Thus, while we make a traffic of what is most sacred, these shopkeepers exhibit a delicacy and loftiness of feeling which would have done honor to the most perfect models of chivalry. It is to industry that they are indebted for this superiority. Our idle cits, not being able to increase their patrimony, are obliged in taking a wife to calculate her portion in order to decide if their joint income will be enough to support a family. The American, having the taste and the habits of industry, is sure of being able to provide amply for his household and is, therefore, free from the necessity of making this melancholy calculation.[14]

If, on the surface, marriage is far less of a business arrangement to start with in America, it becomes a joint working enterprise afterward as the partners divide their spheres and employ their boundless industry. Wealth in France is viewed by Chevalier (or by his countrymen) as static, and so marriage becomes a matter of calculating what proportion of a fixed total will result when wife and husband combine their funds; whereas in America wealth is viewed as unlimitedly attainable, so that the fixed amounts brought to the marriage are secondary to the compatibility of those who will enter into partnership to pursue it. But here also, by inference rather than direct statement, is an absence of the passional. With a commercial marriage arranged, the French man or woman will seek sexual realization in or out of that marriage as is necessary, but for the American, sexual realization will have to become a subdivision of the common industry. When Chevalier likened the delicacy of the Americans to the loftiness of feeling of the models of chivalry, he did not remember that the chivalric tradition, unlike the American, recognized the love relationship as taking place outside of marriage.

With such a high view of the American's ability to be both commercial and yet an uncalculating suitor, Chevalier asked, "Is it possible to doubt that a race of men which thus combines in a high degree the most contradictory qualities, is reserved for lofty destinies?" And Tocqueville was even more emphatic on the same topic:

> As for myself, I do not hesitate to avow that although the women of the United States are confined within the narrow circle of domestic life, and their situation is in some respects one of extreme dependence, I have nowhere seen women occupy a loftier position; and if I were asked, now that I am drawing to the close of this work, in which I have spoken of so many important things done by the Americans, to what the singular prosperity and growing strength of that people ought mainly to be attributed, I should reply: To the superiority of their women.[15]

Even in this concluding paean Tocqueville acknowledges that the American woman exerts her strength from within marriage rather than as a separate person, and, moreover, that her married position is one of extraordinary dependency, so that her influence upon her society is indirect.

The extremity of the dependency was emphasized by the remarkable independence enjoyed by the young woman prior to marriage, as extreme in its way as was the condition that followed in the opposite way. In marrying, the American woman moved from one polar situation to the other, and if she could not in the second discharge the intellect and the energy developed in the first, her discontent would be enormous. That she did so, in the main, is testified to by the many who regarded her as the key to America's success. Avoidance of marriage, of course, was no solution to the dilemma of exchanging self for family, because the self that was retained could make little meaningful connection with society. Harriet Martineau, a forceful unmarried woman herself, but an Englishwoman, admired the capacities of Margaret Fuller highly and therefore regarded Fuller's unmarried life (she married in her late thirties) as a terrible waste of time, since without a marriage Fuller was, as it were, deprived of a power base and dissipated her talents in lectures to women or in journalism in a vain attempt to find some consequential attachment to her society. Martineau wrote, "It is the most grievous loss I have almost ever known in private history,—the deferring of Margaret Fuller's married life so long."[16]

Ideas of absolute social justice or of the scientifically true nature of the differences between the sexes are, of course, applicable to American society in the first half of the nineteenth century. But as a means of understanding the condition of women they are less rewarding than is a sense of the manner in which the discontent of women was connected in great part to the peculiarly sharp contrast in that society between the qualities of independence in single life and those of dependence in married life. This explains why from the European perspective the American woman signaled a new and finer era whereas from her own perspective the situation was an unhappy one. Her society attempted to moderate the sharp contrast by maintaining publicly what it regarded as a pure and wholesome atmosphere, so that the single young woman could move through her entire environment—the streets as well as the sitting room—without having her ear offended by a suggestive remark, her eye offended by a suggestive book, or her person offended by a suggestive man. She was to be as secure in America at large as in her family, because America at large was to be a moral extension of the values of the family home. To be sure, this was somewhat qualified by region and even more so by economic class, as the women of the poor, perforce, were exposed to conditions different from those experienced by the wealthier. But America was a middle-class nation, by and large. Thus, the progress from being a child in a family to being a young woman in society to being a mother of a family was made against a backdrop of unchanged simplicities. This pretence of coherence could only compound the complication noted by Hawthorne: the discrepancy between private condition and what was publicly manifest. The society did not match the stages of a woman's emotional growth by accepting that she could enjoy and benefit from experiences that responded to a greater sexual sophistication than those of her protected girlhood. In America, a decent woman, regardless of age, was not to read a French novel, or converse about sexual relations, or view a nude statue in the presence of men.

What the American woman was offered in place of social correlatives to her maturity was what in that day was most frequently called "gallantry," a recognition on the part of all men she encountered that she was dependent, special, and therefore cherishable. Fanny Fern with her characteristically racing scorn advised young ladies:

> When you enter a crowded lecture-room, and a gentleman rises politely,—as American gentlemen always do,—and offers to give up his seat, which he came an hour ago to secure for himself,—take it as a matter of course; and don't trouble yourself to thank him, even with a nod of your head. As to feeling uneasy about accepting it, that is ridiculous! because if he don't fancy standing during the service, he is at liberty to go home; it is a free country![17]

Harriet Martineau was, of course, more analytic:

> She has the best place in stage-coaches: where there are not chairs enough for everybody, the gentlemen stand: she hears oratorical flourishes on public occasions about wives and home, and apostrophes to woman: her husband's hair stands on end at the idea of her working, and he toils to indulge her with money: she has liberty to get her brain turned by religious excitements, that her attention may be diverted from morals, politics, and philosophy; and especially, her morals are guarded by the strictest observance of propriety in her presence. In short, indulgence is given her as a substitute for justice.[18]

Martineau had observed one too many teas with the minister to believe that they were anything other than lightning rods designed to direct woman's energy along an inconsequential course. But the alliance of the kept classes, women and clergy, had an enormous potential. Daniel Webster patted both on the head when he spoke of Union and urged compromise for its sake. But Charles Sumner, who spoke radically of Free Soil, managed to follow the infinitely more magnetic Webster to the Senate despite his public extremism and his private dullness. His electoral success stemmed in good part from enlisting the persuasive power of the clergy, whose votes were insignificant in number, and of women, who did not vote at all. Edwin Whipple was an acute observer of the phenomenon:

> In a few months after the oration on the Fourth of July, 1845, it became evident that Sumner had established himself as a power among two classes of our New England population which it is never safe for any politician to disregard or despise; namely, earnest, progressive clergymen, and warm-hearted, cultivated women. In speaking of "cultivated" women, it is of course implied that the phrase includes not only those women of large hearts who have been highly educated as to the knowledge of many languages and many literatures, but those women who have been trained in the austere discipline of practical life to regard moral obligations as the most important and permanent of all the ties in which civil society rests, though they may speak no language but their own and have read but few books except the Bible and "Pilgrim's Progress." The influence which Sumner early obtained among these sources of real power went on increasing to the day of his death.[19]

Whipple then felt compelled to offer a psychological explanation for Sumner's appeal in the following predictable terms: "There was from the first something feminine, though not effeminate, in the delicacy of his perception of moral obligations."

If Martineau correctly saw that women were offered indulgence as a substitute for justice, she nevertheless underestimated the political force of the indulged. Indeed, as the success of Harriet Beecher Stowe was to emphasize, women in their dependency could exert a greater social force as women than they would be able to do for some time after they actually gained political rights.

This, however, did not mean that dependency and its attendant, gallantry, were therefore justified, and there was no shrewder observer of the matter than Lydia Maria Child. She saw, as did few other feminist commentators, the terrors of the world the men had reserved for themselves: "It is horrible to see our young men goaded on by the fierce calculating spirit of the age, from the contagion of which it is almost impossible to escape, and then see them tortured into madness, or driven to crime by the fluctuating changes in the money-market."[20] She accordingly believed that no benefit could derive to women who entered the public arena that would compensate for the injury that would be done them. But this did not mean that she condoned gallantry. Located as she was in New York, where increasing social and economic complexity permitted expressions that were muffled elsewhere, she more than hinted that lewdness was on the rise:

> This sort of politeness to women is what men call gallantry; an odious word to every sensible woman, because she sees that it is merely the flimsy veil which foppery throws over sensuality, to conceal its grossness. So far is it from indicating sincere esteem and affection for women, that the profligacy of a nation may, in general, be fairly measured by its gallantry. This taking away *rights* and condescending to grant *privileges,* is an old trick of the physical force principle; and with the immense majority, who only look on the surface of things, this mask effectually disguises an ugliness, which would otherwise be abhorred.[21]

And most impressively Child identified literature's role as a conditioning agent for woman's acceptance of her inferior position. A century was to pass before writers developed the topic that Child incisively etched:

> There are few books, which I can read through, without feeling insulted as a woman, but this insult is almost universally conveyed through that which was intended for praise. Just imagine, for a moment, what impression it would make on men, if women authors should write about *their* "rosy lips," and "melting eyes," and "voluptuous forms," as they write about *us*! That women in general do not feel this kind of flattery to be an

> insult, I readily admit; for, in the first place, they do not perceive the gross chattel-principle of which it is the utterance; moreover, they have, from long habit, become accustomed to consider themselves as household conveniences, or gilded toys.[22]

Among middle-class women protective confinement within the domestic sphere clearly meant arrested development on a national scale. While men prided themselves on shielding women from life's harshness, such women appeared to American men who had seen their European counterparts to be childish,[23] or, as Hawthorne put it, to look like anxious skeletons. Moreover, although spared the brutality of outdoor labor on most farms and the rudeness of the marketplace in the cities, women were exposed to other threats to their health peculiar to their condition. Dr. Holmes exclaimed, "Talk about military duty! What is that to the warfare of a married maid-of-all-work, with the title of mistress, and an American female constitution, which collapses just in the middle third of life, and comes out vulcanized India-rubber, if it happens to live through the period when health and strength are most wanted?"[24]

More pernicious because the causes were less understood were the frequent nervous breakdowns which were accepted as an all but normal result of being born a female. On one hand a future mother needed to be educated because, it was universally agreed, the home over which she would eventually preside was her society's only center of ideality and she had to be prepared to be its "priestess," as Harriet Beecher Stowe untiringly characterized her. Holmes explained the matter thus:

> The education of our community to all that is beautiful is flowing mainly through its women, and that to a considerable extent by the aid of these large establishments [girls' schools], the least perfect of which do something to stimulate the higher tastes and partially instruct them. Sometimes there is, perhaps, reason to fear that girls will be too highly educated for their own happiness, if they are lifted by their culture out of the range of the practical and every-day working youth by whom they are surrounded. But this is a risk we must take. Our young men

> come into active life so early, that if our girls were not educated into something beyond mere practical duties, our material prosperity would outstrip our culture; as it often does in large places where money is made too rapidly.[25]

On the other hand, as Holmes was prepared to admit, the education a girl received in order to make her the carrier of culture in an otherwise material society could so tune her expectations that her subsequent life as a wife would be one of frustration.

Chevalier was amazed at the "jars, disappointments, mortifications" of practical life among America's cultivated classes and noted that "the independence of servants involves the dependence of women, condemns them to household labors little consonant with the finished education which many of them have received, and nails them to the kitchen and the nursery from the day of their marriage to the day of their death."[26] Headaches, faintings, hysterics, and numbed taking-to-beds were regarded as natural products of woman's biological makeup. They were, in good part, the result of the discrepancy between a woman's education for culture and her total subjugation to domestic labor.

It was this discrepancy that Margaret Fuller sought to alleviate in the series of conversational classes for women she held at Elizabeth Peabody's home from 1839 to 1844. Keenly intelligent and thoroughly if harshly educated by her father, with an emphasis on Latin that early led her to identify with the Roman virtues of what she consistently called "manhood," she had "a tendency to robustness, of which she was painfully conscious, and which . . . she endeavored to suppress or conceal." The male friend who noted this could not, for all his knowledge of her outlook, suppress his gallantry, and insisted that her plainness was not "positive plainness," citing her abundant hair, excellent teeth, and eyes that appeared all the more piercing for their being near-sighted.[27]

Fuller edited *The Dial* (1840–42) and wrote on various topics, most notably a book on her travels to the West, *Summer on the Lakes* (1844), and a book that grew in some part from her conversational classes and is the most fully reasoned feminist document to its date in America, *Woman in the Nineteenth Century* (1845). In 1844 she joined the staff of Greeley's *Tribune* in New York, gaining a wide reputation as a critic, and in 1846, thanks to the patronage of friends and a commission from Greeley to act as correspondent, she was finally able to fulfill her lifelong ambition to visit Europe. In Paris she met with George Sand; and she became personally and politically involved with Mazzini and Mickiewicz, each planning a revolution that he hoped would bring democracy to his homeland. Thence she went to Italy, where, because of her friendship with Mazzini, she was soon caught up in the actions that led to the Roman revolution of 1848. In Rome she met the Marquis Ossoli, a minor nobleman for all the grandness of his title. He was a revolutionary (converted to the cause, it is highly probable, by her) while his family was loyal to the Pope, and he was a Catholic while she was a Protestant; marriage to her would jeopardize his and his children's inheritance. Such considerations probably led to the secrecy of their marriage, which, in all likelihood, did not take place until after the birth of their child. Each was active during the revolution, but their duties separated them. When the revolution failed, they decided to come to the United States to work for the next revolution, which they deemed inevitable. They embarked in 1850, and crossed the ocean, only to be caught in a storm off Fire Island. Their ship sank and although a number of passengers were saved, all three Ossolis drowned.

The profile Fuller's career presents is one of enormous intelligent energy seeking some form of social effectiveness. The fact that she spoke better than she wrote, was far more commanding in person than on the page, is indicative of her troubling place in cultural history. She is an undeniably formidable presence and yet that presence is embodied in writings that, though able, lack the attractive power she exerted on the many women who confided in her, on such men as Emerson, Mazzini, and Mickiewicz, and on such events as the development of American literary identity and the war for Italian national identity. What seems clear is that in each successive period of her life—Boston, New York, Europe—her strength grew in direct ratio to her ability to find concrete social and political commitments.

In Boston she was the kind of oddity the town knew how to deal with—the "literary" spinster. She was, consequently, given the kind of role assigned Elizabeth Peabody, secretary to the transcendental literati and maid-of-all-work in the temple of advanced ideas. Only by escaping to New York did Fuller escape Peabody's destiny of kindhearted dottiness. There her journalistic duties gave her much wider and ruder scope, but she was still reporting far more than doing. Even her book on woman was essentially reactive rather than agitative. Nonetheless, she had come out from Boston privacy, where, in exchange for good libraries, literary acquaintances, and a small closed audience, she was required to exercise her talents by pursuing abstractions. She later came to prefer Rome to Florence because Florence, she said, was too much like intellectualizing and undoing Boston. Finally, in Europe she broke through to the feeling that she could be a maker rather than a taker, although she feared the moment had probably arrived too late. She wrote Emerson from Rome, 20 December 1847:

> I find how true was that lure that always drew me towards Europe. It was no false instinct that said I might find an atmosphere here to develop me in ways I need. Had I only come ten years earlier! Now my life must be a failure, so much strength has been wasted on abstractions, which only came because I grew not in the right soil.[28]

What she came to perceive in Italy was that the fundamental evil of sexual discrimination was not so much that it blocked a woman from the pursuit of an intellectual career as that it conditioned her to engage in that career with an undeveloped social consciousness. Insofar as woman responded to political events she did so in assertion of moral or religious truths of which she accepted the guardianship, believing them to be absolute, whereas they were neither truths nor absolute but mere social sentiments. Fuller in Europe came to perceive that history was dynamic and consequently to believe that she had formerly erred in agreeing with her society that her social beliefs were apart from the vulgar political and economic squabbles of the day. In a dispatch to the *Tribune* in 1848, she told her fellow Americans, "You may in time learn to reverence, learn to guard, the true aristocracy of a nation, the only real nobles—the LABORING CLASSES."[29]

Fuller's Boston conversations had been based on the realization that women were not called upon in life to reproduce anything they had learned in school. Her classes would provide such an opportunity:

> My method has been to open a subject,—for instance, . . . the history of a nation . . . and, after as good a general statement as I know how to make, select a branch of the subject and lead others to give their thoughts upon it. When they have not been successful in verbal utterance of their thoughts, I have asked them to attempt it in writing. At the next meeting, I would read these "starts of pen and ink" aloud, and canvass their adequacy without mentioning the names of the writers.[30]

Too many have testified to the value of these sessions with Fuller to permit doubt as to their effectiveness as a kind of local therapy. But Harriet Martineau, for all her strident self-righteousness and despite the fact that her deafness did not permit her to appreciate the power of Fuller's conversation, does not seem entirely misguided in her contemptuous dismissal of them: "While Margaret Fuller and her pupils sat 'gorgeously dressed', while talking about Mars and Venus, Plato and Goethe, and fancying themselves the elect of the earth in intellect and refinement, the liberties of the republic were running out as fast as they could go, at a breach which another sort of elect persons were devoting themselves to repair; and my complaint against the 'gorgeous' pedants was that they regarded their preservers as hewers of wood and drawers of water, and their work as a less vital one than the pedantic orations which were spoiling a set of well-meaning women in a pitiable way."[31]

Fuller herself, had she lived after her Italian experiences to read these remarks, would have agreed with their import. In Rome in 1848 she reflected that she could not when she was at home endure the abolitionists; "they were so tedious, often so narrow, always so rabid and exaggerated in their tone."[32] Now the very thought of them pleased her and she prayed God to strengthen them.

It may well be argued, however, that *Woman in the Nineteenth Century* grew from the conversations not just in the sense that feminist topics had there been broached but also in the sense that Fuller in the book reacted to what Martineau called the "gorgeous" setting in which they took place. Fuller knew at bottom she was engaged as a leisure-class entertainer, and even as she admired women who came out of domesticity to exercise their minds on set occasions, she was baffled by the inconsequentiality of it all when compared with what women were capable of doing. At a fashionable resort, Fuller said in her book, she saw fashionable women with heads full of folly and hearts filled with jealousy or vanity, confirming the low opinion men had of women. How much, after all, did such women differ at bottom from those she addressed in Boston? She met another circle of women when she visited a prison:

> They had not dresses like the other ladies, so they stole them; they could not pay for flattery by distinctions and the dower of a worldly marriage, so they paid by the profanation of their persons. . . .
>
> Now I ask you, my sisters, if the women at the fashionable house be not answerable for those women being in prison?[33]

The concept of sisterhood here developed is perhaps the single most significant theme in *Woman in the Nineteenth Century.* Compared with Fuller's later social awareness the book is confused in its naive tracing of social, political, and economic causes. But it is admirable in its recognition that these, rather than biology, are at the root of the problem, and penetrating in its insistence that the initial step must be the altering of women's awareness. Fuller affirmed that in her time women were the best helpers of one another, and that men had a role only because they were needed to remove arbitrary barriers. In her peroration she said of women, "If you ask me what offices they may fill; I reply—any. I do not care what case you put." Then in a final burst she gave an example that made her book notorious among the unsympathetic many and risible even among the sympathetic few: "Let them be sea-captains, if you will."[34] For all his admiration of her, Horace Greeley thought himself killingly funny when he habitually held the door for Fuller and then shouted as she passed through, "Let them be sea-captains!"

In the less admired *Summer on the Lakes,* the reservoir of Fuller's essentially unused literary powers can be better gauged than in the more significant book on women. Her view of the white man's alienation from nature is completely in keeping with Romantic thinking on the subject: "He loses in harmony of being what he gains in height and extension; the civilized man is a larger mind, but a more imperfect nature than the savage."[35] But the vehemence of the imagery in which she conveyed her sense of the matter reveals a passion for the primitive and a loathing of the materialism of the modern that matches that of Thoreau: "Wherever the hog comes, the rattlesnake disappears; the omnivorous traveller, safe in its stupidity, willingly and easily makes a meal of the most dangerous of reptiles, and one whom the Indians look on with mystic awe. Even so the white settler pursues the Indian, and is victor in the chase."[36]

When she arrived at the obligatory set piece on Niagara Falls—a standardized test in Romanticism so highly regarded that Hawthorne represented himself as at first falling to the ground and refusing to look so that his unworthiness would not be exposed[37] —she wrote:

> The perpetual trampling of the waters seized my senses. I felt that no other sound, however near, could be heard, and would start and look behind me for a foe. I realized the identity of that mood of Nature in which these waters were poured down with such absorbing force with that in which the Indian was shaped on the same soil. For continually on my mind came, unsought and unwelcome, images such as never haunted it before, of naked savages stealing behind me with uplifted tomahawks; again and again this illusion recurred, and even after I had thought it over, and tried to shake it off, I could not help starting and looking behind me.[38]

Poe was much taken with this passage, pointing out that Fuller's properly ingenious emphasis on subjective effect rather than objective sight constituted true descriptive writing. The excited anticipation of being cleaved by a tomahawk borne by a naked man, like the image of the deadly but mystic rattlesnake, flows from a passionate source too deep and too dammed to find sufficient release in the rational flow of her literary criticism or even in her feminist essays. From such fragments one infers that she might have been a powerful creative writer had she been developed by circumstances other than those that surrounded an intellectual Boston female; but the stronger inference to be drawn from her larger career is that she was from the start a social critic and that the forceful imagery expended on stock Romanticism awaited the growth of her knowledge of historical cause.

Mickiewicz wrote from Paris to Fuller in Rome, "Learn to appreciate yourself as a beauty, and, after having admired the women of Rome, say, 'And as for me, why, I am beautiful!' "[39] She took his advice and acted upon it successfully. It was not mere male patronizing but the expression of a just perception of the passion dammed in her, denying her life the strength it should have been able to expend. The imagery such passion found in America was imagery of nature opposed to civilization, the past opposed to the present; but when it finally found outlet in Europe, that passion flowed in political action. As a woman in Boston Fuller assumed she was shut out of history, and her writings, while demanding that women be granted their fullest identity, did not see them as involved in history. In Italy, privileged no doubt by her status as a foreigner, which licensed behavior available only to the women of the nobility, she discovered that the historical forces that attracted her—the democratic nationalisms hurtling toward 1848—were not forces of the past, such as the Indians of America or the orators of ancient Rome, but forces of the present striving to become the future. She responded fully: "Art is not important to me now," she wrote home in 1847. "I take interest in the state of the people, their manners, the state of the race in them."[40] And a year later she wrote, "Here things are before my eyes worth recording, and if I cannot help this work, I would gladly be its historian."[41]

Such exhilaration at finally attaching passion to intelligence, will to action, self to history, was on the ship with her when she arrived off Fire Island. Kindled in Europe it was drowned within sight of the American strand.

Chapter Ten

Brotherhood: Reform, Sentiment, and *Uncle Tom's Cabin*

As early as 1837, John Greenleaf Whittier had written to the Grimké sisters, expressing his concern about their emphasis on the rights of women in their lectures. His abolitionist fervor approved of the fact that they daringly spoke before what he termed "promiscuous" audiences: that is, although they were women they publicly addressed mixed assemblages of women and men. This showed, he felt, that it was "the right and duty of woman to labor side by side with her brother for the welfare and redemption of the world." He was anxious, he wrote them, to have a long conversation with them on "the subject of *war,* human government, and church and family government." His use of the singular—"the subject" —for this awesome mixture of topics is indicative of the omnivorous optimism of the reformers; to set one thing right one must and could set everything right. But he was beginning to fear that the cause dearest to his heart, abolitionism, was becoming attenuated by its entanglement with the intensely personal issue of woman's rights, and he wanted to steer the Grimkés back to the main track. Why enter the lists on the woman's question, he asked them. "Does it not *look,* dear sisters, like abandoning in some degree the cause of the poor and miserable slave . . . ? Is it not forgetting the great and dreadful wrongs of the slave in a selfish crusade against some paltry grievance of our own?"[1]

Angelina Grimké replied that moral reforms could not be kept separate and that the denial of woman's rights was a stumbling block to the success of the united enterprise. Whittier was not persuaded. In the event, the mainstream of abolitionism did isolate the issue of the slave from other matters and grew in strength as a result. Still, in its Garrisonian version, abolitionism was a policy within the larger program of nonresistance, which opposed man's pretensions to govern. "Any intermediaries between the individual and God," the nonresistance people held, "were rivals to God's sovereignty and impeded the coming of the millennium."[2] Theirs was the dogma that Emerson explained to his English friends when asked if there had ever been an American idea.

Before the issue of the slave emerged as *the* issue in the three decades preceding the Civil War, a good deal of reforming thought, energy, and experiment had been spent on a range of social ills—economic, political, religious, and domestic—which, because they were viewed as interconnected, encouraged reformers to respond by conceptualizing model communities. In these, everything from family, worship, and remunerative labor to government could be restarted in a proper fashion, which seemed to make better sense than attempts to remain in general American society and pick at one or another of the threads in its tangled web.

Economically, such communities—Brook Farm being the best known but by no means the only or even the best example—were responding to the loss of control over product and income that the worker experienced as the factory replaced the craftsman in New England. For instance, a textile worker did not by himself make even a square inch of cloth, and the money he received, which used to be called his "price," signifying his identity with his product, was now called his "wages," signifying that it was his labor alone that he marketed. "In the present condition of society," Theodore Parker admitted, "this is unavoidable." With the glimmer that lit utopian communities, however, he added, "I do not say in a normal condition, but in the present condition."[3] Tocqueville's summary view of the matter was this:

> In proportion as the principle of the division of labor is more extensively applied, the workman becomes more weak, more narrow-minded, and more dependent. The art advances, the

> artisan recedes. On the other hand, in proportion as it becomes more manifest that the productions of manufactures are by so much the cheaper and better as the manufacture is larger and the amount of capital employed more considerable, wealthy and educated men come forward to embark in manufactures, which were heretofore abandoned to poor or ignorant handicraftsmen. The magnitude of the effort required and the importance of the results obtained attract them. Thus at the very time at which the science of manufactures lowers the class of workmen, it raises the class of masters.[4]

Social difficulties were compounded by the fact that under such a system the capitalist did not live at the center of his workers, as the European nobleman had lived among his peasants, nor did he have any obligation to them other than paying them wages. He was not bound to come to their aid in their distress as were both the European nobleman and the Southern slaveholder. His accumulated wealth did promise a source for the sustenance of cultural institutions—the support of universities, libraries, artists, churches—but it also powerfully affected the tone of what depended upon it. So the culture told truths and lies in reflection of the powerful class, according to Parker, while true literature and art were in the hands of poor men.

How far utopian communities could go to ameliorate this condition Hawthorne discovered—not far at all. And with regard to the larger economic situation, such communities without exception proved to be conservative rather than radical, in that they fought against modern technology to bring back the good old days in which the craftsman owned his own tools, worked for himself, quit when he wanted, and did not have to fit into a boss's scheme.[5] Even George Lippard, raging against the condition of the urban poor, could not imagine any counter to the exploiting capitalists other than a brotherhood that would restore to labor the fancied harmony of rural craft conditions. Outraged by the actualities of prostitution, debtors' courts, and church proprietorship of slums, he differed from his more bucolic brethren chiefly in that he sought to bring about change conspiratorially, in imitation of what he believed to be the successful methods of the powerful.

Sexual life in Lippard's America was affected by technological and urban conditions in subtler and more important ways than the provision to the bloated rich of concubines from the ranks of the wanting poor. The separation of the total self from its wage-earning activity in the factory resulted in a curbing of the spontaneous, the erotic, and the passional, as Melville reflected after he had seen Typee. Hawthorne recognized that private and public were being driven apart, and from this he derived the lesson that the subject matter of the serious American writer would have to be psychological rather than social. Since the psychological in his day was, as it were, without a vocabulary, the technique would have to be symbolic rather than naturalistic. In this course, it can be said, the mainstream of major American fiction flowed through Henry James to the twentieth century, when Freudianism supplied the psychological with so widely accepted a vocabulary that it could be treated naturalistically.

The question of the true nature of sexual relations was not evaded by the reformers; it was what they meant by "family government." John Humphrey Noyes, notoriously, pursued it thoroughly in his Oneida community. "All experience testifies (the theory of the novels to the contrary notwithstanding)," he said,

> that sexual love is not naturally restricted to pairs. Second marriages are contrary to the one-love theory, and yet are often the happiest marriages. Men and women find universally (however the fact may be concealed), that their susceptibility to love is not burnt out by one honey-moon, or satisfied by one lover. On the contrary, the secret history of the human heart will bear out the assertion that it is capable of loving any number of times and any number of persons, and that the more it loves the more it can love. This is the law of nature, thrust out of sight and condemned by common consent, and yet secretly known to all.[6]

Noyes maintained that the sexual appetite in America was starved not because of the widening split between the passional and the public but because custom, the source of which he did not explain, led to marriage at around the age of twenty-four, "whereas puberty commences at the age of fourteen." Such an unwritten law bore hardest on women because they had less opportunity to control their time of marriage than did men.

Notorious as was the free-love experiment at Oneida, it was conducted, significantly, like a family, those gathered there being brothers and sisters under the parentage of Noyes. In terminology it did not differ from its polar opposite, the Shaker community, in which there was no sexual intercourse whatsoever—its members in coming out of the world renounced their mates as sexual partners and gave their children over to a life of celibacy—but which also visualized itself as a family of brothers and sisters governed by an appointed mother and father. The weakening of the sexual meaning of gender in much literary discourse in the period was accompanied by an extraordinary confusion of family terms. At Oneida brothers and sisters made love with a will, presumably, whereas in the Shaker communities they kept apart and were the children of parents who had never had intercourse. In popular sentimental literature the happy relationship established by a solidly married couple was unhesitatingly characterized as that of a brother to a sister, while in sensational penny dreadfuls the standard avengers of seduced maidens were their brothers, who pursued the vicious Lovelaces with all the vehemence of wronged husbands and lovers. Lippard, for example, employed the device of having a wronged woman take revenge on her faithless lover by disguising herself as a man and then explaining to her lover's new mistress that he had been murdered by her (disguised as a him) because he had seduced his sister (really herself).

It was against such a background that Hawthorne explored the potential benefits of bisexual behavior at Blithedale among a family of brothers and sisters, and Melville's Pierre set up housekeeping with a passionate brunette, who was his half sister, and a passive blonde fiancée, who behaved toward him as a sister, both established in the role of wife. Before arriving at this stage, Pierre had lived with a widowed mother and they had enacted their little domestic scenes, such as meals together, as incidents in the life of a married couple, while addressing each other as "brother" and "sister."

Recourse to the family model as the only one available for any communal experiment regardless of its sexual organization, and recourse to the sibling relationship as the best example of understanding between a man and a woman, whether husband and wife or joint workers in a social cause—these were something more than habits of speech. In a deep fashion they indicated the enormous strain that contemporary life was inflicting upon the society's idealized and simple vision of itself. This is not to deny that incest fantasy was prevalent in the society, but rather to point up its presence. As a response to increasing depersonalization in their daily lives, Americans would appear to have fantasized a fulfillment of the qualities they felt to be missing, and to have done so in terms of family bonds that were, at the time, dissolving. To be married figuratively to one's sibling was to be safe from outside forces. When those forces caused a person to stray, then the counterforce was visualized as familial, most commonly an avenging sibling. Not surprisingly, Coverdale thought of his lust for Zenobia as brotherly love, while he admitted to sexual love only for the sexless Priscilla, who was like a little sister to him. Pierre's sexually charged triangle of mother, half sister, and fiancée resolved itself on the dictional level into his having three sisters. And countless popular works represented married couples as enjoying a sibling relationship.

The reformers were caught in a dilemma. Was sexual fulfillment a necessary part of the freedom they sought to affirm, or was sexual promiscuity the result of conditions which, once removed, would permit men and women to exercise self-control and love monogamously? Abolitionists recognized that the abstract principle of love for one's fellows that fueled their cause also implied greater sexual freedom; at the same time, one of their favorite images was that of the South as a great brothel. In this area of the culture the thinkers and writers of reform had tied themselves into a knot that might well have strangled them. They were saved by the ample outlet of direct political action opened for them by such events as the Mexican War and the passing of the Fugitive Slave Act. Response to such events drew them off increasingly from their theoretical problems, and the master contribution to their cause, *Uncle Tom's Cabin,* came at last from a religiously conservative, fiercely monogamous mother, scribbling in her kitchen in her spare time.

That book was in large part a product of the Midwest, or, as it was then called, the New North, in the strikingly national scope of its scenes and pitch of its tone as well as in its feel for the widening audience for popular literature. When Lyman Beecher moved to Cincinnati in 1832 to lead the struggle against Catholics and infidels for the soul of the region, his daughter Harriet accompanied him, and there, in 1836, she married Calvin Stowe, a professor in the seminary her father headed. The Beechers were among the foremost of those many New Englanders who had come into the new lands, and as a result of their efforts Cincinnati, despite its border location, took on a rigorous Protestant tone. "The moral aspect of Cincinnati," Chevalier noted, "is delightful in the eyes of him who prefers work to everything else, with whom work can take the place of anything else."[7] In emulation of New England's first cities, Cincinnati had its churches, schools, societies for temperance and prison reform, and its proscriptions against a range of amusements that, Chevalier remarked, were condemned as immoral pleasures, although he could not but regard them as innocent relaxations. The Midwest had become a cultural colony of New England.

This development both strengthened and was strengthened by Daniel Webster's efforts in Washington to keep the West from combining with the South on matters such as cheap land, free trade, and states' rights.[8] Calhoun, the definer of the southern position, was not concerned with wage earners or small entrepreneurs. He saw a class conflict coming that, he believed, would bring about an alliance of the big northern capitalists and the southern planters. Webster, however—so manifestly a spokesman for northern property that he was supported by a fund raised in the name of property against numbers—rejected Calhoun's vision of an ultimate America split into the propertied few and the unpropertied many. He envisioned a proliferation of small property owners sufficient to reconcile property government with popular government. The Yankee colonization of the Midwest gave him a strong base for his unionist rhetoric, since it spread the work ethic throughout the new lands and stimulated the aspiration toward small property holdings.

Yankeeism also brought a rage for literacy that descended ultimately from the puritanic distrust of any intermediary between man and his God. The people's right to direct access to the revealed word meant their right to literacy so that each could read his Bible. Illiteracy in the South Atlantic states in 1850 was five times greater than it was in New England, and in the new states south of Ohio it was three times greater than in the northern section of the Midwest.[9] The implications of this grew on northern publishers. Initially they exchanged journals with the *Southern Literary Messenger* and were sensitive to southern reaction to their books. But as western readership grew while the southern remained static, they were emboldened by the new market to disregard southern reactions. In 1849, James T. Fields of Boston removed the *Southern Literary Messenger* from the list of journals to receive review copies of books by such as Lowell, Holmes, and Whittier; and G. P. Putnam concluded that he could ignore the threats of southern readers of his monthly, since his entire sale in the South was smaller than it was in Ohio alone.[10] In the entire period before the Civil War, William Ticknor, Hawthorne's publisher and confidant, recorded sales in Cincinnati alone that totaled only $400 less than in the whole of the South.[11] By the time *Uncle Tom's Cabin* appeared as a book, in 1852, there was no need for uneasiness about offending a significant portion of the book-buying public. Within the first eight weeks 100,000 copies were sold in the Midwest, and, of course, it boomed along in the old North. Richard Henry Dana, reading it on a train journey from Boston to New Haven, noticed four others in his car reading it also.[12]

By the time she wrote *Uncle Tom,* Stowe was back in New England, where her husband had accepted a faculty post in Maine. Her earliest attitudes had, of course, been formed by a Calvinistic New England upbringing—she was twenty-one when the Beechers moved west—but her first writings, sketches and tales, were prepared to be read aloud at the social literary parties of Cincinnati and bind the sentiments of domestic New England to the scenes of the Midwest. In one, for example, "Little Fred, The Canal Boy," a western infant is exposed to moral coarseness that would not have threatened him Down East, but, thanks to timely missionary efforts, he survives with innocence intact. The tales, in the main, are so ridden with the unexamined pieties of the bombazined American bosom that they defy reading today. With the wisdom of hindsight, however, one can note that even as Stowe is in them assimilating the West into the moral climate of the East, so she is also training her eye to the observation of other regional types. When she came to write *Uncle Tom's Cabin,* she peopled it with characters and provided it with scenery drawn from every region of the United States. Although its massive appeal doubtless rested upon her great gift for developing dramatic correlatives for the sentiments she wished to express, the national sweep of the book gave her drama a powerful and impressive scope that enhanced that appeal. No other American work of fiction to date—or for some time after—managed to seem to be set in all America, despite the fact that its political effect was to disunify the country. Indeed, it is in the light of its national scope that one must read George Ticknor's grumbling about it. Loyal to the end to the cotton interests, he naturally disliked the novel's politics, but he also complained, "It is quite without the epic attribute that alone can make a romance classical, and settle it as a part of the literature of any country."[13] No one, perhaps, would bother to refute him; the book had other than epic intentions. But since he chanced to mention the matter, was it not, after all, close to an American epic? The story begins at the midlife point of its central character and focuses on his passion in Kentucky, in New Orleans, and in the hell of a remote Louisiana plantation, introducing a spectrum of characters drawn from all social classes and all regions of the nation. The national identity that emerged both in the readership and in the characters of *Uncle Tom's Cabin* was not political but religious—American Protestantism at its beneficent and sentimental fullest; it was not heroic but domestic—women swayed the plot throughout and Tom's powerlessness as a slave led him to epitomize the finest feminine attributes. When Whitman, some three years later, undertook a far more conscious national epic, "Song of Myself," he too ranged over regions and he too made the central figure hermaphroditic. This was fitting for a culture that, as the popularity of *Uncle Tom's Cabin* indicated, would not recognize a portrait of its finest self unless it included the power of the matron, shaping the consciousness and destiny of the children of the republic.

In scene after scene of maternal right behavior or maternal influence in *Uncle Tom's Cabin,* Stowe's appeal is to mothers who are reading the work, and through them their children. "I hate reasoning, John—especially reasoning on such subjects,"[14] says the matron, Mrs. Bird, when her husband, a state senator, presses her with the constitutionality of the Fugitive Slave Act, a valid argument used in insistent outrage by the South and countered by abolitionists with ultimately illogical or at least unconstitutional arguments drawn from a "higher law." But Stowe was a Christian mother, not a legal theorist, and she disposed of political arguments at length as Mrs. Bird disposed of them in brief: "There's a way you political folks have of coming round and round a plain right thing; and you don't believe it yourselves, when it comes to practice." In the novel

Senator Bird shrugs and assists the fugitives; the sentimental drama of plain right things, there is every reason to believe, elicited at least the private adherence of many a previously unconvinced reader.

Stowe directly addresses "You, mother at home," and says she especially wants to speak to one who knows the loss of a child, an experience she herself had had and one that was common throughout the land. "Why don't somebody wake up to the beauty of old women?"[15] she asks at another point, and does her best to provide the awakening.

On religious ground, southern clergymen had persistently asked their northern brethren to point to any passage in the Bible that declared against slavery, and, for good measure, wondered why women were so unscripturally permitted to have a public voice in the matter. "Let the Northern philanthropist learn from the Bible," Fred A. Ross told an Alabama synod, "that the relation of master and slave is not sin *per se*. Let him learn that God says nowhere it is a sin."[16] He recognized, as did most southern spokesmen, that slavery was a degraded condition and he did not believe it was fastened perpetually on the South, but in the fullness of Providence the matter needed far more time for dissolution. The North, as a further indication of its unnatural and irreligious haste, now encouraged a species that Ross called "convention ladies." He said:

> We of the South are afraid *of them*. . . . When women despise the Bible, what next, *Paris, then the city of the Great Salt Lake,—then Sodom—before and after the Dead Sea*. Oh sir, if slavery tends in any way to give the *honor of chivalry* of Southern young gentlemen towards ladies, and the exquisite delicacy and heavenly integrity and love to Southern maid and matron, it has then a glorious blessing with its curse.[17]

The fustian of the rhetoric indicates the cause is already lost, but this should not mask the fact that Ross's representative appeal to the Bible and his invocation of a society refined by southern chivalry have as valid a base as do the northern reformers' assertion of a higher law and northern society's worship of a maid-of-all-work called mother. The words "bombast" and "bombazine" come from the same root.

The typical southern rhetorical appeal rings false because of the kind of past to which it attaches itself. That past, the age of chivalry, was not one that had developed on southern soil but one that existed only in British fiction. It was adapted by southern fictionalists to a social landscape in need of a self-image that would counter the northern image of the home of honest soil. Slavery preserved the women from degrading duties—that could be said for it; and if the sayers were challenged with the citation of thousands of poor-white women not so freed, the response would have been that southern culture no more took its tone from them than northern culture did from the women in the streets of Philadelphia and New York.

Romanticism in the North sought to harmonize industrial man with a natural moral order. Romanticism in the South, where alienation of work from nature was far less grievous, dwelt upon the nobility of character that emerged from a social gradation that mirrored the scale of natural employments. In response to political threats, such Romanticism glorified a code of manners as the highest proof of social value, and in so doing invoked the tradition of feudal chivalry. Southern writers and speakers answered northern moral righteousness with concepts of honor and character, answered northern glorifications of hard work with examples of the sensitive manners that could be developed by humans freed from debasing toil. There was no sufficiently separate identity among the southern small entrepreneurs and skilled wage earners to impede the construction of such upper-class fictions.

As a result, when southerners protested that *Uncle Tom's Cabin* was an inaccurate picture of plantation life they gained little credence outside their region. However distorted Stowe's picture may have been, it was far more realistic than the improbable portraits available in southern fiction. Only after slavery had disappeared did southern writers capture the old plantation in their fictions in a way that served to correct the view millions took from *Uncle Tom's Cabin*.

Stowe fought the battle in just the right terms. Women knew better, as Mrs. Bird illustrated, than to think the ultimate appeal was to reason. Stowe eschewed political arguments in favor of image after pathetic image of the convincing superiority of the home run by an industrious matron on the best principles of northern thrift, as compared with the home, however gracious, served by slaves. She granted the St. Clare home its full charm, but all her homes, even the most opulent, rested on the foundation of the kitchen, and when she looked, as she frequently did, into that of St. Clare, she found slaves thriftless of time and materials laying a wasteful base for the entire edifice. She did not haggle, did not oppose the condition of the northern wage earner to that of the southern slave. She illustrated, and her appeals against slavery, in melodramatic scenes such as the escape across the ice or the brutal floggings, were held in proportion by key pictures of the northern kitchen that set the norm:

> There are no servants in the house, but the lady in the snowy cap, with the spectacles, who sits sewing every afternoon among her daughters, as if nothing ever had been done, or were to be done,—she and her girls in some long-forgotten forepart of the day, "*did up the work,*" and for the rest of the time, probably, at all hours when you would see them, it is "*done up.*" The old kitchen floor never seems stained or spotted; the tables, the chairs, and the various cooking utensils never seem deranged or disordered; though three and sometimes four meals a day are got there, though the family washing and ironing is there performed, and though pounds of butter and cheese are in some silent and mysterious manner there brought into existence.[18]

Although there has been plenty of hard work, the focus is not on the heated disarrangements of physical exertion but on the cool, tranquil harmony of its result, presided over by a "snowy cap" symbolic of the clime and the virtue that promote such results. There is no secret about nor substitute for the fatiguing churning required to convert milk into butter, yet it is accomplished so efficiently and uncomplainingly in a servantless house that it partakes of mystery. The scene, of course, is idealized, but it does not distort the reader's sense of her own ways or his memory of his mother's ways.

Such women are the emotive answer to Reverend Ross's fears of Sodom, Paris, or worse still, Salt Lake City. Rather than engage in ingenuities of textual criticism, Stowe meets the argument from the Bible through motherhood also. St. Clare defends slavery as suitable for the economy of the region, but when also offered the biblical support for it, he says:

> The Bible was my *mother's* book. . . . By it she lived and died, and I would be very sorry to think it did [justify slavery].

> I'd as soon desire to have it proved that my mother could drink brandy, chew tobacco, and swear, by way of satisfying me that I did right in doing the same. It wouldn't make me at all more satisfied with these things in myself, and it would take from me all the comfort of respecting her; and it really is a comfort, in this world, to have anything one can respect.[19]

When death approaches, St. Clare senses the presence of his mother, not the sainted little Eva, and his last word is "mother."

Even the vicious characters are gauged in terms of motherhood. Cassy, Legree's concubine, turned wicked only after her children were sold. Legree himself is most terrified when he involuntarily recalls that he rejected his mother's pious teachings. The institution of slavery as represented by Stowe separates slave mothers from their children, who are sold, and slaveholding mothers from their children, who are given to the care of slaves. Tom assumes maternal qualities in his cultural guidance of motherless slaves, all of them, in effect, orphans, and in his care of the children of his successive owners. While the southern writers were struggling to find in their society actual scenes that validated their fictive creations of a chivalric homeland, Stowe was taking a widespread feeling and shaping it into a fiction of powerful effect.

The same Walter Scott who provided the feudal model for the South had first opened to Stowe the glories of fiction. It was a memorable day in the Beecher household, where the children had available to them a library consisting of such items as Bell's sermons, Horsley's tracts, and Toplady on predestination, when Lyman Beecher announced to his children, "You may read Scott's novels. I have always disapproved of novels as trash, but in these is real genius and real culture, and you may read them."[20] Harriet promptly went through *Ivanhoe* seven times in the course of one summer.

Still, such an activity was confined within an outlook informed by a clear sense of the religious nature of life. Wandering thoughts had long been a concern of Puritan preachers acutely aware of the mind's tendency to stray from focus on its eternal condition into fantasies of earthly ease. Lyman Beecher said:

> Reverie is a delightful intoxication into which the mind is thrown. It is extempore novel-making. I knew a person who

> was wont to retire into this garden of reverie whenever he wished to break the force of unwelcome truth. I told him he must break up the habit or be damned.[21]

Harriet Beecher Stowe's art was shaped in accordance with these thoughts. Although she found a better justification for her art than any provided by her father's philosophy, nevertheless she said, and in her fiction after *Uncle Tom's Cabin* dramatized the conviction, that "the great fundamental facts of nature are Calvinistic, and men with strong minds and wills always discover it."[22] If Melville himself was not to say amen, certainly his principal characters were. Her aesthetic reasoning was tangled and even contradictory in its terminology, but from it emerges the doctrine that guided her. Citing Plato because God forbid that Christians need be any narrower than he, she maintains that there are two beauties, the celestial Urania and the terrestial Venus.[23] The latter represents the outward grace of art and nature, which was sufficient for other cultures. But in America, committed as it is and should be to disinterestedness, faith, patience, and piety as exemplified in the heroic lives of the Puritan founders, Venus is relegated to the role of being Urania's priestess, attracting men to earthly beauty only insofar as it guides them to divine intentions. By desexualizing Venus and casting her in the role of priestess rather than goddess, Stowe equated her with the American mother, whose duty it was to make of the home a shrine: "Priestess, wife, and mother, there she ministers daily in holy works of household peace, and by faith and prayer and love redeems from grossness and earthliness the common toils and wants of life."[24] Stowe herself accepted her place as mother-priestess and art-priestess. She claimed that *Uncle Tom's Cabin* first came to her in a vision she had of its climactic scene, and at other times she also seemed to justify art by claiming its divine inspiration. After her first exposure to the masterpieces of painting in Europe, she was a bit shaken and came close to admitting that creative genius may have followed rules of its own, apart from morality. She rallied, however, at the price of saying something silly, a price she was always unconsciously paying, and stoutly affirmed among other things that Shakespeare received his image of Desdemona from memories of his mother.[25]

Such silliness did not weaken the force of purpose she acquired from a sense of her dual role as priestess. With mother and artist reconciled she felt justified in focusing in detail upon the local scene. Hawthorne, somewhat ironically to be sure, maintained that a better book than he would ever write was happening each day outside his window, although he lacked the perspective from which to capture it. Stowe's equation of the home with art gave her the perspective to record the actual, and the result, in such works as *The Minister's Wooing* (1859), *The Pearl of Orr's Island* (1862), and *Oldtown Folks* (1869), was descriptive realism of a force and charm to match the genre paintings of the same period by George Caleb Bingham and his contemporaries.

In an early sketch of a minister, Stowe wrote, "The Bible in his hands became a gallery of New England paintings,"[26] and she was herself emboldened to add directly to that gallery. In her works we see babies suckling on a rag stuffed with carraway seeds and dipped in milk, find that a perfect baby is one that weighs just eight and three quarters pounds and has hair that parts with a comb, and learn that no young woman is fit to be married until she is able to boil an Indian pudding of such durability that it can be thrown up chimney and come down on the ground outside without breaking. An hour lost in the morning will not be found all day; those who sing before breakfast will cry before night. Such folkloristic detail must be watched sharply if the larger meanings are to emerge, because, for example, "Love in Puritan families was often like latent caloric,—an all-pervading force that affected not a visible thermometer . . . , seldom outbreathed in caresses."[27] Dreams must be ignored because dreams belong to the old dispensation which Jesus abrogated.

Stowe believed that her pictures of New England life and manners could not be experienced properly unless the viewer understood their hidden causes, but these for her were not psychological. Rather, they were theological:

> The clear logic and intense individualism of New England deepened the problems of the Augustinian faith, while they swept away all those softening provisions so earnestly clasped to the throbbing heart of that great poet of theology. No rite, no form, no paternal relation, no faith or prayer of church, earthly

> or heavenly, interposed the slightest shield between the trembling spirit and Eternal Justice. The individual entered entirely alone, as if he had no interceding relation in the universe.[28]

Accordingly, the agony of a young man's mother and fiancée when he is reported lost at sea is occasioned not so much by the thought of the death itself as by the strong possibility that he died unregenerate. Personality in such a theme was secondary, and the best is noted of Stowe's New England fictions as well as the worst when it is said that she was the great delineator of the New England type, the portraitist of Puritans become Yankees, unemotional but sentimental, living practically and thinking abstractly, dour in mien and tender at heart.

Hundreds of thousands of Americans accepted the reconciliation of strict piety and indulged feelings that Harriet Beecher Stowe offered in *Uncle Tom's Cabin.* For all the pro-North effect of that novel and for all the local content of her New England fictions, her region was social rather than geographical—the region of the anxious, well-intentioned, unquestioningly religious literate classes who formed the main part of America. She was a national writer.

Chapter Eleven

The Fool Killer: George Washington Harris and Sut Lovingood

The great popular success of *Uncle Tom's Cabin* increased desire in the South for a literature distinctive of that culture. It was not a desire of long standing. Before Garrison started his weekly, *The Liberator,* in 1831, southerners took pride in all American literature, regardless of regional origin, as their literature.[1] But the hostility of such publications as the abolitionist journal led to a concern that southern opinion have a literary outlet, and the more southern men of letters reflected on the matter, the more they were struck by what Poe had announced as a fact: the literary products of New England were a sectional literature masquerading as a national literature. The most prolific, and some would say the only, southern writer of note based in the South, William Gilmore Simms of Charleston, complained that not only were the Yankees regional in their writing, what was worse, they were not manly. The highest praise he could find for their work was conveyed in phrases such as "nice taste," "clever imitator," "delicate," "unobtrusive humor." But there was a native character the opposite of this, rough, original, and above all manly, and this he felt the North had evaded in its feeble writings.[2]

Simms himself attempted to capture such original native flavor in his novels, but nativism to him meant adherence to the code of manners practiced in the South, and the more urgent the political pressures from the North, the more refined became that code in his pages. By the 1850s he was, without quotation marks or qualification, calling his plantation owners "aristocrats" and entering into detailed illustration of the circumstances under which overseers might safely be honored with the friendship as well as the indulgence of their employers. James Fenimore Cooper, who also followed Scott in the framework of much of his fiction, had argued that there were real social distinctions in a democracy and undertook the task of demonstrating them in his novels. But Simms accepted the existence of a social hierarchy as fixed as the planets—elegant aristocracy, knightly retainers, sturdy yeomen, fiercely loyal slaves—and within that static frame was unable to start a resonant action because all human and social issues had been settled. He was left with the melodrama that could be stirred by sheer villainy, and his novels' better moments are generally those devoted to recording the talk of the low characters—deliberately staged in response to a formula by Shakespeare out of Scott—where his ear for speech, far finer than Cooper's, keeps such characters from becoming, like Cooper's, massive bores. Simms lacks, however, the dynamic sense of social issues that Cooper possessed so surely.

And Simms stood just about alone. His fiction was the sharpest kind of realism when compared with the confections of southern life as feudal idyll that were baked in answer to the threatening North. In these lesser novels characters named Iolia, Manolia, Roscius, and Cassanio moved languidly beneath the southern moon, exercising in speech and action an exquisite courtesy toward one another. The diction was Latinate and the syntax frequently periodic, although there were happy intervals in which the whole collapsed into a comic mélange that was unintended. A mountaineer, asked if he knows where Roscius is, stands at the door of his cabin and manfully attempts to maintain the standard of lofty speech set him by his acknowledged betters: "I have heard tell of no such youth. Them ravens you hear screaming over yon chasm can give you some account of him likely."[3]

The culture that was forced into such literary reaction had a high respect for learning, but was also separated from a good part of its own social reality. On one hand there is the illiteracy rate five times greater than that of New England; on the other, by 1860 there were twenty-three colleges in Virginia, enrolling 2,824 students, in contrast to eight colleges in Massachusetts, enrolling 1,733 students, some of them Virginians. Annually Virginia spent $50,000 more on her colleges than Massachusetts did.[4] The failure of southern literature to match northern in either quantity or quality did not stem from the absence of an educated class, but from the aspirations to which that class put its learning, as well as from the fact that status and therefore identity were withheld from a literate middle class of tradesmen and mechanics, who should have served as traffickers in ideas as well as goods.

Law, politics, and religion attracted the learned, and the verbal arts were aimed at oral delivery rather than a written literature. Indeed, a literary reputation was considered damaging. Augustus Baldwin Longstreet's *Georgia Scenes* (1835) initially made him a hero in a state which, in 1835, was strongly set off from its neighbors because of the New England origin of its settlers; Georgia was called the Connecticut of the South. At the time he wrote the sketches he was a lawyer. But as he moved on to being a judge, a clergyman, and then a college president, and in the process moved throughout the South—he headed, in turn, Emory University, Centenary College, the University of Mississippi, and the University of South Carolina—he found that his well-known book was more hindrance than help. By the midpoint of his life he abandoned all fiction other than the didactic.

Frederick Law Olmsted, traveling through the South in the early 1850s, was amazed at the "singularly simple, child-like ideas about commercial success" he found even among educated Virginians. They looked on the agency by which goods were transferred from producer to consumer as a swindling operation and spoke angrily of New York "as if it fattened on the country without doing the country any good in return. They have no idea that it is *their* business that the New Yorkers are doing."[5]

Olmsted traced the reasons that led southerners to place so high an emphasis upon professions such as the law and to withhold status from the skilled worker:

> The idea that a muscular or handicraft occupation, if directed with the genius and thought it always may and should be, is lower or less fortunate and less likely to be attended with honor in a free country, than the occupations of transfer,

> scheming, copying and adapting for forms and precedents, is a most false and pernicious one. It is true, only, that a man without any education may be a bad workman, while he cannot well be even a bad clerk, lawyer, or physician. But genius, taste, energy and dexterity, as well as capital in general knowledge and culture of mind, are even more valuable, and are at this time more wanted in our market, and are better paid for in the artisan and mechanic, than they are in the tradesman and the professional man. The only basis for the contrary notion that I know of is, that slaves are excluded from trade and "the professions," and that therefore, wherever the influence of Slavery extends, those occupations to which slaves are condemned are considered to belong to a lower *caste* of the community, and so to degrade those who engage in them.[6]

The paradox of a high density of colleges and a high rate of illiteracy among the white population is clarified by such an observation, and the failure to emerge of a self-respecting middle class, so vital to the spread of literature in nineteenth-century America, is explained also.

Emerson, brooding upon the contrast between the timid, prudent, calculating Yankee, unable to fight until his cold blood had been subjected to a long process of heat and even then finding complicated obstacles in his conscience, and the chivalrous, passionate, haughty Virginian, quick to defend honor and avenge insult, predicted the course that events were to take when he said in 1842 of the young abolitionists vaporing in the streets of Boston, "The Virginian . . . beats them today, & is steadily beaten by them year by year."[7]

In the border states at some distance from the homes of the feudal ideal, however, a literature of the plain folk was beginning to find expression, a literature that surpassed that of the North in its expressive colloquialism, skillfully shifted points of view, and vital presentation of spontaneous feeling. The yarns and sketches from this region that began to find their way into local newspapers and thence into the sporting journals of the Northeast, not regarded as reading suitable for the home, were southern in their dialect, and southern in their undisguised hatred for the North (while genteeler southern writers disagreed or remonstrated, the writers in this tradition refreshingly hated). But as tied to the South as this region was by its acceptance of slavery, the energy of its literature came in some good part from a contempt for the ideal southern hierarchic social vision. Hill farmers, copper miners, and river men had their own version of southern culture, one that scorned authority and ridiculed sentiment. The fantasies that grew straight up from the roots of their anarchic culture were so passionate as frequently to be sickeningly sadistic, and the writing of their greatest creator, George Washington Harris, is so centered on cruel if comically intended scenes of revenge, detailed with such physiological precision, that the pleasure of his achievement is forever mixed with distaste for his climactic scenes of discomfort and dismemberment. But the ferocious antisentimentalism of Harris's sadistic scenes provides a valuable, one might almost say a relieving, contrast to the unexamined pieties of even so accomplished a moralist as Stowe. His celebration of the primal, his ability to slide persuasively into the epic and out again, his keen eye for animation, his subtle ear for the offbeat, anticlimactic, comic line, and his capacity to symbolize in incident the nexus of antiintellectualism, sexual vigor, antiauthoritarianism, and cruel physical force buried in the psyche of his folk make him one of the greatest American writers of his day, albeit one who has not written more than ten consecutive pages that can be read without wincing.

The paradox in his achievement is matched by the paradox in his life.[8] Born in Allegheny, Pennsylvania, in 1814, Harris migrated to the West, where by the age of nineteen he was captain of a steamboat on the Tennessee River. He went on to speculation in glassworks, supervision of a copper mine, and another spell as a steamboat captain, and in the course of his activities began writing sketches of local incidents and manners. In 1854 he seems to have encountered in extreme southeast Tennessee a man who served him as the basis for the character of Sut Lovingood, the "born fool" through whose eyes and voice the finest of his tales are realized.

Harris became a Presbyterian elder in Knoxville, was a sabbatarian and a hard-working machinist. Sut was irreligious and expressed strong doubts about his even possessing a soul; he was free with women and with the bottle, and shiftless. Harris was a Democrat, although his half brother Samuel Bell, who was mayor of Knoxville and stood to him as a father, was a pro-union Whig, as was his close friend William Crutchfield, to whom he dedicated *Sut Lovingood's Yarns* (1867). But Sut was an unthinking, anarchic Yankee-hater, more apt to set a mortal trap for a Whig than to talk to him. Sut is not developed ironically by Harris nor is he patronized by him. Rather he is a free spirit, the true alter ego of his creator; he expresses the passionate subrational forces repressed in the mechanically skilled Presbyterian elder, and he expresses them all the more forcefully for Harris's successful repression of them in his own life.

"It's an awful thing, George," Sut tells Harris, "to be a natural-born durned fool. You's never experienced it personally, have you? It's made pow'fully agin our family—and all owin to Dad."[9] But, of course, because he is a fool, Sut is free to act out what Harris must control, and throughout the accounts of his adventures Sut emphasizes his reliance in tight spots on the length and speed of his legs rather than on his wits: "I tell you . . . that running am the greatest invenshun on yearth when used keerfully."[10]

In Sut's world women are objects of sexual desire, and motherhood has no special aura, meaning, as it does, the end of the first flush of headlong youth. Jule Sawyers hugs Dick Harlan tightly as she rides behind him on the pony carrying them to the dance: "She says she didn't mind a fall but it mought break hir leg an then good bye frolicks—she'd be fit fur nuthin but to nuss brats ollers afterwards."[11] Even Sut's own mother is presented without the pieties that glossed over the matron in northern literature; since she is a woman, her basic characteristic for the male who contemplates her is sexual force, even though that male is her son. When Sut considers that neither of his parents has the long legs that are his most distinctive feature, he explains the matter thus:

> My long legs sometimes sorta bothers me. But then Mam took a pow'ful scare at a sand-hill crane a-sittin on a peeled well-pole, and she outrun her shadow thirty yards in comin half a mile. I expect I owes my legs and speed to that circumstance and not to any fraud on Mam's part.[12]

The explanation is vigorously unprudish, and the visualization—the sharpness of "peeled well-pole"—the unforced alliterative rhythms, and the ease with which hyperbole is accommodated through its presentation in precise detail—"thirty yards in runnin half a mile"—ground the outlook in a comprehensive and coherent perception of reality.

Sut's celebration of the sexual attraction of women is detailed in images drawn from his ragged environment, and the frankness of his physical observation is all the more welcome for this. Decades before Mark Twain attempted through the concrete, nature-bound diction of Huck Finn to elicit a feeling larger than the homely details in which it was expressed, Harris, whose work Twain knew well, was experimenting with shabby American circumstances:

> She shows among women like a sunflower among dog fennel, or a hollyhock in a patch of smartweed. Such a bosom! Just think of two snowballs with a strawberry stuck butt-ended into both on 'em. She takes exactly fifteen inches of garter clear of the knot, stands sixteen an a half-hands high, and weighs one hundred and twenty-six in her petticoat tail afore breakfast. She couldn't crawl through a whiskey-barrel—with both heads stove out—nor sit in a common armchair, while you could lock the top hoop of a churn, or a big dog collar round the huggin place.[13]

The object of this rhapsody is Sicily Burns, a young woman who does not reciprocate Sut's desire for her and who plays a cruel practical joke on him to underline her preference for another man. Sut, in turn, will have his revenge upon Sicily with equal physical cruelty, and notable in such incidents is the perfect social and psychological equality of the sexes. Unlike the tender domestic creatures to the north and the pale, elegant, objects of chivalry to the south, women in Sut's country are as forthright as men and can be treated in the same way. His description of Sicily was a description of the only way women differ from men.

In the culture he so closely observes, Harris is able to construct similes of a scope to match those in the folk epics of other and older lands. They are genuine, unaffected for all their far-reaching nature, because they grow, as did the folk epics' similes, from an oral tradition in which emotion is likened to what is physically perceived, rather than being explained in a vocabulary created by the literate:

> I'se heard in the mountains a first-rate, fourth-proof smash of thunder come unexpected and shake the earth, bringin along a string of lightnin as long as a quarter-track and as bright as a welding heat, a-racin down a big pine tree, tearin it into toothpickers, and raisin a cloud of dust and bark and a army of

> limbs with a smell sorta like the Devil were about, and the long, darning-needle leaves fallin round with a *tith-tith* quiet-sorta sound and even then a-quiverin on the earth as little snakes die. And I feel queer in my innards, sorta half-comfort, with a little glad and right smart of sorry mixed with it.
>
> I'se seed the rattlesnake square hisself to come at me, a-sayin "Z-e-e-e-e" with that noisy tail of his'n, and I feel queer agin—monstrous queer. I've seed the Oconee River jumpin mad from rock to rock, with its clear, cool water . . . white foam . . . and music. . . . "Music." The rushin water does make music. So does the wind, and the fire in the mountain, and it gives me an uneasy queerness again. But every time I looked at that gal Sicily Burns, I had all the feelins mixed up—of the lightnin, the river, and the snake.[14]

At the other end of his spectrum of the sexual world is Sut's earthy recognition of male physiology. To look at Jule Sawyers's legs is to make a man "feel sorter like a June bug was crawlin up his trowses and the waistband was too tite for it to git out."[15] In the agonies of springtime love, Wat Mastin, the blacksmith, blunders about with "his hands socked down deep into his britches-pockets like he was feared of pickpockets"; but after his wedding night, "His coat . . . and his trousers looked just a scrimption too big, loose-like, and heavy to tote. I asked him if he felt sound. He said 'yas,' but he'd welded a steamboat shaft the day afore and were sorta tired-liked."[16]

And in his hymn to widows Sut exposes in fine detail the objects of his material culture, the manners of courtship in his society, and above all, in contrast with other regional cultures, the avidity with which greater experience is pursued:

> Gals and ole maids ain't the things to fool time away on. It's widders, by golly, what am never-kickin, willin, spirited smooth pacers. They come close't up to the hoss-block, standin still with their purty, silky ears playin and the neck-veins a-throbbin, and waits for the word—which of course you give after you find your feet well in the stirrup—and away they moves like a cradle cushioned on rockers, or a spring buggy runnin in damp sand. A tech of the bridle and they knows you want 'em to turn, and they does it as willin as if the idea were their own. . . .
>
> They has all been to Jamaicy and learnt how sugar's made,

> and knows how to sweeten with it. And, by golly, they is always ready to use it. All you has to do is to find a spoon, and then drink comfort till you're blind.
>
> If you understands widder nature, they can save you a power of trouble, uncertainty, and time; and if you is enterprisin, you gits monstrous well-paid for it. The very sound of their little shoe-heels has a knowin click as they tap the floor.
>
> When you has made up your mind to court one, just go at it like it were a job of rail-maulin. Wear yer workin clothes; and, above all, fling away your cinammon-oil vial and burn all your love songs. No use in tryin to fool 'em, for they sees plumb through their veils. No use in a pasted shirt; she's been there. No use in borrowin a cavortin fat hoss; she's been there. No use in hair-dye; she's been there. No use in cloves to kill whiskey breath; she's been there. No use in buyin closed curtains for your bed, for she has been there. Widders am a special means . . . for ripenin green men, killin off weak ones; and makin 'ternally happy the sound ones.[17]

Harris's diction is impressive, nouns and verbs effectively carrying the descriptive burden loaded by others onto the backs of adjectives and adverbs, and his syntax is equally effective, duplicating the drawn-out sentences of the storyteller but keeping their units in so simple and rhythmic a relation to one another that the reader visualizes what is said effortlessly and never has to trace back to fix the scene aright.

In addition to his sure gift for aural and visual effect, Harris developed a technique of shifted point of view that serves as an unforced reminder that the primal world of Sut is a world of magic. One tale centers on an all too typical practical joke played on Stillyards, an avaricious lawyer and congressman, Connecticut-born, as Sut is quick to explain, although he puts it more feelingly—"hatched in a crack in the frosty rocks, whar nutmaigs am made outen maple, an whar wimmin paints clock-faces." Sut comes upon him in the road just after he has taken as fees the dog and grandfather clock of a man for whom he lost a case and the big mare of a widow for whom he lost another. Stillyards wants to hire Sut to help him with the transport of his goods, but Sut persuades him to mount the mare, tie the dog's rope around her neck, and place the clock along his back and belt it to his waist. As Sut anticipated, the mare bolts, Stillyard jounces violently and helplessly, the clock begins an endless striking, further accelerating the horse, and the dog is jerked into so swift a run that, in a detail Harris typically refuses to withhold, his entrails stream behind. The scene is sharply set in motion before the reader, but it can no longer be expected to raise the hilarity it once provoked in barbershops.

Harris's literary tact, however, is superior to his sporadic tastelessness. The point of view shifts. Sut strolling homeward well satisfied with himself passes a cabin "whar a ole 'oman dress'd in a pipe an' a stripid apron wer a-standing on the ash-hopper lookin up the road like she wer 'spectin tu see somethin soon." Her words pour out. "Say yu mister, did yu meet anything onkommon up thar?" Sut shakes his head and she unwinds:

> Mister, I'se plum outdun. Thar's sumthin pow'ful wickid gwine on. A crazy organ-grinder cum a-pas' yere jis' a small scrimpshun slower nur chain litenin, on a hoss wif no tail. His organ wer tied ontu his back, an' wer a-playin that good tchune, "Sugar in the Gourd," ur "Barbary Allin," I dunno which, an' his monkey wer a-dancin Hail Columby all over the road, an' *hits* tail wer es long as my clothes-line, an' purfeckly bar ove hare.[18]

Sut suggests that it was either the advance guard of a circus proclaiming its coming or the arrival of the millennium, "durn'd ef I know'd which." But the woman, with a shrewd eye for detail, disagrees and advances sounder theories:

> She 'lowed hit cudent be the merlennium, fur hit warnt playin hyme-tchunes; nur a sarkis either, fur the hoss warn't spotted. But hit mout be the Devil arter a tax collector, ur a missionary on his way tu China; hit look'd ugly enuf tu be one, an' fool enuf tu be tuther.[19]

The sudden sight of a spectacle that, however uncommon, has nevertheless been naturalistically explained to the reader as it erupts into the field of vision and assaults the understanding of a simple bystander endows it with a memorable and magic effect and provides Harris's yarn with a studied anticlimax that exceeds the actual scene in comedy, as was intended. It was a technique that William

Faulkner, an enthusiastic Harris reader, was to use, for example, in *The Hamlet,* where naturalistically explained runaway Texas horses dash into Tull's carriage in apocalyptic furor. The comedy is fulfilled and its fulfillment partakes of a visitation of the supernatural into the lives of the folk, who believe in its imminent presence.

Harris's sure sense of the folk imagination, moreover, led him to techniques that were not again to be widely employed until the development of the twentieth-century comic strip and animated cartoon aimed at the imagination of the masses. No matter how his characters are maimed in one episode, they are soundly reassembled and ready for use in the next, like cartoon characters. And more impressive from a literary point of view, Harris animates in such a way as to be able to stop his frame and see what takes place in nature too swiftly for the eye to notice: "Bart loaned the parson a most tremendous contusion right in the bull curl. I seed the parson's shoe soles a-goin up each side of Bart's fist afore Bart had time to move it after he struck."[20]

The cruelty that Harris lovingly constructs time and again is the eruption of an omnipresent outrage at the sentimental view of life, which he equated with the hypocritical moralizing of the dominant culture. Like Harriet Beecher Stowe, he was a Calvinist, but unlike Stowe and with the ruthless thoroughness of one who has been exposed to the elemental facts of a world governed by sin, he presses home the inherent viciousness of all creatures. Acceptance of universal corruption enabled him to be comic, as temporizing with it led Stowe to be sentimental. Sut was the mouthpiece of his perception of the bottom of creation—deeper even than the teachings of the Presbyterian Church—and perhaps no scene of cruelty is more discomfiting and yet more courageous than is Sut's outburst on the subject of innocence. Man is perverse, he broods; if something happens to your best friend you feel sorry for him, yet you sense a deep-down satisfaction:

> Or say a little calf, a-buttin first under the cow's forelegs and then the hind, with the point of its tongue stuck out, makin suckin motions, not yet old enough to know the bag-end of its mam from the hookin end . . . don't you want to kick it on the snout, hard enough to send it backwards—say fifteen foot—just to show it that buttin won't allers fetch the milk? Or a baby

> even, rubbin its heels a-past each other, a-rootin and a-snifflin after the breast, and the mam doin her best to git it out over the hem of her clothes: don't you feel hungry to give it one percussion-cap slap right onto the place what some day'll fit a saddle or a sewin-chair, to show it what's atwixt it and the grave; that it stands a pow'ful chance not to be fed every time it's hungry or in a hurry?[21]

Sut's perception of depravity goes beyond Calvinism to the soil that nurtures it. His world is one of poverty, illiteracy, and physical exertion, one in which sexual activity is a welcome outburst of the troubled self. It is a world of barely repressed passion, and reason is its enemy because reason comes from without to thwart or to manipulate it. The agents of reason are elected officials, clergymen, or lawyers, who exploit rather than improve, and Sut's anarchic hate of this condition leads him to attack authorities in all his practical jokes. His constant rage is, finally, the unconscious reaction of the proletarian in a society in which the rules operate to make him pay while others profit. His only weapons are force and flight; his principal expression is sexual love.

"Rare Ripe Garden-Seed," perhaps the greatest of Harris's stories, still finds its way into modern anthologies because of its relative freedom from sadism and because of the mythic quality of the folklore it develops. Sut approaches the tale through a monologue that explains why he hates sheriffs and was therefore willing, in the tale to follow, to assist friends in their revenge on one. Here with understated mastery he blends the elements of a class hate born of economic circumstances, elements that lie deeper than a mere desire for revenge against a particular personality.

> I tell you now, I minds my first big scare just as well as rich boys mind their first boots or seein the first spotted-horse circus. The red top of them boots am still a rich, red stripe in their minds, and the burnin red of my first scare has left as deep a scar onto my thinkin works.
>
> Mam had me a-standin atwixt her knees. I kin feel the knobs of her joints a-rattlin a-past my ribs yet. She didn't have much petticoats to speak of, and I had but one—and it were calico slit from the nape of my neck to the tail, held together at the top with a draw-string and at the bottom by the hem. . . .

> Mam were feedin us brats onto mush and milk—without the milk—and as I were the baby then she held me so as to see that I got my share. When there ain't enough feed, big childer roots little childer outen the trough and gobble up their part.[22]

Onto the scene comes the sheriff to levy the bed and the chairs, and Sut's mother hisses like an animal in danger and the children scatter. No piece of writing from honestly concerned prewar socialists matches the proletarian eloquence of the scene created by the alter ego of the conservative Presbyterian elder of Knoxville.

As the war drew nearer, Sut turned more and more vicious on the subject of the North, and as Stowe on her level matched arguments with sentiments, so Harris on his matched them with violence. His outlook is summarized in Sut's haunting if terrible myth of why his region takes the stand it does:

> When we elects our Governors, we elects a fool-killer for every county and furnishes him with a gun, some arsenic, strychnine, and a big steel trap; and it is his duty to travel, say about one day, ahind the circuit rider. You see, the circuit rider gathers the people together, and it makes it more convenient, and the fool-killer kills off the stock of fools to a considerable extent every round he takes. Our fool-killers have done their duty, and consequently the South have seceded.[23]

Sut, the natural-born, damned fool, ends his career by celebrating the fool-killer. In a sense, Harris is now finished with his alter ego as the times move to put a finish to the conditions that spawned him. But from a broader point of view, Sut is no such fool as the fool-killer seeks out—these are sympathizers with abolition, idealistic philanthropists, and moral sentimentalists—and he survives to tell his tales because, of course, in them the fool and fool-killer are one. And though his culture went under during the war, it did not disappear; such folk were used to the shifts of survival constantly forced upon them from above.

The world of Sut Lovingood reappeared censored after the war as a region of charming local color, and survived into the twentieth century as the tobacco-road culture of sexual degeneracy and menacing violence that blended into blue-collar brutality as natives of the border states moved into the factories. But the art and outlook of George Washington Harris are not in such literature. Rather his comic vision born of a sense of universal depravity and his mythic celebration of the debased human condition can be seen in the writings of Faulkner, who valued his work and whose ultimate point of view was not that of the aristocracy of Simms but of the suspicious, pawky, lower-class observers of the spectacle. And Harris's voice, transmitted by another admirer, Mark Twain, and purified in the transmission, is present in the work of Hemingway, whose narrators distrust the words applied to actuality and seek the words actuality wears.

Like all writers, the American writer in the prewar period had to find his reader before he could find his voice and his genre. He did not need a large audience, but he had to be satisfied in his mind that there existed the kind of reader for whom he wrote. Harris was thwarted by this necessity, able only to imagine a readership that fell short of the full stretch of his genius, and consequently he warped his best work as he accepted the sporting journal as his medium. With far more modest literary powers but with a sure sense of a wide, middle-class audience, Stowe was encouraged to write better than she knew how to do, even as Harris wrote worse than he could.

The suspicion that American literature was really New England literature disguised is, finally, misfounded. The region of origin is secondary to the culture of the reader who is imagined, and American literature in that age attempted to speak to Americans.

Chapter Twelve

Imagining What Exists: Henry David Thoreau and the Language of Literature

No American writer so tried the proposition that to be thoroughly rooted in region was to discover the source of universality as did Henry David Thoreau. Alone of Concord's eminent literary personages, he was a native, and his boast that he had traveled widely in Concord was meant both as the amusing remark that it was and as a warning that the egotism of his writings—his two books *A Week on the Concord and Merrimack Rivers* (1849) and *Walden* (1854) are concerned with the doings of "I" and his essays on politics or nature keep "I" at the center—was to be justified not by the comprehensiveness of his worldly experiences but by his superior ability to make natural experience stand for everything valuable that need be known. Emerson, his friend and cautious patron (Thoreau was guarded about both intimacy and dependency, regarding them, in the last analysis, as identical), said, "No truer American existed than Thoreau."[1] He insisted that Thoreau's preference for his country, and a rather small slice of it at that, and for his condition as a surveyor and handyman available for day hire (despite his Harvard education) was positive, not defensive. It was from a conviction of the superior worth of what he had chosen, Emerson implied, that Thoreau felt contempt for English and European manners and was even fatigued by Emerson's reports from the literary capitals of the world.

Emerson made these observations in one of the finest pieces of sustained prose he ever wrote, an essay composed shortly after Thoreau's death in 1862. He seems still to have been thinking of Thoreau when after the Civil War he wrote of New England culture, "I please myself with the thought that our American mind is not now eccentric or rude in its strength, but is beginning to show a quiet power, drawn from wide and abundant sources proper to a Continent and an educated people."[2] Rudeness and eccentricity were badges Thoreau chose to wear, and Emerson, his own powers sadly failing with age, relinquished his hopes for any great posthumous effect Thoreau would have. The postwar world was one of confident material expansion requiring various kinds of political, social, and industrial combinations. In it, Thoreau's consistent manner of shunning community would have been anomalous. "If I only knew Thoreau," Emerson once told his journal, "I should think cooperation of good men impossible."[3]

Thoreau's severe apartness from others may have been called rudeness, but Emerson worried that eccentricity was on display in his prose: "A certain habit of antagonism defaced his earlier writings,—a trick of rhetoric not quite outgrown in his later—of substituting for the obvious word and thought its diametrical opposite. He praised wild mountains and winter forests for their domestic air, in snow and ice he would find sultriness and commended the wilderness for resembling Rome and Paris."[4]

What Emerson calls a trick of rhetoric is certainly present, spread upon all the unpublished manuscript pages Thoreau left as well as on those he published (fourteen of the twenty volumes of his *Writings,* 1906, were previously unpublished journals). It is not, however, antagonism for the sake of novelty alone that informs the technique, but a ceaseless attempt to develop a literary style that freshly conveys the wonder to be experienced when one confronts life without the intermediaries of society or literature, and in isolation pursues it to its burrow. From early manhood, Thoreau severely measured the reality of his experience against the written records of what life was supposed to be. He kept essentially to himself because it was *his* life he was examining, and, as a result, he appeared to be carrying Emersonian individualism to a point not far short of absurd. To keep to his rigorous self-examination, he developed a habit of hypothesizing the opposite to the accepted formula for any situation, and he found that he could make a significant number of such propositions good. Moreover, by keeping his consciousness on tireless alert, he discovered tropes in nature, unobserved by others, that expressed better, if at first glance more slantly, what was generally accepted.

This unflagging experiment with life originated in Thoreau's agreement with the Emersonian view of man as an original unit whose value depends on how he can penetrate the form of appearance and attach himself to the flux of transcendent reality. Thoreau, too, sought to rise above his fate and considered history undetermining. Nevertheless, he was consistently political in the goal of his writing. A notorious shunner of society, he still believed that the lessons taught by his life and his writings were about how to live in communities as well as with oneself; how, in the last analysis, to make an American nation. The apparent egotism of his style arose from a conviction, carried to an extreme that Emerson was too civilized to pursue, that in testing life anew he was a representative man and therefore could teach men. If he had merely lived his experiment, the record of his life would have been that of an antisocial, occasionally engaging, eccentric. But he converted his experiment into a highly conscious literary creation—far from a mere report of his doings—and in so writing converted selfishness into selflessness, private conception into a major public statement of the nature and conduct of life.

Since the conditions that he seized, an abundance of outdoors nature and a freedom to say no to custom, were particularly American, Thoreau specifically believed he was constructing a program for Americans. Emerson saw the potential social consequences of Thoreau's genius, but felt that in materialistic America they were to be realized only if Thoreau actually made something of himself in life, was some kind of a recognizable success. He lamented that Thoreau, "instead of engineering for all America . . . was the captain of a huckleberry-party,"[5] because such flagrant countercultural behavior undermined the influence of the ideas it symbolized. He could not anticipate the effectiveness of Thoreau's transmutation of an intensely private life into a great public document because, ultimately, he had little faith in the formal power of literature. Voices speaking through the forms of literature he heard with avidity. But that the form and the voice could be one, that the life of a prose style could exceed in vitality the life that it translated, this he did not believe. The measure of Thoreau's difference from Emerson is that Thoreau was an artist, capable of risking all on the creation that incorporated his perceptions; Emerson felt always the need to speak apart from or in destruction of form.

At Harvard, Thoreau studied rhetoric with Professor Edward Tyrell Channing, whose course had been the training ground for many other writers, among them Emerson, Holmes, and Dana. Professor Channing was not the man to brook eccentricity, and Thoreau's exercises reveal scant signs of the remarkable style that was to distinguish his writing in the next twenty years. His sentences march forward with propriety: "Each successive defeat afforded the Carthaginians new lessons in the art of war, till at length, Rome herself trembled at their progress."[6] But in so practicing he acquired a standard that would inform his departures from it and govern the rhythm of his narratives.

In argument, on the other hand, Thoreau's exercises suggest the author who was to emerge. In the main, they are on what can loosely be termed the Romantic side of whatever question Channing set for the theme; one such, for example, is "Advantages and disadvantages of foreign influence on American literature." But they successively contain an increasing vehemence of assertion on behalf of native as opposed to imported literary values, or of nature as opposed to art itself. His mature literary career was to be a labor of converting such convictions into style rather than mere subject matter.

The voice of Emerson had early reached Thoreau's ear. A year before Emerson's "American Scholar" address, Thoreau was writing at the age of nineteen, "We are, as it were, but colonies . . . we have dissolved only the political bands which connected us with Great Britain; though we have rejected her tea she still supplies us with food for the mind."[7] In the same essay, he is a bit defensive about the raggedness of the American landscape, and his diction, responding doubtless to the demands of the professor, runs counter to the nativistic thrust of his remarks: "The devotee of literary fashion is no stranger to our shores; true there are some amongst us who can contemplate the bubbling brook without, in imagination, polluting its waters with a mill-wheel, but even they are prone to sing of skylarks and nightingales, perched on hedges, to the neglect of the homely robin red-breast, and the straggling rail-fences of their own native land."[8]

But the vehemence increases, and in the following year, his last at Harvard, Thoreau is asserting that "the civilized man is the slave of matter," and claiming that it is a mockery for one who walks on pavements and lives within walls—a "wigwam of bricks and mortar"—to set the standard for Americans. If such a setting makes civilized literature, then civilized literature must be disregarded. "So much for the influence of life," he writes with a youthful bravado that will fuel his mature convictions. Thanks to Emerson, a basis for his feeling is now at hand:

> A nation may be ever so civilized and yet lack wisdom. Wisdom is the result of education, and education being the bringing out, or development of that which is in man, by contrast with the Not Me, is sager in the hands of Nature than of Art. . . . Learning is Art's creature; but it is not essential to the perfect man—it cannot educate.[9]

The concept of the Not Me is from Emerson's *Nature,* published the year before, but a more potent if less obvious effect of that essay governs Thoreau's entire argument. Words are signs of natural facts, Emerson had written, and even those that express intellectual facts can be traced to some physical condition. The young Thoreau, in affirming that nature is the true educator, takes his clue from this. He does not supply a defense of his theory of education beyond deriving it from the natural reality behind the word—education, a bringing out—and makes that the thing the word stands for. This preference for the concreteness behind even conceptual, latinate diction was to be shaped in time into the cornerstone of his distinctive prose style.

In pursuing his peculiar course as teacher, surveyor, day laborer, and tramper of the woods after his graduation, Thoreau was well aware of the road he did not choose. The young Americans of his day were outward bound to cheap land in the West or new markets in the Pacific, where whalers were charting the trade routes that merchantmen were following. It was, Thoreau said, "a filibustering *toward* heaven by the great western route," and he declined it: "No; they may go their way to their manifest destiny, which I trust is not mine."[10] But the frequency of his allusions to voyaging, trading on distant shores, and discovering new species as well as new markets reveals his consciousness of the enormous amount that New England nature would have to provide him as compensation for his electing not to move outward.

It was one thing to say the following:

> Most whom I meet in the streets are, so to speak, outward bound, they live out and out, are going and coming, looking before and behind, all out of doors and in the air. I would fain see them inward bound, retiring in and in, farther and farther every day, and when I inquired for them I should not hear, that they had gone abroad anywhere, to Rondout or Sackets Harbor, but that they had withdrawn deeper within the folds of being.[11]

But it was another to demonstrate the contention that one's native conditions could more than sate one's hunger for life's possibilities. When Thoreau set about doing this, he made clear in *Walden* that the truth to which experience led would compensate for the limits of that experience only if the imagination made a tremendous leap over them:

> The migrating buffalo which seeks new pastures in another latitude is not extravagant like the cow which kicks over the pail, leaps the cow-yard fence, and runs after her calf in milking time. I desire to speak somewhat *without* bounds; like a man in a waking moment, to men in their waking moments; for I am convinced that I cannot exaggerate enough even to lay the foundations of a true expression.[12]

By the time he came to write this, Thoreau was habitually organizing his prose as an exposition of the natural fact behind the abstract idea connoted by a word. In this passage the word on which he plays his variation is "extravagant"—from *extra,* outside, and *vagari,* wander—so that his picture of the cow that jumps the fence is a picturing of extravagance even as it delivers a deliberate comic shock. The reader, accustomed to the picture of wasteful expenditure conveyed by the word "extravagance," is asked to reconcile it with the drama of a cow with heavy bag somehow clearing a fence.

Such seeming incongruity is at the bottom of what irked Emerson, although it flowed from a theory he had advanced, and it may still irk a reader who attributes it to contrived imagery rather than to an unearthing of the physical underpinning of thought, the corporeality of abstraction. The ultimate validity of the etymology, even though it may not be consciously present to the reader, makes the unexpected image as right as it is surprising.

Thoreau goes on to advance his argument by translating into Anglo-Saxon English the word that has already been translated into a picture: "*without* bounds." His underscoring of *without,* moreover, emphasizes the double meaning that is there available—he himself is extravagant enough to wander outside the limits and thus also to have no limits. Those like the buffalo who merely wander from pasture to pasture—be those new pastures in Kansas or Canton—are the unextravagant, for they have kept within the limitations placed upon them by their restlessness. Without straying from Walden's vicinity, however, he has passed limits.

In such a fashion Thoreau attempted to make the very phrasing of his argument the argument itself, as a means of justifying the capacity of America, and especially of her nature, to meet the capacity of her children's imagination. He did not think that the American language, which had to be the vehicle of their perception of their reality, was, in vocabulary, different from the British language. Unlike Whitman, although attracted to the speech of the folk, he did not see in it an ultimate fountain of new language. New effects, from time to time, yes, and he could when he would play the pawky, straight-faced Yankee droning by the cracker barrel. So his unexpected encounter with a dog with porcupine quills in his nose roaming the Maine woods far from any town can launch him on a Down East soliloquy:

> If he should invite one of his own friends up this way suggesting moose-meat and unlimited freedom, the latter might pertinently inquire, "What is that sticking in your nose?" When a generation or two have used up all the enemies' darts, their successors lead a comparatively easy life. We owe to our fathers analogous blessings. Many old people receive pensions for no other reason, it seems to me, but as a compensation for having lived a long time ago. No doubt our town dogs still talk, in a

> snuffling way, about the days that tried dogs' noses. How they got a cat up there I do not know, for they are as shy as my aunt about entering a canoe. I wondered that she did not run up a tree on the way; but perhaps she was bewildered by the very crowd of opportunities.[13]

There is a lot that is pithy and a lot that is amusing happening here: the vigorous effect of yoking "moose-meat and unlimited freedom"; the surprise insight of attributing old-age pensions not to having lived a long time, but—what is more to the point so far as community values are concerned—to having lived a long time ago; the putting of the patriotic rhetoric of Tom Paine's times that tried men's souls, debased in countless Fourth of July orations, into its proper contemporary perspective; the simile of the cat shy as his aunt; and the punch line delivered not with emphasis but as a seeming, brooding afterthought, in the yet to be perfected manner of the inspired idiot of Artemus Ward or Mark Twain. But Thoreau shows what he can do in this line in order, finally, not to do it.

Rather, for him the American language was to differ in its radical return to the natural physical base. The English tongue as filtered through British history had become a highly cultured variant of the root stock. A new history in America meant the refounding of language on the new reality. This did not mean rudeness rather than civility, and certainly not commerce rather than art, although both replacements are secondary effects in the imagery. But centrally it meant an apprehension of the common language as being healthiest and most serviceable when employed with a full sense of its organic connection to natural surroundings. The very nature of America must draw Americans back to this dictionary which supplied the dictionary on their desks.

In a frequently quoted passage, Thoreau wrote:

> Let us spend one day as deliberately as Nature, and not be thrown off the track by every nutshell and mosquito's wing that falls on the rails. Let us rise early and fast, or break fast, gently and without perturbation; let company come and let company go, let the bells ring and the children cry—determined to make a day of it. Why should we knock under and go with the stream? Let us not be upset and overwhelmed in that terrible

rapid and whirlpool called a dinner, situated in the meridian shallows.[14]

The word that first keys this elaboration is "perturbation," containing at its heart *turbo,* disorder. But at the heart of the heart is the natural fact also denoted by the Latin *turbo,* whirlpool, so that when the word "whirlpool" is actually used to designate noon-hour dinner it comes as an echo of "perturbation," and as the Latinate word contained the sense of "whirlpool" in its effect, so "whirlpool" when it arrives suggests an intellectual disturbance also.

After the initial use of "track," carried in transition from the preceding paragraph ("the track is laid for us"), the day is likened to a voyage down a stream. Opposed to movement is fixity, the key term for which is "fast." When one arises and starts the day he goes into motion, one meaning of "break fast," the other, of course, being the eating of the first meal of the day. The morning meal is a breaking of fixity and the noon meal threatens to be the height of the disorder thus commenced. But we must be determined (that is, in root terms we must fix limits), and thus although the apparent controlling image is that of a voyage, the key terms are used in disapproval of movement. Coherently rather than as a mixed metaphor, therefore, we learn the voyage will be successful not to the extent it flows along but to the extent it can get stuck fast. We can, that is, conquer the flux of time and arrive at a reality beyond time's appearance:

> Let us settle ourselves, and work and wedge our feet downward through the mud and slush of opinion, and prejudice, and tradition, and delusion, and appearance, that alluvion which covers the globe, through Paris and London, through New York and Boston and Concord, through church and state, through poetry and philosophy and religion, till we come to a hard bottom and rocks in place, which we can call *reality,* and say, This is, and no mistake; and then begin, having a *point d'appui,* below freshet and frost and fire, a place where you might found a wall or a state, or set a lamp-post safely, or perhaps a gauge, not a Nilometer but a Realometer, that future ages might know how deep a freshet of shams and appearances had gathered from time to time.

As the voyage image contained its opposite in the way in which fast was opposed to perturbation, so now this marvelous sentence of fixity against the wash of time is carried on as a voyage through cities, institutions, and ideas. It is not a geographical or horizontal journey from home to a new terrestrial haven, but a vertical rooting movement through which the self attaches itself to ultimate reality, and as abstract as is the concept of reality, it here also has a tactile, rocky feel to it.

With a language so conceived and employed, Thoreau gave to the Emersonian theory not only the corporeality it lacked in Emerson's explications but also a mythic power. His prose carries in its texture the validity of his contention that at Walden he escaped chronological and inhabited cosmogonic times. The book he makes of that prose demonstrates that a similar experience is available to his fellow Americans, both by their sharing in the venture of his imagination through reading *Walden* and by their now being able to perceive that part of their life that is life, as distinct from the greater part that is not living.

Emerson too often confused his trenchant views of a possible escape from history—of a true American beginning—with his excited sympathy for the constant series of startings that he saw around him: the founding of frontier communities, the initiation of immigrants into the cities, the turn of fortune in established families. He weakened the radical potential of his vision of America as mythic possibility by sometimes representing it, albeit most movingly, as little more than the conventional land of opportunity for the future capitalist. But Thoreau made of Walden Pond the metaphor of America as a sacred place, a hallowed ground on which reality retained its connection with the super-real that initiated it, sustained it, and was constantly accessible to it. In comparison with this primal reality, historical actuality is mere insect-scurrying.

When Thoreau recommended that once we have penetrated through shams and delusions we set up a Realometer, not a Nilometer, he was punning. A Nilometer is a gauge for measuring the rise and fall of a river and derives its name from the Nile, on which it was originated. He puns on *nihil,* nothing, and urges us to measure something real in our fixity rather than what has only seasonal, apparent meaning. Such wordplay is another of the characteristic strategies whereby he endeavors to make abstractions concrete. He gives words meaning as a poet does, both by uncovering the thingness at their core and by attaching thingness to them through their sound when it is absent from the core. In talking against the emphasis men put on fashion, for example—the opinion that clothes make the man—he says, "Dress a scarecrow in your last shift, you standing shiftless by, who would not soonest salute the scarecrow?"[15] To be shiftless is to be lacking in resources. A distinctly different meaning of shift is shirt. The pun combines these meanings by presenting a picture of a man who, because he is unclad, is also regarded by his fellow men as without ambition or abilities. A social idea is attached to and expressed in a picture of a shirtless man standing beside a scarecrow.

In *Walden* Thoreau advanced the linguistic ideas first opened in his Harvard theme when he complained that American art could not come from those who blocked their view of nature with walls of brick and mortar. Speaking of language he said: "Our lives pass at such remoteness from its symbols, and its metaphors and tropes are necessarily so far fetched, through slides and dumb-waiters, as it were; in other words the parlor is so far from the kitchen and the workshop," that it is in danger of degeneration. He refused to believe that "only the savage dwelt near enough to Nature and Truth to borrow a trope from them."[16] In reinforcement of *Walden*'s constant theme that morning, the time of awakening and origins, is cosmogonically the time in which we live, he drew the majority of the book's literary allusions from the classical epics and the bibles of the Orient as well as of the West. "There is more day to dawn. The sun is but a morning-star,"[17] he said in the book's concluding sentences; hence his preference for literature that stemmed from the dawn of civilization and spoke of the exchange between gods and men. Once we awaken to our true selves we realize we are contemporaries of the mythic heroes, not the pallid heirs of history.

As Thoreau continued his experiment with life beyond his Walden years, he became increasingly aware that this aspect of it, his identification of vital existence with the dawn of human history and the primitive in nature, was understated. Whereas in *Walden* he had said that he loved the wild no less than the good, thereby admitting an ethical value opposed and equal to that of wildness, he later came to believe that in wildness is the preservation of the world. He thought further about the Bible as a document of the human condition, and concluded:

> Surely, it is a defect in our Bible that it is not truly ours, but a Hebrew Bible. The most pertinent illustrations for us are to be drawn not from Egypt or Babylonia, but from New England. Natural objects and phenomena are the original symbols or types which express our thoughts and feelings. Yet American scholars, having little or no root in the soil, commonly strive with all their might to confine themselves to the imported symbols alone. All the true growth and experience, the living speech, they would fain reject as "Americanisms."[18]

When speech is seen, as Thoreau here sees it, as having no life and identity of its own, being dependent constantly on nature, then, in effect, he sees language as but a minor ripple on the great pool of wordless silence which is our fullest environment. He recognized this. In *A Week on the Concord and Merrimack Rivers* he reworked an essay on Sir Walter Raleigh he had written some five years earlier, and said:

> The word which is best said comes nearest to not being spoken at all, for it is cousin to a deed which the speaker could have better done. Nay, almost it must have taken the place of a deed by some urgent necessity, even by some misfortune, so that the truest writer will be some captive knight, after all. And perhaps the fates had such a design, when, having stored Raleigh so richly with the substance of life and experience, they made him a fast prisoner, and compelled him to make his words his deeds, and transfer to his expression the emphasis and sincerity of his action.[19]

This being so, Thoreau had to consider the relation of his act of book-writing both to the deeds he could better have performed and to the silence he would thereby have better recognized. As to the former, he must have seen his life in materialistic Massachusetts as trivial, himself a captive of his culture. Hence his need to translate his deeds into words. As to the latter, he kept reminding himself that silence was the ideal form that lay beyond creation, both *the* creation and his literary creation: "Creation has not displaced her, but is her visible framework and foil."[20] At times, he admitted, he had forgotten this truth and felt he had made a promethean inroad upon silence, but "a man may run on confidently for a time thinking he has her under his thumb, and shall one day exhaust her, but he too must at last be silent, and men remark only how brave a beginning he made; for when he at length dives into her, so vast is the disproportion of the told to the untold that the former will seem but the bubble on the surface where he disappeared."[21]

As early as 1843, Thoreau had said, "As for me, I would never speak more," explaining that when heaven spoke to men it did so as follows: "Its motion is its language; it reduces the seasons to their time; it agitates nature; it makes it produce. This silence is eloquent."[22] When he did speak he hoped he did so as a translator of silence rather than an opposer; ultimately, by making words for the tropes nature provided, he claimed to affirm the silence in which they rested.

At the close of *Walden,* Thoreau reaches almost desperately to express the way in which his book comes from and must rest in silence. The penultimate chapter is concerned with spring, but the description of its advent is unexpectedly intestinal. Spring does not first announce itself in the arrival of the robin or the budding of trees, those well-known, cheerful, all-but-shouting signals. Rather, Thoreau first notes the thawing of the ice on a railroad bank. Loosened sand begins to flow, and in the flowing takes the form of "sappy leaves or vines." He comments:

> This sandy overflow is something such a foliaceous mass as the vitals of the animal body. You will find thus in the very sands an anticipation of the vegetable leaf. No wonder that the earth expresses itself outwardly in leaves, it so labors with the idea inwardly.[23]

He then elaborates this vision of spring as the delivery of the innermost principle from the womb of earth, and in so doing he functions as the midwife to the process. Leaf-shape in the sand becomes leaf-shape in the vitals of reviving animals, leaf-shape in the wings of soaring birds, and leaf-shape on the trees themselves. But his constant counting over of leaves is not an interruption of silence because his very words, he contends, grow from the force that compels the shape:

> *Internally,* whether in the globe or animal body, it is a moist thick *lobe,* a word especially applicable to the liver and lungs and the *leaves* of fat (. . . *labor, lapsus* to flow or slip downward, lapsing; . . . *globus,* lobe, globe; also lap, flap, and many other words); *externally,* a dry thin *leaf,* even as the *f* and *v* are a pressed and dried *b.*[24]

The conceit here advanced is perhaps the most extended ever elaborated by Thoreau, his fullest attempt to capture the way in which sensory things are but the forms of nature's innermost idea. Words, as has been seen, are for Thoreau but one form that the natural principle takes, but to drive home the point in this remarkable passage he insists not just upon the physicality of the denotation of words but also upon the actual physical correspondence of the shape of a word's oral utterance to what it signifies: the liquid *l* starts a flow that is rounded by the *o* and closed by the *b* as the drop suspends itself, so that the word "lobe" *is* a lobe. From such a perspective words do not interrupt silence but take their place among its myriad manifestations.

For Thoreau language is not human in the sense of human differentiated from other forms of life—man, the rational animal. It is an utterance determined by the same force that drives through the tree to make it utter leaves. Thoreau was conscious that if he fell short of the credulity of primitive men in such assertions—and he felt a deep affinity with the somewhat pantheistic responses to nature of the Indians—he was, nevertheless, well beyond the confines of scientifically verifiable truth. Modern linguistic science, of course, must regard his contribution as mere fable. Even in his own day he was regarded as a naturalist, as distinguished from a scientist: he was a keen observer of wild life, but the inferences he made from the data were not of great significance as botanical or zoölogical laws. He did not quarrel with his exclusion from such sciences, but staked out the ground he chose to occupy:

> Surely the most important part of an animal is its *anima,* its vital spirit on which is based its character, and all the

> particulars by which it most concerns us. Yet most scientific books which treat of animals leave this out altogether and what they describe are, as it were, phenomena of dead matter. What is most interesting in a dog, for instance, is his attachment to his master, his intelligence, courage, and the like, not his anatomical structure, and even many habits which affect us less. . . . A history of animated nature must itself be animated. The ancients, one would say, with their Gorgons, Sphinxes, Satyrs, Mantichora, etc., could imagine more than existed, while the moderns cannot imagine so much as exists.[25]

The final emphasis on imagining what exists applies to his linguistic theory. As he was not a scientist but a naturalist, so he was not a linguist but a poet, and a poet of the highest order, perhaps the greatest maker of language in the history of America's literature.

"I think that the one word which will explain the Shakespeare miracle," Thoreau wrote in his journal, "is unconsciousness. If he had known his own comparative eminence, he would not have failed to publish it incessantly. . . . There probably has been no more conscious age than the present."[26] Whatever questions may be raised by his characterization of Shakespeare, he was certainly accurate in his view of his own time—especially as it was taken in the vicinity of Concord, with Emerson receiving transcendental pilgrims, Alcott spinning out schemes for the moral perfection of mankind, horticulturists conducting experiments that led to the Concord grape, and radicals planning abolitionist tactics. Thoreau himself as a writer is the epitome of self-consciousness, from the relentless employment of "I" in all his writings to the calculations he visibly makes for each leap over the fence of experience into the vastness of the imagination. In its extraordinary consciousness, his language-making is, indeed, the opposite of Shakespeare's, displaying a craftsmanship that always leaves its marks on the product, rather than manifesting spontaneity, either true or illusory. He forcefully restated the principles of organic art held by Emerson and the sculptor Horatio Greenough and gave them an embodiment that they did not receive from the others. As he practiced the organic theory, however, he revealed that its rules were as demanding and as artful as were the rules of "civilized" aesthetics that he scorned. *Walden* is obviously and unashamedly shaped both in its entirety and in the shapes within that entirety.

Whitman was to practice organic art also, but for him the show of spontaneity was essential. So far as the example of Thoreau serves, however, it goes to indicate that American art in its first, great upsurge could not escape self-consciousness because it had no implicit conventions on which to rely. American writers were driven toward manifestly artful constructions far more than their transatlantic colleagues were, and driven thus to the discovery of new forms. What is the genre of *Typee* or of *Walden*? Why was Hawthorne compelled to launch into an explanation of what he meant by romance every time he started a novel? Why did Thoreau promptly disabuse his readers of any notion that his account of what happened at Walden would actually be a record of his days there?

Edgar Allan Poe had praised Margaret Fuller for the writings of hers that resembled his: description that focused on subjective effect rather than objective sight. So far as he was concerned, all the individual artist had to rely on in America was his own feelings—the society was lumpish and nature had been alien since the days of Eden. Obviously, Thoreau's controlling approach was opposed to Poe's both in his idea of the relation of man to nature and in his aesthetics of literary execution. Thoreau's notebook comment on the topic of expository writing may today be read as predictive both of Poe's future success on the European continent and of the contrasting suitability of his own method for American writers:

> Nature never indulges in exclamations, never says ah! or alas! She is not French. She is a plain writer, uses few gestures, does not add to her verbs, uses few adverbs, no expletives. I find that I use many words for the sake of emphasis, which really add nothing to the force of my sentences, and they look relieved the moment I have cancelled these, words which express my mood, my conviction, rather than the simple truth.[27]

That simple truth only began in nature. It was heated, shaped, cooled, filed, and polished in the workshop of a totally conscious artist. The nearer the wild woods, the greater the labor required to translate their message.

Chapter Thirteen

Concentrated Summer: Thoreau, Nature, History, and the Art of Composition

As his writings from his earliest days make clear, Henry David Thoreau was keenly aware of the ways in which his countrymen reacted to the provincialism of America. In the area of high culture, observers such as George Ticknor and Richard Henry Dana argued for patient anticipation of the establishment of a leisure class, which could support the arts. In the meantime, they encouraged writers who accepted the conventions of English literature and attempted to knit their work to that great fabric. Such an attitude Thoreau dismissed almost contemptuously. A new reality meant for him a radically new art.

In the area of popular life, Americans were as vigorously pressing beyond the oceanic frontier as beyond the western frontier, and although such enterprises were principally commercial, the published reports of them expanded American awareness of how many ways there were to lead life and how many wondrous things filled up the globe. These attitudes Thoreau recognized and assumed into his larger purpose, as is indicated by his many allusions to accounts of travel and discovery and by his rhetorical habit of paralleling his own activities with more adventurous and exotic voyages.

When Poe made his single attempt to write a full-length novel, he turned to the travel narrative as his genre and used published accounts of oceanic exploration for topics and incidents. In the event, the voyage of Arthur Gordon Pym quickly turned into an intense inner journey of discovery. Pym sailed into an area unconnected with any mapped part of the physical world, and his quest was for fulfillment of his capacity to undergo extreme sensations; he wanted to discover his feelings by pursuing the sharpest stimuli. Another generation, at the end of the nineteenth century, would represent the same inner journey without the need to invent stimuli that could not be found in Paris.

When Thoreau constructed his first book he also followed the popular theme of voyage and discovery. *A Week on the Concord and Merrimack Rivers* is, superficially, a record of one week's travel on two very tame New England millstreams. But it is conveyed rhetorically as if it were the equal of a danger-laden journey into exotic landscapes. Thoreau's intention was, of course, ironic; he wished to point up the miraculousness of what was near at hand and yet difficult of access, as compared with the cheapness of what was at a distance and yet available merely by getting there physically. To seek true meaning on the Merrimack River was to engage in as daring and complex a quest as to seek yet another set of circumstances on the Congo or the Amazon.

A Week is very unlike *Pym* in that the self that is sought is to be discovered in terms of its location in transcendent reality rather than in terms of its experiencing every last sensation of which it is capable. But both assert that nothing is so mysterious as the life of man that lies beneath or beyond appearances, and both use the metaphor of the voyage to sail into that territory. Any good travel account, of course, teaches the observer something about himself, at least in passing, but it also proceeds from the assumption that the world being explored is different from us and that acquaintance with it adds to our store of known facts. Neither Poe nor Thoreau contributes to such an inventory; for them the relative geographical and cultural isolation of the American justified his descent into himself rather than demanded an attachment to other places and peoples.

Accordingly, there is good basis for the contention, advanced by William Carlos Williams among others, that Poe was the first writer to speak from America, because he proceeded from cultural isolation to examine the mystery of the self—in parallel with the widespread native consciousness of being surrounded by a secret, wild continent—rather than to borrow a civility from his European background with which to silence the primal voice of his landscape. As attention to his language and his style reveal, Thoreau, too, speaks from America in this radically original fashion. He set about his task for different conscious reasons, believing, as Poe did not, in man's ultimate identity with his natural environment, but once launched on his enterprise, like Poe he speaks of sources of identity deeper than the intellect. No writer of the generation that succeeded Poe's is more concerned with the demands of insistent corporeality and the artificiality of denying them. He was repellent—you would sooner think of taking the arm of a tree than of taking his arm when you walked with him, said Emerson—and yet his writings release a stronger passion for the tactile than do the novels of his contemporaries, who were, presumably, concerned with passion as subject matter.

In his efforts to hear the message of the wild, Thoreau was well within the Romantic philosophy that insists on the moral superiority of the natural to the artificial. But he went beyond the conventions of that outlook as they were practiced in the literature of his day. By contrast Cooper's Leatherstocking, the man of unspoiled nature, expurgates what the environment he so incessantly champions has to tell him. Murderous doings between and among human and inhuman species he either ignores or accounts for as ultimately having little to do with "white" nature. Sexuality he sees far more as the result of manners than as a natural condition—he is apter to see that it is natural to want companionship than that it is natural to want sexual intercourse. In speaking of the superior morality of nature, Cooper, like almost all other Romantic writers, meant that inartificiality was to be preferred in the best human community and that a preservation of the untamed natural setting in America would provide the best social environment for inartificiality. Voracity of appetite and violence in its gratification were not inevitable features of the nature he portrayed. As a result, he Europeanized the wild to at least the same extent as he Americanized the tame. His Leatherstocking symbolizes this, ever fleeing the corruptions of society only, paradoxically, to be the pathfinder into the wilds for society; the trail along which he retreats is that which others follow to advance.

Thoreau, however, did not begin with a social vision, as did Cooper, but attempted to arrive at one only after confronting the unexpurgated facts of nature. If he too argued the morality of nature, then he was compelled to account for the seeming viciousness within it—and thus within himself—that Cooper evaded. He was aware of the vulnerability of his endeavor. Was he not simply beginning again with primitivism? Would he not eventually waste his life rediscovering what the history of man could already teach him about the evolution of the human condition from nomadism to fixed community, from savagery to civility, from immediate, unthinking gratification of appetite to sublimation and refinement of desire? His career of self-discovery was dominated by the need to reconcile the whole self—not just the spiritual part, since nature spoke through thingness—with the conduct of life, and in so doing to accept his culture's nineteenth-century location rather than advocate a reversion to precivilized behavior. Many an earlier democratic theorist had answered similar questions by assuming a fixed agricultural future for the United States, a permanent suspension between the savagery of the western wilds and the artificiality of the European city, a sort of recapitulation of the history of civilized man to the halfway point of rural living and then a magical, permanent arrest. But Thoreau confused neither the yeoman farm with the essential values taught by nature, nor hard labor with the fulfillment of the imagination.

Five years out of college, serving as a handyman at Emerson's and watching his closest friend, his brother John, die horribly of lockjaw, Thoreau in 1842 attempted to resign himself into God's hands. His life, he concluded, would have to come to him as a plant's life came to it, and yet this did not satisfy his reason: "Why, God, did you include me in your great scheme? Will you not make me a partner at last? Did it need there should be a conscious material?"[1]

As he worked on *A Week,* devoted to the memory of the brother who had been his companion on the journey, he increasingly sought to account for life led in the unsettled regions as superior to life led in the civilized centers. The issue was linked to his need to accept his purely natural existence and yet to see it as not merely passive but also an engagement of his best, conscious self. In 1848 he told his journal:

> The deeper you penetrate into the woods, the more intelligent, and in one sense, less countrified do you find the inhabitants; for always the pioneer has been a traveller, and, to some extent, a man of the world; and, as the distances with which he is familiar are greater, so is his information more general and far reaching than the villager's. If I were to look for a narrow, uninformed, and countrified mind, as opposed to the intelligence and refinement which are thought to emanate from cities, it would be among the rusty inhabitants of an old-settled country, on farms all run out and gone to seed with life-everlasting, in the towns about Boston, even on the high road in Concord, and not in the backwoods of Maine.[2]

The fear of provincialism haunted him because it marked him as imbalanced, a utilizer only of his unthinking side. There was such a thing as civilization and its measure seemed to tell against the rough clothes he wore, the rough people he met, and the rough way in which his days were spent. He protested to himself:

> No people can long continue provincial in character, who have the propensity for politics and whittling, and rapid travelling, which the Yankees have, and who are leaving the mother country behind in the variety of their notions and inventions. The possession and exercise of practical talent merely, are a sure and rapid means of intellectual culture and independence.[3]

There is some point to his claim, a point that was lost on those observers who, from his day to this, have watched the Yankees' movement into central roles on the world stage and smiled at their naive lack of a sense of political actualities. Such observers fail to perceive that a new political reality had been shaped by a talent for whittling and rapid travel and was thus more responsive to these skills than to a knowledge of the classical political maneuvers of history.

But still his provincialism and that of his countrymen nagged Thoreau, and he dealt with his doubts finally by a characteristic reversal of values. Yes, the Yankees were, after all, provincial, not because they lacked the tone that prevailed in civilized cities but because they aped it and in so doing put their consciousness to borrowed tasks rather than to a realization of their true condition:

> With respect to a true culture and manhood, we are essentially provincial still,—not metropolitan,—mere Jonathans. We are provincial, because we do not find at home our standards,—because we are warped and narrowed by an exclusive devotion to trade and commerce and manufactures and agriculture and the like, which are but means, and not the end.[4]

Such a view of the matter delivered him into the clearing where he wrote *Walden*. Nature was not opposed to culture, but there was a culture of nature that grew as the consciousness came to terms with unadorned existence, and this culture was so immediate and yet so universal as to beggar what was called civilization.

He tested his perception against the culture of Great Britain, which, as Emerson had so well demonstrated in *English Traits,* was not only splendid in itself but perhaps the sum of human society. But consider the unnatural and therefore inhuman manner of it, Thoreau insisted. With his eye for the telling, unconventional image he did not cite crowded London nor the etiquette of high tea to support his judgment but looked at Britain's relations with the wild: "Think how many musquash and weasel skins the Hudson's Bay Company pile up annually in their warehouses, leaving the bare red carcasses on the banks of the stream throughout all British America; and this it is chiefly which makes it *British* America." The violence of civilization's use of splendid nature is here scored together with its wastefulness, and the red carcasses speak of colonial exploits in other parts of the world as well. North America, says Thoreau, "is the place where Great Britain goes a-mousing,"[5] and in so trivializing an uncultivated continent civilization reveals the poverty of its imagination.

Hawthorne was impressed by Thoreau's radical insights. For all his distrust of the Concord bores and for all his feeling that Thoreau in person could be tediously trying, he proposed in England that admirers of Emerson and Longfellow pay more attention to the unknown Thoreau. Despite his dislike of novels, Thoreau had given Hawthorne the germ of the ill-fated *Dolliver Romance,* and when Hawthorne planned (prematurely, as it turned out) to publish that novel after Thoreau's death, he wrote his publisher that he wanted to prefix a sketch of Thoreau. He said, "It seems the duty of a live literary man to perpetuate the memory of a dead one," yet thinking of the burrlike Thoreau he knew, he added, "but how Thoreau would scorn me for thinking *I* could perpetuate him."[6] Hawthorne had the feeling for the man that Emerson had tried to express when, noting that no college ever offered Thoreau a professor's chair and no academy a membership, he mused, "Perhaps these learned bodies feared the satire of his presence."[7] Thoreau had so succeeded in his rendering of what natural culture meant that already for his contemporaries he represented what he was to symbolize for generations of Americans who followed: that one could disregard a world not of one's making and, in returning to the nature in terms of which one was made, could realize one's finest self.

This message, misunderstood in Thoreau's day and afterward, seemed to be simply an advocacy of living in nature rather than in cities. Thoreau sent and continues to send people to seek fulfillment in the woods. But to spend a day *as deliberately as* nature does not necessarily mean spending it *in* nature, because the nature ultimately to be followed is the essential self, which retains its rhythms independent of location so long as one is alerted to listen to them. Once rendered in *Walden,* this model so inescapably assaults the imagination, affirming the potential of the path that civilized readers have not taken, that their consciousness of it achieves the status of conscience itself.

After a summer seeking the civility of nature in the Adirondack wilderness, W. J. Stillman concluded, almost with relief at not having to pursue the course further, "My quest was an illusion." The men and women who lived there got drunk frequently to ease the harshness of their condition and most had degenerated into brutality. The best specimen he encountered was a hunter, but if this man was not brutal he was at least animalized. "He had drifted back into the condition of his dog, with his higher intellect inert."[8]

Thoreau would have told Stillman that the animal in man was an important part, which had to be realized, and that a reattachment to it was not, in nineteenth-century America, a relapse but a recognition from which good things could be expected. He would not have defended a mere animal existence, because man was a conscious beast, but despite the attractions of the purely spiritual life as explored in the Higher Laws chapter of *Walden,* he finally declared for the saving power of savagery. His most remarkable announcement of it comes not as explanation but as revelation, the outburst of an ecstasy that had seized him in the Maine woods:

> What is it to be admitted to a museum, to see a myriad of particular things, compared with being shown some star's surface, some hard matter in its home! I stand in awe of my body, this matter to which I am bound has become so strange to me. I fear not spirits, ghosts, of which I am one,—*that* my body might,—but I fear bodies, I tremble to meet them. What is this Titan that has possession of me? Talk of mysteries!—Think of our life in nature,—daily to be shown matter, to come in contact with it,—rocks, trees, wind on our cheeks! the *solid* earth! the *actual* world! the *common sense*! *Contact! Contact! Who* are we? *Where* are we?[9]

This fervor seems connected with his tubercular condition in its flushed celebration of the physical and its fierce appetite for the objects of the here and now. The ultimate relating of such physicality to a transcendental reality is all the more persuasive in that, unlike Emerson, Thoreau reaches supernatural reality by going through the body—through the things that crowd the sight and press the touch—to what truly is and always has been.

It is not surprising to discover that Thoreau alone among the New England authors of his day is comfortable with, indeed hungry for, the uncontrolled fecundity of nature and that he constantly seeks summer. Although he extolls the severities of cold weather and the opportunity winter provides for the reflective faculties, his fundamental stance is always that of this journal entry made on a bleak December day:

> Our eyes go searching along the stem for what is most vivacious and characteristic, the concentrated summer gone into winter quarters. For we are hunters pursuing the summer on snowshoes and skates all winter long, and there is really but one season in our hearts.[10]

The wasteful, rife voracity of nature thrilled the man under a death sentence from the tubercles that teemed within him. We need the tonic of wildness to explain our deaths to us and thus to sharpen our lives.

One illustration of such a perception begins with the bracing effect of marshes where the mink crawls with belly close to the ground and the bittern lurks in sedges, and goes on to celebrate the healthiness and sanity of nature's lavish dealings in death as well as life:

> We need to witness our own limits transgressed, and some life pasturing freely where we never wander. We are cheered when we observe the vulture feeding on the carrion which disgusts and disheartens us, and deriving health and strength from the repast. There was a dead horse in the hollow by the path to my house, which compelled me sometimes to go out of my way, especially in the night when the air was heavy, but the assurance it gave me of the strong appetite and inviolable health of Nature was my compensation for this. I love to see that Nature is so rife with life that myriads can be afforded to be sacrificed and suffered to prey on one another; that tender organizations can be so serenely squashed out of existence like pulp,—tadpoles which herons gobble up, and tortoises and toads run over in the road; and that sometimes it has rained flesh and blood![11]

Although the tendency kept thrusting itself forth, Thoreau in the main resisted converting his positive view of natural savagery into a romanticizing of the superiority of the Indian to the white man. The latter he saw as "knowing well what he knows, not guessing but calculating; strong in community, yielding obedience to authority; of experienced race; of wonderful, wonderful common sense; dull but capable, slow but perceiving, severe but just, of little humor but genuine; a laboring man, despising game and sport; building a house that endures, a framed house."[12] This was not to be dismissed in favor of a celebration of the nobility of the savage, which, in the final event, simply invested him with manners idealized by society. But it was to suggest the incompleteness of the white man, an incompleteness that Thoreau symbolized when he said that the white man, in cutting himself off from true, natural time, had cut himself off from the sun and so was "pale as dawn." If he abandoned history and yielded to the truths of his origin, represented by the sun, exposing his body as well as his mind, he would attain the more natural human colors of red and black.[13] Cosmic awareness would return him to a state lost in historical progress, one of harmony with his terrestrial location.

If this had the flavor of too elaborate a conceit, still Thoreau was deliberate and serious when, surveying human history, he decided with Emerson that the American condition need not be constrained by the past. All that human culture required was available from natural history, he affirmed, but what he meant was something different from the sentimental view of such as Stowe, who implicitly replaced notions of social and political history with the faith that all the history that mattered was the history of the human heart.[14] Her school of sentiment reacted to the harshness of masculine doings in the forum by asserting that finally such bustlings were not equal in their effect on American life to the constant domestic pieties practiced by women. By natural history such writers meant woman's life; her role as child bearer and child rearer was seen as a natural one compared with the male's role as breadwinner. In their sentimentalizing of this outlook, they were, at the least, ignorant of the ways in which society's idealization of the family was economically determined, and were, at the worst, the willful spinners of banalities that kept their readers from the truth of their condition.

The natural history Thoreau opposed to social history was not that of "the heart," in this sense, but of radical existence. Pondering the probability that the Norsemen, not Columbus, had discovered America, he wrote, "Consider what stuff history is made of—that for the most part it is merely a story agreed upon by posterity."[15] If a fact has been so lost that it needs to be formally commemorated—called to mind by history books, monuments, or national holidays—of what moment is it? he asked. Only that past life which present life feels or is compelled to imagine by the facts that surround it is of consequence. "Strictly speaking," he said, "the historical societies have not recovered one fact from oblivion, but are themselves instead of the fact that is lost."[16] This, if they only realized it, was a good thing insofar as it substituted living men for dead shards. But the viewpoint of historical societies was blind to the true source of what informs life from beyond the present:

> The Anglo-American can indeed cut down and grub all this waving forest and make a stump speech and vote for Buchanan

> on its ruins, but he cannot converse with the spirit of the tree he fells—he cannot read the poetry and mythology which retire as he advances. He ignorantly erases mythological tablets in order to print his handbills and town meeting warrants on them.[17]

Walden is a handbook on how to avoid such ignorance and live fully in the true present, natural, mythological, and sacred, instead of submitting to the factitiousness of the past and to ideas of progress that maim reality.

Such views did not absolve Thoreau from political commitment but placed that commitment in perspective. He believed:

> Those things which now most engage the attention of men, as politics and the daily routine, are, it is true, vital functions of human society, but should be unconsciously performed, like the corresponding functions of the physical body. They are *infra*-human, a kind of vegetation.[18]

He acted accordingly. Going about his own business was a political expression, not an escape from politics; his anarchism was a considered policy. One characteristically independent gesture flared up so notably that he was imprisoned for a night, but his refusal to pay the poll tax was not the result of his belonging to any party, nor did his stay in prison drive him to join any group. Indeed, when he engaged a hall to lecture in praise of John Brown, the abolitionists warned him that he was injudiciously harming the cause of the slave, but he replied that he was giving them notice of the talk, not consulting them about its advisability. Moreover, although he spent but one night in prison and although the lectures on Brown and on civil disobedience are his only explicitly political writings—and even these are, in Aristotle's sense, more ethical than political—he sincerely intended that all his writings illustrate the truth that his entire life was political. He knew that his doctrine and his practice, if accepted—and he took great pains to make them acceptable through converting them into literature—would lead to clashes with the state. But when conscientious action clashed with government, then one must conclude that there was no need for government. Living in a time and place that were as yet innocent of techniques of mind control, he affirmed that all the state could do was imprison dissenters until the untenable point was reached at which dissenters would outnumber the imprisoners and would definitively explode the falseness of their policy. There was a constant need, therefore, for complete, "vegetative" individual political behavior rather than a historical need at specific moments for organized political tactics. He likened the action of a government that incarcerated a man while leaving his thoughts free to the mean and petty revenge boys took upon the dog of an owner whom their spite could not reach. The more there were who followed his example, making political gesture a coherent and unpremeditated aspect of their total conduct of life, the surer would it be, not that chaos would ensue, but that government would retreat to that Jeffersonian optimum point at which it governed least.

When he extended his ideas of minimal government and maximum individualism into economics, Thoreau on the surface appeared to be a laissez-faire capitalist run wild:

> This government never of itself furthered any enterprise, but by the alacrity with which it got out of its way. *It* does not keep the country free. *It* does not settle the West. *It* does not educate. The character inherent in the American people has done all that has been accomplished; and it would have done somewhat more, if the government had not sometimes got in its way. For the government is an expedient by which men would fain succeed in letting one another alone; and, as has been said, when it is most expedient, the governed are most let alone by it.[19]

So far as the conduct of life was concerned Thoreau was indeed committed to unrestrained enterprise, and this extended to economics. In his time, however, such a view was not associated with the conservative money lords but with the radicals. The members of the financial community favored the Bank of the United States, protective tariffs, federal highways, and other governmental intrusions into the economy, while their opponents saw these as unfair favors granted to a few, favors that led to sharp inequality in the market and to social conflict. They believed that removal of the government from the economy would permit a more equitable distribution of property. They drew their political strength from artisans, shopkeepers, and small business men,[20] and it was to these that Thoreau was allied in the no-government principles he asserted. If the consequences of unrestraint threatened a devastation of nature, the conversion of pines, as Thoreau put it, into pine-tree shillings,[21] the remedy had to be informed consciousness rather than mere statute.

The first and longest chapter of *Walden* is titled "Economy." In part its intent is satiric. As Thoreau in seeming commercial pride presents his ledgers so as to prove that his experiment at Walden was financially profitable, he is parodying the penny-catching success manuals that followed in the wake of Franklin's *Autobiography* (first published in America in 1818). He does indeed deal in pennies and even half-pennies. The minuteness of the sums finally calls attention to the fact that some other kind of profit was at stake in his experiment. But his economic discussions are not parodic as a whole. He is seriously addressing "the mass of men who are discontented and idly complaining of the hardness of their lot or of the times, when they might improve them," and this, while it finally applies to a wide audience, takes its rise from a specific one, the economically marginal farmers and the morally marginal tradesmen of New England, such men as young students are likely to become for want of other examples:

> On applying to the assessors, I am surprised to learn that they cannot at once name a dozen in the town who own their farms free and clear. If you would know the history of these homesteads, inquire at the bank where they are mortgaged. The man who has actually paid for his farm with labor on it is so rare that every neighbor can point to him. I doubt if there are three such men in Concord. What has been said of the merchants, that a very large majority, even ninety-seven in a hundred, are sure to fail, is equally true of the farmers. With regard to the merchants, however, one of them says pertinently that a great part of their failures are not genuine pecuniary failures, but merely failures to fulfill their engagements, because it is inconvenient; that is, it is the moral character that breaks down. But this puts an infinitely worse face on the matter, and suggests, beside, that probably not even the other three succeed in saving their souls, but are perchance bankrupt in a worse sense than they who fail honestly.[22]

Although not concerned with the mechanics of getting rich, Thoreau is very serious about getting a livelihood, and that, he insists, is now being achieved in his society by "a formula more complicated than the problem itself." Once a livelihood is secured —and that, he shows, is quite simple—then the crucial matter to be pursued is the improvement of the self rather than of material possessions, and his basic rule is that "the cost of a thing is the amount of what I will call life which is required to be exchanged for it." The application of this rule reveals that the poor are endlessly so and the rich have given up life.

In 1847 Thoreau had written a review of the works of Thomas Carlyle and in it noted that for Carlyle, nature had so greatly receded that "as we read his book here in New England, where there are potatoes enough, and every man can get his living peacefully and sportively as the birds and bees, and need think no more of that, it seems to us as if by the world he often meant London."[23] After *Walden* the rejoinder might well have been that by the world Thoreau meant even less, just Concord. But since nature had not receded from Concord as it had from London, Thoreau's insistence would have been that his claims upon posterity were better founded than Carlyle's. He admired much of Carlyle and in his essay noted that Carlyle gives justice to the giants of the will such as Mahomet and Cromwell, whereas Carlyle's American friend Emerson gives justice to the giants of moral greatness such as Plato and Jesus. "But above all and after all," Thoreau wrote, "the Man of the Age, come to be called working-man, it is obvious that none yet speaks to his condition."[24] *Walden* takes root here, and if it has served in its considerable audience fewer workingmen than intended, it is not because of some fault in Thoreau's economic arithmetic but because the desire for wealth, or, that failing, luxuries relative to necessities, continued to dominate national behavior against the best interests of the workers. For Thoreau, America was the New World because it was a setting in which man could again arrive with ease at the takeoff point into the spiritual; material concerns need not enthrall him as they did perforce in societies where the land was poor or where the many were compelled to pay rent to the few. If he failed finally to alter consciousness on a wide scale, Thoreau succeeded in becoming a widely felt conscience.

In his theory he relied upon the cheapness of American land, but basically he did not believe in proprietorship at all. In 1838 Emerson wrote:

> Henry Thoreau walked with me to Walden this P.M. and complained of the proprietors who compelled him to whom as much as to any the whole world belonged, to walk in a strip of road & crowded him out of all the rest of God's earth. He must not get over the fence: but to the building of that fence he was no party. Suppose, he said, some great proprietor, before he was born, had bought up the whole globe. So he had been hustled out of nature. Not having been privy to any of these arrangements he does not feel called on to consent to them & so cuts fishpoles in the woods without asking who has a better title to the woods than he.[25]

Retaining this attitude, Thoreau did not press it in parallel with his advocacy of radical political behavior, did not endorse trespassing to the point at which trespassers would so crowd the jails that ownership would be exploded.

He did, however, believe that America meant not so much freedom from want as a freedom to want other than the material. Recognizing the desperate condition of the Irish immigrants, whose presence alarmed many older settlers, he refused to be dismayed even at their encroachments upon the ground he loved. While sojourning on Staten Island, he wrote to Emerson in response to such news:

> Let them hack away. The sturdy Irish arms that do the work are of more worth than any oak or maple. Methinks I could look with equanimity upon a long street of Irish cabins, and pigs and children reveling in the genial Concord dirt; and I should still find my Walden wood and Fair Haven in their tanned and happy faces.[26]

He did not oppose using nature for human life, but condemned abusing it for profit beyond sustenance.

In *Walden,* Thoreau describes his attempt to make John Field, an Irish head of family, conscious of the economic good sense of his way of life:

> I tried to help him with my experience, telling him that . . . I lived in a tight, light, and clean house, which hardly cost more than the annual rent of such a ruin as his commonly amounts to;

> and how if he chose, he might in a month or two build himself a palace of his own; that I did not use tea, nor coffee, nor butter, nor milk, nor fresh meat, and so did not have to work hard to pay for them; again, as I did not work hard, I did not have to eat hard, and it cost me but a trifle for my food; but as he began with tea, and coffee, and butter, and milk, and beef, he had to work hard to pay for them, and when he had worked hard he had to eat hard again to repair the waste of his system—and so it was as broad as it was long, for he was discontented and wasted his life into the bargain; and yet he had rated it as a gain in coming to America, that here you could get tea, and coffee, and meat every day. But the only true America is that country where you are at liberty to pursue such a mode of life as may enable you to do without these, and where the state does not endeavor to compel you to sustain the slavery and war and other superfluous expenses which directly or indirectly result from the use of such things.[27]

But he confessed the failure of his effort, recognizing a resistance that he could not overcome in a consciousness formed by other conditions: "With his horizon all his own, yet he is a poor man, born to be poor, with his inherited Irish poverty or poor life, his Adam's grandmother and boggy ways, not to rise in the world, he nor his posterity, till their wading webbed bog-trotting feet get *talaria* to their heels."[28] Those who had greater familiarity with American living and so an unease that persisted after the stomach had been filled would have to be his most vital audience.

The unsuccessful tutelage of John Field occurred some time in the period from 1845 to 1847 when Thoreau lived in a cabin by Walden Pond. The book on his experiment with life was not completed until some seven years later, by which time the failure of his influence on such as John Field had been assimilated into a literary structure that stood in place of the lived experiences as the true expression of what it meant to grow *talaria*. The art of composition transformed history into myth, organizing events in keeping with the seasons of one year, and offering its lesson as an integrated whole that was self-validating, a metaphor the reader found applicable through experiencing it as art rather than learning it as the regimen recommended to John Field.

Thoreau had long experimented with the conversion of history into myth, as he had long experimented with a vascular language. It had cost him an immediate audience in part because of the time he took to perfect work before he considered it publishable, but in greater part because that publishable work struck publishers as dense. He concluded at one point that even editors who would publish just about anything drew the line at a well-formed sentence —that they were afraid of. "I can sympathize, perhaps, with the barberry bush," he wrote a friend in 1848, "whose business it is solely to *ripen* its fruit (though that may not be to sweeten it) and to protect it with thorns, so that it holds on all winter, even, unless some hungry crows come to pluck it."[29] With a greater degree of severity at the disparity between what he had written and what of his was available in print, or, when available, was read, he remarked in the year he published *Walden* that to be popular is "to go down perpendicularly."[30]

In his first and spectacularly unsold book, *A Week on the Concord and Merrimack Rivers,* Thoreau conducted an intense, explicit experiment on the conversion of history into myth, a test of how to value a moment from the past not because it affected the present but because it was present. Without preliminaries, he begins one section: "On the thirty-first of March, one hundred and forty-two years before this, probably about this time in the afternoon, there were hurriedly passing down this part of the river, between the pine woods which then fringed these banks, two white women and a boy, who had left an island at the mouth of the Contocook before daybreak."[31] He then retells the story, legendary in New England, of Hannah Dustan of Haverhill, who, having been kidnapped by Indians who murdered her infant, arose before dawn in the camp of her captors and in company with a white woman and a white boy killed two men, two women, and five children with tomahawks; she fled, but fearing she would be disbelieved at home, returned to take the scalps of the dead as evidence, and with them recommenced her successful voyage to the white settlements.

Hawthorne had treated the same story with great sympathy for the Indians, whom he pictured as devout believers in Providence, and with great horror at Hannah Dustan, whom he pictured as a "bloody old hag," in contrast with her husband at home, a "tender-hearted yet valiant man."[32] But Thoreau does not evaluate the episode morally. He recounts it in slow, drawn-out, dozing sentences, seeing it through the haze of a September afternoon on which he occupies Hannah Dustan's stretch of the river. Before he is halfway through, so thoroughly has the story permeated his present that he slips out of the past tense: "Early this morning this deed was performed, and now, perchance, these tired women and this boy, their clothes stained with blood, and their minds racked with alternate resolution and fear, are making a hasty meal of parched corn and moose-meat, while their canoe glides under these pine roots whose stumps are still standing on the bank. They are thinking . . ."[33] He is thus rendering his present, not Dustan's past, and in making her history something that has been assimilated into and exists in his natural environment he asserts that it counts for something.

In his next unit, reflecting on the scene he has presented, Thoreau ponders chronology and admits that the Dustan episode did not happen very long ago in view of the length of human history, in view of what Europeans would consider antiquity. But, he insists, for Americans it is a tale of antiquity, "for we do not regulate our historical time by the English standard, nor did the English by the Roman, nor the Roman by the Greek."[34] The age of the world, he says, is great enough for our imaginations and the age of the American world can well serve Americans. Hannah Dustan, like a demigoddess of prehistory, looms as the presiding spirit over that stretch of the river.

What Thoreau attempted in *A Week* was what he called "a true account of the actual," and as he pondered its difficulties so he came to appreciate its dangers. The greatest writing comes finally from so deep a source—the area of the intermixing of man's thoughts and actions with nature—that it is a perilous undertaking. It taps the unconsciousness, and "the unconsciousness of man is the consciousness of God." Thus, uncontrollable forces are at play and all of creation is at risk. Plan and plan as one may, the perfection, if achieved, finally comes from the invisible contact point—submission to the vegetative is not, after all, a denial of consciousness but a feeding of it—of our oneness with the wholeness that sustains it. Into such ruminations, startlingly, comes an echo of the Dustan episode: "The talent of composition is very dangerous—the striking out of the heart of life at a blow, as the Indian takes off a scalp."[35]

Twelve years later the notion was still strong. Writing of John

Brown, a man of deeds, Thoreau noted that the time of his trial coincided with the time of the death of Washington Irving, but that Brown's fate so absorbed public attention that the death of the country's greatest literary idol went almost unobserved. He agreed with the scale of values this implied. Consistent with his youthful view of Raleigh, in which he maintained that the greatest writing came, at last, from captive knights who could no longer act, he preferred Brown the actor to Irving the writer. He wrote:

> Literary gentlemen, editors and critics, think that they know how to write, because they have studied grammar and rhetoric; but they are egregiously mistaken. The art of composition is as simple as the discharge of a bullet from a rifle, and its master-pieces imply an infinitely greater force behind them.[36]

The bullet and the tomahawk symbolize Thoreau's ultimate view of the savage source and violent consequences of true literature. It bursts upon the consciousness as a reminder of identity deeper than the consciousness. *"Contact! Contact! Who* are we? *Where* are we?"

Chapter Fourteen

Public Son, Private Native: Theory, Style, and Content in Whitman's Poetry

For all his Concord roots, his transcendental affiliations, and his antislavery feelings, Thoreau still could not like the ponderous, amiable, misty Bronson Alcott. Thinking of him after his death, Emerson noted of Thoreau that "he liked sufficiency, hated a sum that wouldn't prove." So he "loved Walt and hated Alcott."[1]

Thoreau had visited Whitman in 1856 after the publication of the second edition of *Leaves of Grass*. It was something of a scouting trip on behalf of headquarters in Concord. Whitman had sent Emerson a copy of the first edition (1855), and Emerson, flooded though he was with offerings from disciples and from those hopeful of the lift his approbation would give their careers, took time to read the unknown New Yorker's book, acutely noted its importance, and generously sent a congratulatory letter saluting the unknown poet at the beginning of a great career. Some friction was eventually to follow when the rude Whitman, raised in the rough-and-tumble of political journalism, immediately made use of Emerson's words, without seeking permission, as the best possible advertisement for his next edition. That wasn't gentlemanly. Still, the words could not be taken back, embarrassing as they could be made to seem when prefaced to a volume that spoke among other things of "hips, hip-sockets, hip-strength, inward and outward round, man-balls, man-root."[2]

The congratulatory letter was, after all, only the seal of what Emerson had been saying all along while Whitman's strengths were gathering: that he whose sympathy went lowest and was so alive to every presence, however mean, was a man to be dreaded by kings because the world would convert itself into him; that it was not meters but a meter-making argument that made the poem; that the American genius would arrive when the entire society somehow managed to sublimate itself into a hero or a bard.

And the Emersonian approbation so vulgarly paraded was, finally, most valuable for Whitman not as a potential sales-catcher but as the ringing echo that told him he had struck the anvil truly. *Leaves of Grass* emerged from a physical and social environment farther from Emerson's than Brooklyn was from Concord—fleshy, turbulent, lower-class, boastful, gaudy, leering—and yet sprang up in response to Emerson's sowing of his doctrine. To no greater extent was Emerson's close friend and neighbor Thoreau the heir of the master's preaching, which he had heard and discussed in person, than was the Brooklyn ex-carpenter, hack writer, and Broadway loafer whom the words reached in print. Despite his self-insistence and public self-confidence, Whitman, having written the first batch of poems just about single-handedly, needed sorely that one echo beyond any other response. It made continuation possible for him.

Thoreau was greatly impressed by Whitman in person, more than he cared to admit. The force of the impression lies in the words of a letter he sent his friend Harrison Blake; that it was deeper than the words express can be inferred from the uncharacteristic length and somewhat rambling nature of his remarks. "That Walt Whitman . . . is the most interesting fact to me at present," he wrote on 7 December 1856. He went on to say that he was struck that Whitman in his poetry did not celebrate love at all, but "it is as if the beasts spoke." This was a trial for Thoreau, who was shocked, despite his commitment to the *anima* in animal. Still, he reasoned, such doings took place in the world, and if fault there was, it resided not in being told of such matters but in seeing ourselves engaged in them—"if we are shocked whose experience is it that we are reminded of?" Even here, Whitman "spoke more truth than any American or modern I know." "America" or "American" then rang in each succeeding paragraph: "very brave and American" and no sermon equal to it for preaching; "an alarum or trumpet-note ringing through the American camp"[3]—how his fellow New Yorkers must shudder when they read him.

Thoreau, with his sturdy, porcupine nature, felt compelled, however, to tell Whitman that he himself didn't think much of "America or of politics, and so on,"[4] thus putting, he felt, a damper not on Whitman's claim to represent America but on what it was he bothered to represent. For all his unease at Whitman's sensuality, Thoreau preferred it to the social; it reached closer to the source of poetry, was more natural. Whitman was to recall the December 7 meeting, and that Thoreau asked: "What is there in the people? Pshaw! What do you (a man who sees as well as anybody) see in all this cheating political corruption?" They were walking Brooklyn streets, and Whitman remembered, "I did not like my Brooklyn spoken of in this way."[5]

Yet four years later, when the war was inevitable, Whitman too was willing to speak of political corruption—in his way, at least—and to bring the impending horror home to the truckling, vote-cadging cheaters of the North far more than to the arrogance of the South:

> What deepening twilight! Scum floating atop the waters!
> Who are they, as bats and night-dogs, askant in the
>   Capitol?[6]

This was meant to identify the administrations of Fillmore, Pierce, and Buchanan. Forcing America to hold a mirror to its face, Whitman pointed out that "flashing eye," "sonorous voice," and "springy step" were gone: "No brain, no heart left—no magnetism of sex." From his own outset as a poet in 1855 to 1860 the change in the land was terrible: "Such a result so soon—and from such a beginning!"[7]

But Whitman's own beginning came from waterfalls so high and his genius flowed so powerfully that this reaction was, finally, but the pressure felt by "pent-up aching rivers," which were to modify their channels in the coming years but maintain their flow—more calmly to be sure—after their first tumble out of their sources. Those sources were American, yet no American writer had been able to accept their intermixture.

Walter Whitman was the son of a quick-tempered, violent father, an unsuccessful builder whose failure deepened his gloomy nature. Whitman's mother was his gentle sustenance throughout his young manhood, but she was illiterate, and Whitman's love for her, even adoration of her, could not be communicated to her in his poems. If he would have addressed anybody in a lyric vein it would have been she, as, say, Wordsworth addressed Dorothy, but this outlet was closed by her inability to read, although he could, of course, recite his verses to her. To this circumstance must in some small part be attributed the public as opposed to the lyric nature of his verse. He wrote what could be chanted aloud to an assumed audience (an assumed audience; he knew perfectly well his poems were going to be read) of nonreaders, and he placed before their eyes the objects of which he spoke, frequently heaping them, naming each item as it was added to the collection in such a fashion that it stood forth as an illustration in the text. If it were attached to a concept, that concept kept its place awaiting inference. But the illustrations were not pictures from a child's book, for all the similarity they bore them, because no writer more than Whitman intuitively grasped the pushiness of words, their refusal to stay fixed in a composition. Accordingly, at their frequent best, his illustrations, each a completed little scene, press upon one another in their containment of both force and resistance, the tension of which runs from scene to scene:

> Where the panther walks to and fro on a limb overhead
> —Where the buck turn furiously at the hunter,
> Where the rattlesnake suns his flabby length on a rock
> —Where the otter is feeding on fish,
> Where the alligator in his tough pimples sleeps by the bayou,
> Where the black bear is searching for roots or honey
> —Where the beaver pats the mud with his paddle-tail.[8]

The nervous pacing of the panther, tinged with menace in his being overhead, is joined to a scene of actual antagonism as man hunts food. In the next line there is no explicit motion or opposition, but rattlesnake means a tense and deadly coiling, so that his flabby, torpid extension is quick with its opposite; in repose the threat is not reduced but charged with a potential energy that crackles. The more peaceful otter follows, engaged in a perfectly mild yet direct killing for food—the *f*'s of his "feeding on fish" picked up from the preceding "flabby." Then, in parallel with the rattlesnake, the deadly alligator also rests, his instantly available energy marvelously conveyed by "tough pimples." Again a shyer beast follows, the black bear, and again the concern is motion and food, and the beaver in characteristic motion closes the group of animal pictures with a thump as paddle echoes pat and reminds us of panther. Illustrations all, and yet each with motion or what is even more dynamic, the menace of it, the sense of life feeding and life at rest but capable of leaping out and killing.

"There is that indescribable freshness and unconsciousness about an illiterate person," Whitman wrote, "that humbles and mocks the power of the noblest expressive genius." Plain people see beauty in the heavens, the forests, the mountains, and the rivers as readily as does the poet. What they do not see, as he does, is that they are as good as he is. They do not need him to point out beauties, but they do need him "to indicate the path between reality and their souls."[9] The poet is the man who knows what it is to be complete and can thus show others that they too are complete. He must share with others what he is, how he perceives, in order to bring them to recognize the fullness of what is already there within them. "What is commonest, cheapest, nearest, easiest, is Me,"[10] he says, not as clownish self-abasement or as proletarian brag, although both tendencies are there and contribute to his charm and force when so controlled (while in his lapses they distort his verse). Rather, all the commonest "is Me" because as Me presents the parts that form him he is presenting the items that constitute the reality of even the humblest.

Emerson had a strong influence on such views in his insistence, for example, on the reclamation in America of the whole man, not just a walking part of him. His assertion of the "I" as microcosm of the All released creative energies in those who were hesitating on the shores of action, rendered fearful by their own provinciality and by the crude simplicity of their environment as compared with the life pictured in the books they read. Because of Emerson, Thoreau could affirm, "I should not talk so much about myself if there were anybody else whom I knew as well,"[11] and in so saying not express narcissism but proclaim that he was going to give an account of life rather than an account of accounts of life. And so Whitman could start his book by saying, "I CELEBRATE myself,"[12] with confidence that he was celebrating the life of each of his countrymen, not making peculiar claims for his own differences. The persona of each of these "I's" was, indeed, distinct, but it was whole, independent of the focused requirements of the lyric mode. Thoreau and Whitman wrote politically in the sense that they addressed an audience envisaged as fellow citizens of their American world, and in consequence they were political in that they were engaged in telling people how to manage their lives.

Perhaps conscious of the pun, Emerson had emphasized the eye of "I" as the dominant sense, that through which his transcendent relationship to the oversoul would most manifestly flow. His claim that he was a transparent eyeball was notorious in his day, causing laughter even among his friends. Whitman followed. The poet was a seer, he claimed, and he meant that first and foremost with literal reference to eyesight: "The other senses corroborate themselves, but this is removed from any proof but its own, and foreruns the identities of the spiritual world." Indeed, as eyesight stood to the other senses, so, Whitman believed, the poet stood to other men, his words finding instant validity, even as seeing is believing, and thus capable of pushing beyond the observations accessible to others, onto the path between sight and soul.[13]

Finally, this is prophecy, and Whitman accepted his role as prophet so long as it was not narrowed to prediction. "It means," he said, "one whose mind bubbles up and pours forth as a fountain from inner divine spontaneities revealing God."[14] He claimed that this was the doctrine of the Friends among whom he had been raised, but it was compatible with Emerson's doctrine and was reinforced in Whitman, even as Emerson himself may very well have been influenced by his reading in Quaker theology. Such prophecy, however, also came from the connection it had with literal seeing, and it is notable that Whitman's omnivorous ability to swallow and digest all ugliness and evil encountered by Myself on equal terms with all beauty and good extends only to his dominating use of sight. Once he hearkens to other senses—hearing and touch—his prophetic power becomes entangled in self-doubt.

The doubtings, of course, are plotted. It is through a marvelous series of sights that he arrives at the middle point of *Song of Myself,* where he can stand up and, after naming so much else, name himself: "Walt Whitman, an American, one of the roughs, a kosmos." As he compiles those sights he brushes aside the opposition to his gathering strength that comes from sound and touch: "Trippers and askers surround me." But they are not the "Me myself," and when he affirms, "Apart from the pulling and hauling stands what I am," he does so by showing that he "looks."

This dismissal of doubters occurs in stanza five, immediately before his mystical intercourse with the soul is dramatized as physical intercourse in which he submits in ecstasy to sound and touch. Even in surrender, however, he proportions those senses. He invites the soul to loaf with him on the grass and "loose the stop from your throat." He does not, however, want words: "Only the lull I like, the hum of your valved voice." And when the tactile meeting takes place it is shifted to the past, "I mind how once we lay," and the return to the present tense is not in terms of touch but of vision:

> And I know that the hand of God is the promise of my own,
> And I know that the spirit of God is the brother of my own,
> And that all the men ever born are also my brothers, and the
>   women my sisters and lovers,
> And that a kelson of the creation is love,
> And limitless are leaves, stiff or drooping in the fields,
> And brown ants in the little wells beneath them,
> And mossy scabs of the worm fence, and heaped stones,
>   elder, mullen, and pokeweed.

The passage moves from an inner vision to outer sights intended to corroborate it, and the discrepancy between the items of the first and the items of the second is so extreme as to appear ludicrous if abstracted: hand of God or spirit of God versus ants and scabs; brotherhood and love versus insect life on the lowest plane of observation. But Whitman makes good the connections, shows, that is, the path from the ground-level shabby reality to the ethereal perception, through extraordinary artistry. That, after all, as he had said, is what men need the poet for. The seven lines pivot on the middle one—"And that a kelson of the creation is love"—and this line is balanced by joining two terms, each of which refers to but one half of the whole revelation: "creation" to the spiritual and "kelson" to the physical. Phonemically the two words are stressed through alliteration and further emphasized by the fact that the alliterative sound, *k,* has not occurred previously in the passage. Its only subsequent occurrences, moreover, are in the finely tuned echo of "scabs" and "pokeweed" that blends even the shabbiest bits of reality to the transcendent whole. Kelson, literally and figuratively, gives base and balance to the soaring vision, a physical floor to spirituality on which bugs and weeds can flourish.

The *k* sound that announces the key link stands forth also because the movement toward it is dominated by initial consonant sounds that are sonorant and continuant. The *g,* a voiced *k,* occurs in but one word, and that a presage of the vital linkage, "God."

As phonemic values move surely in keeping with the ideas and give the gigantic contentions a conviction beyond reason, so the duration of the word gives it an air of rocklike certainty. Of the eighty-eight words only nineteen contain more than one syllable, and the monosyllables create a cumulative effect of solidity of affirmation. Moreover, only two of the nineteen polysyllabic words are as long as three syllables; one is "creation" and the other stems from it, "limitless," but moves on to suggest infinity through releasing creeping, crawling, terrestrial life rather than soaring into space.

The vision follows from a scene of sexual intercourse, albeit the partners are the poet and his soul, and is a consequence of that act. But in a strong undercurrent the passage on the vision also repeats that act. The flow of long lines, building from fifteen to sixteen to twenty-four syllables, followed by the abrupt fall to lines of twelve, thirteen, and eleven before the final normalization at eighteen, conveys this in one way; the "stiff or drooping leaves" phrase does so in another; and the dying movement in using such words as "scabs," "worm," and "pokeweed" in yet a third, suggesting as they do a postcoital sadness tinged slightly with shame. Such a fusion of idea, sound, pitch, and extension speaks of Whitman's rightness in breaking the rules that governed his day's poetry. Growing from his meter-making arguments are measure, meaning, and tonality that give a rule.

Emerson, of course, was in agreement with the doctrine of Whitman's vision—it was his own. Its texture, however, may well have given him pause. To be sure, the soul was joined to the body, but even one's own body was to be considered as the Not Me, that part of our environment which obeys laws we do not and cannot make. Whitman may have been shocking but he was not wrong when he celebrated the body as one might celebrate other objects in nature. When he named sexual organs and described sexual acts in his poems he was doing no more than Adam did when he named the beasts in the garden and thereby placed them in the field of thought. There was a sanity in this, and it quite rightly showed the insanity of the conventions that governed conversation and literature in American society and thereby removed so much of elemental vitality from the area of understanding.

Fanny Fern, another brash New York journalist, was quick to realize this. *"Leaves of Grass,"* she wrote, "thou art unspeakably delicious, after the forced, still, Parnassian exotics for which our admiration had been vainly challenged." Then, in a telling remark, she went on, "Walt Whitman, the effeminate world needed thee." It is telling because Fern had no sense of Whitman's homosexual bias; his recognition of the central place of sex in the world appeared to her to be the opposite of the lying, sentimental avoidance of the topic in her day. So perverse was the culture she deplored that its constrained vocabulary afforded her no better word than "effeminate" to designate everything Whitman was not. She took Whitman's point about bringing good health to his readers:

> My moral constitution may be hopelessly tainted or—too sound to be tainted, as the critic wills, but I confess that I extract no poison from these "leaves"—to me they have brought only healing. Let him who can do so shroud the eyes of the nursing babe lest it should see its mother's breast.[15]

But where Whitman did depart from Emerson was in an imagination that gave corporeality to the soul—and more important, because such corporeality might be taken simply as a dramatic device as old as allegory—that gave consciousness to the body. Thoreau felt that parts of Whitman's verse were like the animals speaking, and accordingly he disapproved. The disapproval was not inconsistent with his manifest admiration elsewhere for the life of animals. What he was asserting was that life was unconscious, nonverbal, and therefore to be spoken about but not itself to be heard speaking. Whitman, however, was reviving in America a sense of consciousness in sexual desire and sexual coupling that was far more stunning than his guileless naming of "hair, bosom, hips, bend of legs, negligent falling hands . . . / . . . love-flesh swelling and deliciously aching."[16]

When "prurient provokers" stiffen his limbs in his encounter with touch, "straining the udder of my heart for its withheld drip," Whitman launches a psychological drama of the body's consciousness. As his clothes are unbuttoned and he is held by the bare waist, all senses but touch immediately slide away. The rational self sees and disapproves, claims his "fellow-senses" were bribed to desert "and go graze at the edges of me." That rational self insists, at the risk of massive self-pity, that he is not implicated, that he is the victim of a plot:

> No consideration, no regard for my draining strength or my
> anger,
> Fetching the rest of the herd around to enjoy them a while,
> Then all uniting to stand on a headland and worry me.

The mood accelerates into a frenzy of paranoia, the self being deserted by its sentries, left helpless before a "red marauder," "given up by traitors." Then, from the core of the frantic dissociation of the rational Me from the terrible, delicious thing that is happening, bursts forth the splendid confession of complicity in desire:

> I talk wildly—I have lost my wits—I and nobody else am
> the greatest traitor,
> I went myself to the headland—my own hands carried me
> there.[17]

Nothing in the literature of Whitman's America matches such a rendering of the psychology of sex. It accepts the social shamefulness of the act; there is a viciousness in the seduction—a betrayal of a fortress from within—and the traitor's name is "touch." But the victim at the height of his delirium cannot deny the sweetness that it is and confesses that victim and villain are one. The truth of the senses emerges from Whitman's truth to the senses. The animal speaks because body is not a detached chamber the soul inhabits, but holds the soul by a hundred filaments that reach to the very core whence speech issues.

Whatever contrariness attaches to the recognition that the natural sanity of sexuality finally arose to expressiveness in American literature through the poetry of one whose preferences were homosexual quickly dissipates when the literature contemporary with Whitman's poetry is placed by its side. The verbal denial of sexual polarity implicit in the tortured abuses of "feminine" and "masculine" to convey every attribute save that of biological gender, and the tyranny of psychological trepidation revealed by citations of the sibling relationship as symbol of the most harmonious way in which a man and a woman could cohabit, form so global an irony that the irony of Whitman's sexuality is converted to forthrightness. Perhaps the knot could be undone only by one whose deepest sense of being in his life was apart from accepted norms, and who was thus driven to establish identity with others and in that drive told the others the truth about themselves. He could see heterosexuality as clearly as he could see trees and houses when he looked back from his headland. Presenting himself as burly, bearded, rowdy, he knew that neither "feminine" nor "effeminate" expressed female. He won his persona as an American, a son of Manhattan, one of the roughs, a member of the crowd, who not only looked on but suffered through his overcoming in imagination his felt sense of difference, and from the struggle this entailed he gained strength. He is the charming and exhilarating poet of brag and lustiness because he is the great poet of limitations and vulnerability.

In "Crossing Brooklyn Ferry" Whitman demonstrates the firmness of his assurance that he is a poet for the future as well as for his time. He moves from his present when he writes the poem to the present of the reader when he reads it, and in so doing shifts his tenses and treats his own time as past while his voice goes on living—"Just as you feel . . . so I felt." He thus alters the mythic emphases of Thoreau, who in retelling the Hannah Dustan story made her past his present. Whitman the cosmic poet insists that his present coexists with the time of any possible reader.

"The glories strung like beads on my smallest sights and bearings" are described in a list of vigorous scenes, each characteristically pictorial and yet kinetic. The reader and he have identity. Neither time nor distance "avails" because just as he experienced his physical world, so the reader experiences his own physical world made up of the same elements and invoking the same sensations. Moreover, to clinch that identity, here is the poem of the physical world shared by poet and reader at different times to compel a sharing between them at the same moment. The splendid assertion has as its goal not just the demonstration that Walt Whitman is a great poet, but, equally, that we are a great audience. He believed that to have great poets the world must have great audiences, but this did not mean great poetry awaited such audiences; rather it went out into the streets and cohered them. Finally, the plenum of the proof is the poem.

But with this recognized, only the large first movement (stanzas 1–4) and the large last movement (stanzas 7–9) of the poem are characterized. At its heart are two stanzas that validate the grand claims for identity of past and present, death and life, the near bank and the distant bank, the poet and his reader, through a confession of the shared fears and vices that eat at human life. Our worst weakness is the strongest bond of our common identity.

"I too felt the curious abrupt questionings stir within me," the poet says; and further, "It is not upon you alone the dark patches fell"; and then he illustrates how full was his experience of the dark patches he too had, how he knows what it is to be evil. His remarkable confession, which becomes our confession, exhausts the parts of speech: verbs—"blabbed, blushed, resented, lied"; abstract nouns—"guile, anger, lust, hot wishes"; modifiers—"wayward, vain, greedy, shallow." In its relentless drive toward catharsis it reaches a thrilling point at which the line thickens, with only the article to relieve the stress, and at that point only concrete nouns, the names of lowly, vicious animals, will serve—"the wolf, the snake, the hog"—to effect the release that is signaled as the line trails out: "The wolf, the snake, the hog, not wanting in me." This is the shared vulnerability that Whitman renders splendidly in every major poem of mighty claims for the transcendent self, the foundation sunk so deep that the spire is enabled to soar.

In "Crossing Brooklyn Ferry" the core section has at its heart of hearts a remarkable image that is so intense as to generate paradox—it wells up coherently and irresisitibly from what is being said, expressing it at a blow, and yet it spouts forth with such power that it goes beyond its function to suggest its own opposite: "I too had been struck from the float forever held in solution."

The immediate picture is that of being thrown from a raft into water. It is an image of how we can be converted in a trice from a balmy sense of merging our separateness into the All to a terrible awareness that at every point along our bodies we end and something else begins. Melville too centered on the deliciousness and treachery of such a sense of merging, in scenes such as those of Ishmael at the masthead and Ishmael squeezing hands with others in a vat of sperm oil.

As the Whitman who was raised by the shore on Long Island and frequented the ferryboats knew, the "float" is also the flow of the sea into a tidal river. To be struck from it in this sense was to be tossed from the womb of the fierce mother, sea, into one's own terrestrial body; or, with the same sense of "float," to have been made from the primal saline world only to have to pursue one's consciousness in a more developed world. In this latter respect the poem "The World Below the Brine" invites comparison, and Whitman's known interest in Darwinism offers confirmation.

But mixed with such meanings is an opposed one. The major symbol of the poem is the ferry crossing at close of day and close of year and thereby suggesting the classic crossing of the Styx from the world of the living to the underworld of the dead. Time is being spanned as well as space, and the spanner of the time is the poem itself, the correspondent of the ferryboat that binds two shores. For Whitman to proclaim that he too had been struck from the float is to force to the surface a subconscious awareness that he is detachable from his poem and knows an identity apart from that with the reader which his poem embodies. The poem is his vehicle but there is a he who can be thrown from it and is none the less real for all that.

The awareness that flashes forth momentarily in the line in "Crossing Brooklyn Ferry" eventually seeks fulfillment in poems also, but on its own terms rather than those of the larger poems. Such fulfillment occurs primarily in the poems of the *Calamus* section, which date from 1860, four years after "Crossing Brooklyn Ferry." This was the period of Whitman's temporary retreat from nationalistic enthusiasm, when he recognized that the northern crowd whose badgering good cheer he so enjoyed was deeply implicated in the coming disaster because of its thoughtless complicity in the corrupt policies of the power-seekers. The *Calamus* poems withdraw from the streets of cities into secret places in nature: "paths untrodden/In the growth by margins of pond-waters,"[18] or "back of a rock,"[19] or "solitary, in a wide flat space."[20] They reveal the poet who is not expressed in the larger poems that speak for American experience. In other poems Whitman boisterously stands forth as

American, but in these he talks of a coming away from America to a place that is truly native to him:

> Native moments! when you come upon me—Ah you are here now!
> Give me now libidinous joys only![21]

The suggestion one takes from the *Calamus* poems is that the great sojourner of the open road could pace it with alert avidity because he was drinking in the sights of a land that he was adding to rather than spinning from himself. Just as he perceived heterosexuality more clearly from his apartness, so he perceived America more clearly from his feeling that he was a native of something other than that country.

Chapter Fifteen

Poet of Death: Whitman and Democracy

In 1867 Whitman added to *Leaves of Grass* an inscription which began:

> One's-Self I sing, a simple, separate Person;
> Yet utter the word Democratic, the word *En-Masse*.

As the nation imperfectly groped toward reconciliation, so he, too, returned to being a poet, however altered, of the widest American experience. The key word in the lines is, strikingly, "yet." There is a conflict between individuality and equality; one cannot sing the self *and* utter the word "en masse" but must do so in counterpoint. After the war Whitman intensified his singing of "en masse," coming more and more to mean by it not the crowds on city streets nor the gatherings in the barn at husking time but an imperial political entity. Americans in their geographical position spanned Atlantic and Pacific and in their temporal position spanned the high civilization and technological advancements of Europe and the cradle of man and the primal myths of Asia. They were a race of races destined to regenerate humanity, not, as Emerson had it, by providing models of what individual man released from the prejudices of history could do, but as a swarming collectivity. This, however, was a postwar Whitman. In the flush of his first early power in the fifties his concern was far more with the separate person than with "en masse."

Thomas Carlyle, in 1867, contemplating the growing influence of the proletarian mass in Britain, felt it needed authoritative leadership from above if it was to realize its best self. "One often wishes," he wrote, "the entire Population could be thoroughly drilled; into cooperative movement, into individual behaviour, correct, precise, and at once habitual and orderly as mathematics; in all or in very many points."[1] For their own and the nation's best interests people should be disciplined to submerge themselves in a common enterprise. Individualism as it was worshipped in America, in name at least, was anarchic, and Carlyle, in common with most European political thinkers, had no difficulty in advocating its integration into a regulated collectivity. Even the crowd in Hyde Park on holiday from work suffered from its want of someone to organize it:

> I believe the vulgarest Cockney crowd, flung out millionfold on a Whit-Monday, with nothing but beer and dull folly to depend on for amusement, would at once kindle into something human, if you set them to do any regulated act in common. And would dismiss their beer and dull foolery, in the silent charm of rhythmic human companionship, in the practical feeling, probably new, that all of us are made on one pattern, and are, in an unfathomable way, brothers to one another.[2]

Only when relieved of the ennui of their own imaginations, Carlyle says, will the populace become "something human," and only when engaged in an organized activity such as military drill will they discover what otherwise is known only to the more thoughtful—that we all are "brothers to one another." Whitman, thinking of an American crowd in a Sunday park, said, "I believe in all that—in baseball, in picnics, in freedom: I believe in the jolly all-round time—with the parsons and the police eliminated."[3] Some brotherhood and humanity, he knew, were stirring and they could only be destroyed by regulators.

With no history of implicit class rule, the crowd in America was all too ready to gather into an undistinguished herd, Whitman knew. It was good, therefore, to see it break out into spontaneous play. One of the crowd himself, Whitman in his first poems opposed the anonymity that could swallow its members; he did not fear the anarchy that could result from lack of regulation. When Thomas Wentworth Higginson, Cambridge-born, intellectual, liberal, earnest, got a glimpse of Whitman in Boston around 1859, he reported, "the personal impression made on me by the poet was not so much of manliness as of Boweriness."[4] His immediate reference was to the fact that Whitman, although physically burly, did not seem physically fit, but his observation also serves to point up the ineradicability of the mark of the beery crowd on Whitman. This mark he carried unabashedly into his poetry. For all his swift changes of perception, Myself has always about him an engaging nonchalance and his diction can swoop to catch up slang with unaffected ease. The mark is also present in the vulgarity of the ill-considered use of foreign terms and the tastelessness of his all-too-easy dismissal of certain British authors: "Perhaps we will have to import the words Snobs, Snobbish, &c., after all."[5]

But although he had this Boweriness, or more likely because he had it, Whitman was as concerned as Emerson to bring to the members of the crowd a sense of their individuality. "En masse" was a given and meant crowds at fires, on ferryboats, in political meetings; he would call forth the ones who might otherwise pass into anonymity. He named them ("Kanuck, Tuckahoe, Congressman, Cuff"[6]); placed them ("in cabins among the California mountains . . . on the Columbia . . . on the banks of the Gila or Rio Grande"[7]); activated them ("The pure contralto sings in the organ loft,/The carpenter dresses his plank"[8]). Whenever he showed a gang he showed an individual blazing forth from it:

> The hurrahs for popular favorites, the fury of rous'd mobs,
> The flap of the curtained litter, a sick man inside, borne to
> the hospital.

The recognized violence of the mob is thus balanced by the recognized vulnerability of its individual constituents.

> The western turkey-shooting draws old and young—some
> lean on their rifles, some sit on logs,
> Out from the crowd steps the marksman, takes his position,
> levels his piece.[9]

Against the grouped leaning and the grouped sitting, the individual leveling. And Whitman himself is the marksman who sights a crowd and draws a bead on the individual in it.

When Whitman in the poetry of the fifties looked at massed Americans from a distance too great to permit the distinguishing of individuals, he did not see—as his later cultural imperialism was to see—a political nation; he saw a yearning common consciousness, the equality of soul in each. In his visionary wandering into and out of the dreams of the sleepers who themselves flow into and out of one another across the continent as the sun trails darkness in its wake, he descends into the death suggested by the sleep of night to say:

> It seems to me that everything in the light and air ought
> to be happy,
> Whoever is not in his coffin and the dark grave, let him
> know he has enough.[10]

But he cannot shake the thought of death, toward which all life and beauty drive—the beautiful, gigantic swimmer with undaunted eyes holds out while his strength holds out, but at last the slapping eddies turn him and bear him away, a corpse. The poet's resistance to the cruelty of the death of beauty is resolved by the awareness that in sleep not just the swimmer and the dancer, not just the perfectly formed and the red squaw are beautiful, but that the stammerer, the sick, the idiot, and the wronged are beautiful also:

> The antipodes, and every one between this and them in the
> dark,
> I swear they are averaged now—one is no better than the
> other,
> The night and sleep have likened them and restored them.
> I swear they are all beautiful.

The poet pictures himself as a commuter between day and night, between particular perceptions of specific physical beauty and a comprehensive perception of the universal beauty of the soul. That equality of soul is why democracy makes utter, irrefutable sense to him. It is a principle that rests not on political theory but on spiritual reality.

The democracy of death is an old literary truism. But the fact that kings and cobblers are equaled in the grave does not necessarily imply that they should not be distinct in life for the welfare of the community. Nor does Whitman's democratic faith rest here. It is located, rather, in the commonplace historical observation that those who emigrated to America did so because the point in the world's history had arrived when monarchy was obsolete. The natural plenty of the new land validated their perception, permitting them equal economic opportunity, which fostered political equality. Such historical confidence was the stock in trade of almost every newspaper of Whitman's day, and he had worked on more than one of them.

But from that observation Whitman moved on to the spiritual equality that he discovered at the base of political equality, and as a poet he committed himself to revealing it as the ultimate human bond. He talked in this respect of identity, but from the perspective of the universality of the soul, identity became a matter somewhat different from the individuality of the contralto, the trapper, or the idiot:

> It is not to diffuse you that you were born of your mother
> and father—it is to identify you,
> It is not that you should be undecided, but that you should
> be decided.[11]

Although he was not so dependent upon etymology as Thoreau, Whitman here seems definitely to be looking to the root meaning of "decide"—cut off—to shape his sense. One received identity through being cut off from all-pervading immortality and assuming, for a moment, mortality. Finally Whitman says, "I swear I think there is nothing but immortality!" and the image that dominates his poem is one of the earth, and especially the American earth, covered by one vast funeral procession: "Slow-moving and black lines creep over the whole earth—they never cease—they are the burial lines."

In his view of the brevity of the mortal span Whitman did not in the fifties force his optimism; he earned it. He recognized that if death was all-encompassing, then the very earth on which men trod and whose beauties they celebrated was one great compost heap. In a remarkable poem, "This Compost," he accepted the image. "O how can the ground of you not sicken?" he asks. "Are they not continually putting distempered corpses within you?" And he goes on to indulge his revulsion, tallying "sour dead," "carcasses," "foul liquid and meat."

Yet, "What Chemistry! / That the winds are really not infectious." There is indeed an amorous "green-wash of the sea"; "melons, grapes, peaches, plums, will none of them poison me"; and no disease is caught "when I recline on the grass." This organic chemistry, however, this conversion of stink to perfume, decay to bloom, only secondarily suggests rebirth. The primary emphasis in the closing stanza, as signaled by attributing the process to the science of chemistry, is on the fearfulness of it all:

> Now I am terrified at the Earth! it is that calm and patient,
> It grows such sweet things out of such corruptions,
> It turns harmless and stainless on its axis, with such endless
> successions of diseased corpses,
> It distills such exquisite winds out of such infused fetor,
> It renews with such unwitting looks, its prodigal, annual,
> sumptuous crops,
> It gives such divine materials to men, and accepts such
> leavings from them at last.

Impersonal process is emphasized: the earth turns "harmless," but the word's connotation seems to be more that the earth cannot be affected by man than that it cannot affect him; it is metallically stainless; and its look masks no intelligence. The poet's assertion of the symbols of rebirth is dominated by his unasserted consciousness of the terrible impersonality of the chemical operation that converts death to life. In the face of so inhuman and inescapable a process, the human response must be a seizing of man's difference from it—his capacity to love and his capacity to die.

When Whitman arrived at this outlook he saw that the great poet of democracy had to be the writer of the great poems of death. Democratic practice did bring together all men into a featureless mediocrity that justified the laments of Cooper and the ironic amens of Hawthorne. Whitman, to be sure, brushed in the features that others did not so much fail to notice as fail to regard as expressive. But finally the marvelous stage drivers, clam diggers, or friendly matrons who start from his lines are not engaged in any drama personal to them. They are not characters in a novel, although the instinct leading Whitman to vivify them leads him also to introduce what was to be the stuff of novels—"The blab of the pave, the tires of carts, sluff of boot-soles."[12] They are, rather, faces burning from out the crowd so fiercely that, once glimpsed, they will never again permit us to think of the crowd as mere mass. Still, what they express turns us toward a new realization of the nature of the democratic whole, not toward a drama of individual careers. There is only one individual character in constant development before our eyes in these poems—"I," "Myself," the poet—and his constant refrain is that he represented us when he wrote the poem, and even as we read his pages he now stands for ourselves. Emerson's controlling view was that representative men represent us by showing that what caused them—the oversoul—can cause us, so that the greater the man, the more representative he is of our potentiality. Still, he was chagrined at times to think that he had written of Napoleon and Goethe but could not directly grasp the greatness of his neighbors. Whitman attacked essentially the same problems. For all that Myself is one of the boys and can also be one with the most degraded, he shows Myself subsuming these and standing forth, finally, as so thoroughly drenched in everything human that he is superhuman. Whitman, too, shows us our potential far more than our actuality. And the drama in which he acts for us is ultimately not that between individuals, because he is all individuals and there is no one to play antagonist to his protagonist; it is the drama of the vital all-in-one and ultimate reality. The great poems of democracy are the poems of death.

Democratic identity depended practically on what human life depended upon—ideally, love. Whitman was its constant exponent, singing not only the love of comrades but the sexual love that underlay it and the love that drove on procreation and furnished further splendid democrats. But identity, as the condition of being cut off during life from the eternal wholeness, also fostered love, a desire for completion in union with another, which in its ultimate unattainability becomes desire for a merger with the unknown. The earthbound solitary singer throbs "Loved! loved! loved! loved! loved!" The poet, who knows he is projected in the song, seeks a further clue, since the word itself is an expression of incompleteness. He receives it in the murmur of the sea, which surrounds the land as the dark does the light, "Death, death, death, death, death." The two fused become the song of the poet.

In "Out of the Cradle Endlessly Rocking," the outsetting poet sought a word and, having received it, was equipped to realize his vocation. But, of course, a poem is many words, not a word. Whitman especially is the issuer of a cataract of words, visibly as well as aurally spilling in lines that stretch across the page only to continue after reaching the margin. His delight in periphrasis and his binding through alliteration and internal rhyme and half-rhyme rather than through ended units further contribute to the effect of torrential flow.

To follow Emersonian linguistic theory was to see the inescapable fitness of each word rightly used; to deal, ideally, in an image and a complete idea each time one dealt with a word. Whitman was not a close adherent of this theory. His words do not seem as tactile as Thoreau's, and the apprentice writer can learn far more about his craft from Thoreau than from Whitman. The phrase is more frequently Whitman's basic unit than is the word—"kelson of creation," "blab of pave." He is fond of compounding—"love-flesh," "palate-valves"; who else would echo "trouser-leg" with "chowder kettle"? To some extent this verbosity deliberately follows from Whitman's literal application of the notion that the magnitude of America must be mirrored in her mightiest poems. More precisely, it arises from Whitman's enormous appetite for motion as a fundamental feature of the poem's assertion, its vital beating against arrest, as if to assume a form, to remain in an enclosed space, would be to contradict the argument of the universe—its urge, urge, urge. So central a feature of his imagination is animation that even when he envisages that part of himself which transcends the Me Myself, the part that is above the pulling and the hauling, the oversoul that ultimately links reader and poet, even then, when baffled and yearning he addresses it in poignant outcry, "You, up there," he must add, "walking or sitting."[13]

One sense that emerges from words so used is the sense of there being an unspeakable word of which the words spoken are but appearances, a word so potent that it spawns the many words. Such a notion was held by the Puritan dissenters from the elegant constructs of the Anglican preachers (such as John Donne and Launcelot Andrewes) who, the Puritans insisted, preached the wisdom of words rather than the word itself in their witty discourses. The Puritans did not say this in order to curtail preaching. Quite the reverse. They replaced the altar with the pulpit; no people were quite so avid for a constant feast of preaching as they were. The sermons on which they continually fed without seeming to glut themselves were plain in diction and built up of expository units each of which so focused on the particular matter to be expounded that an image arose solely to illustrate the point at hand and was quickly abandoned, or succeeded by another image, as the next point followed. Such sermons convey a sense that there is a word behind the preacher's words, of which he is but the spontaneous and fallible mouthpiece.

Whitman was, to be sure, at the farthest remove from what is conventionally called Puritan. But he was shaped in the verbal tradition of the Friends, which was an extension—to the point of lunacy, the Puritans believed—of the Puritan perception. Serious utterance was the imperfect eruption into visibility of the perfect and invisible—an inner light which outer light but shadowed. It was a fragment broken off from silence, and it was followed by the silence intended to reintegrate it. Like Emerson in one way and Thoreau in another, Whitman, too, had reasons to see his words as children of the silence, and, as his Quaker intimacy with the sacredness of silence was deep, so the words with which he translated it were copious.

In *Song of Myself* Whitman offers his reader not a poem but "the origin of all poems." He claims to be not so much speaking as releasing through his voice a preverbal condition that is the structure behind his seeming formlessness. In later editions he was to make this notion more explicit by adding such lines as "I permit to speak at every hazard, / Nature without check with original energy." Although he is the maker of the poem, what he is making is different from the words of which he makes it. He tells the reader, "You shall not look through my eyes," and promises him that he will be able to "listen to all sides, and filter them from yourself." The aspects of nature that can be fixed in words are the aspects that have been charted by the lexicographer, the chemist, the geologist, and he shouts, "Hurrah for positive science! long live exact demonstration!" But he moves beyond such precision, or, what is the same, proceeds from the wholeness that precedes it: "I am less the reminder of property or qualities, and more the reminder of life."

His words must be plentiful because they are the outgrowth of a mighty source, and because no one or two of them can fix, but all of them must suggest. As Thoreau in spring saw life first stir in the dirt and push forward as words contained in natural forms, so Whitman offers an image of the arriving sun quickening words:

> Do you not know how the buds beneath you are folded?
> Waiting in gloom, protected by frost,
> The dirt receding before my prophetical screams,
> I underlying causes, to balance them at last.

But he is here not proclaiming the adequacy of words; he is insisting upon their fragmentary nature. They are a small part of the underlying cause. When speech tells him, *"Walt, you understand enough—why don't you let it out, then?"* he believes the remark to be sarcastic. "You conceive too much of articulation," he replies. His pun on "conceives" says both that speech spawns more than is justified and that it overvalues talking—there are other powers, such as vision.

Still, the poet reveals himself, of course, in words. As he looses them in admission that he is indeed using them as speech, "My own voice, orotund, sweeping, final," so he also recognizes that he is verging on the intolerable:

> I know perfectly well my own egotism,
> I know my omnivorous lines, and cannot say any less.

In a series of lines he attempts to reconcile the opposition between his belief in the limited value of speech and his continual speaking. In each the fixed appearance is given, to be followed by the vital fluidity of which it is but the shadow:

> The printed and bound book—but the printer and the
> printing-office boy?
> The well-taken photographs—but your wife or friend close
> and solid in your arms?

> The fleet of ships of the line, and all the modern improvements—turrets—but the craft and pluck of the admiral?
> The dishes and fare and furniture—but the host and hostess, and the look out of their eyes?

These lines tell us why the multifarious pictures in the poem are so animated. To have offered still lifes would have been to offer the photograph rather than the embrace it arrested. They also provide a version of what is meant by the origin of poems as distinct from poems.

As unsparing as he is in the provision of images, Whitman is noticeably sparing in his use of similes. "The glories strung like beads upon my smallest sight and hearings," to employ one of them, are fragments issuing from an invisible wholeness. They strike the senses as unique. Their likeness to one another results from their origin in a common source, and poetry is consequently not so much a matter of illuminating each by comparison with others as it is a matter of granting each its peculiarity, reveling in it, and then accounting for it by reattaching it to its common origin. On the sensory plane uncommonness is the prominent characteristic of the actualities that greet the senses, as alikeness is on the spiritual plane. By day all objects are distinct; only at night do they suggest the common flow that merges outlines.

The act of poetic creation is the act of generating from silence (the night, the oversoul, immortality) the show that will reveal it, not destroy it. It is to apprehend forms as the "dumb, beautiful ministers" they are, agents of an invisible process that tend to our mortal needs. In one of his most remarkable images Whitman describes the poet's intercourse with silence: "Putting myself here and now to the ambushed womb of the shadows."[14] The key word points two ways. The womb is ambushed in that it is concealed from the senses—literally and physiologically it is hidden and protected. But this concealment of the womb motivates the furtiveness of the poet who would have intercourse with it. He attacks it from hiding and it is thus doubly ambushed. The act of creation is necessarily an act of treachery, an assumption of the cover of silence in order to force it to leave some progeny in the brief, mortal light.

Death and love are two versions of the word behind all words. Another is "a word of the modern—the word En-Masse." Yet another is democracy, which, however, is not quite offered vocally: "I speak the pass-word primeval—I give the sign of democracy." The sense that democracy is primeval, coupled with the assertion that "en masse" is the modern word, is one of a number of oppositions that come into being when Whitman in the fifties deals with history.

On one hand, America is clearly the heir of the ages, formed by all that is past and accepting the lesson with calmness, not repelling it. Nothing so strongly marks it off from the past as the fact that it is moving, incomplete, and so presents its poets with another reason for experimental forms that are open-ended (besides that other reason taken from the sprawl of the new continent). The expression of the American poet "is to be indirect, and not direct or descriptive or epic,"[15] Whitman says.

Thus he frequently sees America as the product of progress. The myths were great but so are liberty and equality, which follow after in history. Youth is great but so is old age, its historical continuation. Day is great but so is its chronological consequence, night, and material wealth is great but so is the spiritual wealth it generates. And language is great but English speech of the nineteenth century "is the mother of the brood that must rule the earth with the new rule."[16] The latter halves in these progressions—liberty, age, night, spirit, English—are improvements on their forebears.

Treating the old myths in *Song of Myself,* Whitman said that man had now replaced the gods and was effortlessly creating reproductions of them, affordable by all: "Taking myself the exact dimensions of Jehovah, / Lithographing Kronos . . . / Buying drafts of Osiris . . . / In my portfolio placing Manito loose, Allah on a leaf." As Currier and Ives sent art into every American home, so the poet distributes whatever was of merit in the once-rare but now easily duplicable deities.

Yet:

> The friendly and flowing savage, Who is he?
> Is he waiting for civilization, or past it, and mastering it?

Primeval simplicity is not only succeeded by the civilized; it may very well master it in turn. History follows on from myth but may also be absorbed by it. Buried in the same stanza that cheapens the gods are images recalling the Christ story, suggesting its daily reenactment in common American life:

> By the mechanic's wife with her babe at her nipple, interceding for every person born,
> Three scythes at harvest whizzing in a row from three lusty angels with shirts bagged out at their waists,
> The snag-toothed hostler with red hair redeeming sins past and to come.

Fire-engine lads emerge from the flames unscathed like Meshach, Shadrach, and Abednego; the poet says he does not object to special revelations. He is willing to admit, after all, that the "bull and bug" were never worshipped half enough, although his reduction of the sacred scarab to a bug prepares us for the second half of his breath: "Dung and dirt more admirable than was dreamed." The stanza ends with his assertion, on his own behalf as poet and on ours as he represents us, that he is as good as the best—meaning the gods of the past—and in fulfillment of the claim he puts himself to the ambushed womb.

Whitman thus frequently suspends us between a view of history as a progressive force that replaced myth and myth as the indomitable force that history only masks. The values of our temporal location alternate as they are illuminated by the flash of infrared from one or the flash of ultraviolet from the other. But the supreme Myself could not have emerged to dominate the scene save as the conventions of the past gave way to the freedoms of the present. That Myself is clearly close kin to Emerson's Me.

For Emerson he was the human being leaping at a bound back into a throne lost since Eden, winning back dominance through an intuitive grasp rather than fighting for the lost kingdom inch by inch through intellectual advances such as those of science.

For Whitman, on the other hand, the same all-dominant individual is far more social. His kingdom includes nature but it is finally a kingdom peopled with fellow men. Thoreau, Whitman complained, had an "inability to appreciate the average life. . . . He couldn't put his life into any other life." He "had an abstraction about man—a right abstraction: there we agreed." But for all that agreement, "we could not agree at all in our estimate . . . of the men we meet, here, there, everywhere—the concrete man."[17] And, indeed, when Thoreau gave poor John Field advice, he did so from his knowledge of what John Field, as abstract man, could become. He was not without sympathy for Field, but that sympathy led him to attempt —with little anticipation of success—to help Field come out from his life into a different life. Whitman, with the same high view of man in the abstract, but from the midst of the jostle in the street, did not call forth that man to a different way of life but revealed to him the strength that lay hidden in what he was.

The quality of Boweriness connected Whitman more closely than Emerson and Thoreau with the determinations of history, although he shared their transcendentalism in good part. His voice is from the crowd, and in making it the voice of the physical man rather than the voice addressed to him from Olympus, he clarified and modified the myths but kept the procession of chronological time at the fore. His concern for the texture of time is not as detailed as Hawthorne's; he was not a novelist although he dealt in some details of social reality that are called novelistic. His perception of the presence of myth, moreover, is not grounded in natural history, although daily and seasonal cycles support it; he was not a persuasive expository writer, although he explicated a philosophy.

He was a poet, but not such a one as had previously claimed that name in America. John Greenleaf Whittier, like Whitman in his proletarian identity, his Quaker upbringing, his antislavery convictions, was one of the day's better poets—perhaps its best. He believed a poet must be "part and parcel" of what he sings.[18] To him, this meant region, and to him this meant applying rhyme and meter to rude, native scenes in order to make them expressive. At the close of his long poem, "Snow-Bound," he speaks of his relation to the reader:

> And thanks untraced to lips unknown
> Shall greet me like the odors blown
> From unseen meadows newly mown,
> Or lilies floating in some pond,
> Wood-fringed, the wayside gaze beyond;
> The traveler owns the grateful sense
> Of sweetness near, he knows not whence,
> And, pausing, takes with forehead bare
> The benediction of the air.

The simile likens the breath of the reader's gratitude to the air perfumed by hidden flowers.

At the end of *Song of Myself* Whitman does not remain to walk the trail as Whittier does once he is freed of his poem. He does not await the returning air of the reader but becomes that air, and the dirt, and the herbage under the reader's feet:

> I depart as air—I shake my white locks at the run-away sun;
> I effuse my flesh in eddies, and drift it in lacy jags.
>
> I bequeathe myself to the dirt, to grow from the grass I love;
> If you want me again, look for me under your boot-soles.

The completed poem went forth from Whittier to become another object among the sweet things of the world. He who for so long and so intense a period had been causing the poem could, in seeing it complete, take pleasure in its independence from him and look forward to its now being a cause and affecting him.

But Whitman cannot let go of the poem without himself dissolving. The imagery of that dissolution reflects his belief in the transmigration of the soul in a final reaffirmation of a body of doctrine that, as Malcolm Cowley has shown, belongs to the mainstream of Indian philosophy and affects the poem throughout.[19]

This diffusion of the poet is also consistent with his poetic theory. His self had body only while the poem was forming, just as nature pre-exists the many forms it takes and does so in formlessness. With the ending of the poem, the poet himself drifts off to the condition of the origins whence the poem issued. He won't linger to take the reflex of his work from the reader because for him the poem is not really a creation but the process of creating, and once stopped, he is no longer in a particular place outside the poem—he is both in it and everywhere else, but he has no objective location as Whittier does. No air can waft a benediction back to him because he is the sanctifying air.

Whitman might agree that the poet is "part and parcel" of what he sings, but what he sings is not region. "The direct trial of him who would be the greatest poet is to-day," Whitman wrote. "If he does not flood himself with the immediate age, as with vast oceanic tides—if he be not himself the age transfigur'd . . . let him merge in the general run and wait his development."[20] He was right. But his was not the only strategy for transfiguring the age. Different as they are, *Walden, Leaves of Grass,* and *Moby-Dick* are forms taken by the swimming shape of one country at one time.

Chapter Sixteen

Landlessness: Melville and the Democratic Hero

Walt Whitman's contention that the greatest poet would be the age transfigured was very much the claim that Herman Melville made when he said that "great geniuses are part of the times, they themselves are the times, and possess a corresponding color."[1] This shared outlook was not the one Alexis de Tocqueville had foreseen for the American writer. Projecting the consequences of America's fundamental ideology, he predicted that among democratic nations, "the destinies of mankind, man himself taken aloof from his country and his age and standing in the presence of Nature and of God, with his passions, his doubts, his rare propensities and inconceivable wretchedness, will become the chief, if not the sole theme of poetry." He based this on his observation that legends and old traditions are not agreeable to a democratic people even when they do exist, because fundamentally the people have ceased to believe in the meanings conveyed by the legends, however much they may be delighted by their picturesqueness. And more important, since democratic language, dress, and daily action are resistant to literary idealization and since men ask of great literature that it give them the ideal behind the apparent, the great American writers, when they arrived, would treat of the "hidden depths of the immaterial nature of man."[2]

Although Whitman and Melville both explicitly expressed a

contrary notion, their major works may very well be read as evidence on Tocqueville's behalf. For all the pictures drawn from daily America, *Song of Myself* dramatizes Myself and every reader he contains, against the backdrop of ultimate reality; and a novel in which representatives of the many nations of mankind combine upon a ship to pursue a whale of metaphysical dimensions seems more of a piece with the literature of man standing in the presence of nature and of God than with the literature of man as a creature of his times. Emerson and Thoreau even more starkly seem to fulfill Tocqueville's prophecy, and Poe, as strikingly different from them as he is, nevertheless studiously avoided the settings of his actual American world. Hawthorne alone appears to be apart, but his insistence on the license of romance, while it does not make him an exception that proves the rule, certainly goes far toward qualifying his exclusion from it.

It may be said, however, that just as Tocqueville in the 1830s was prophesying for the coming decades, so Whitman and Melville in those decades were prophesying for the ones ahead, not speaking of their own or their contemporaries' work. There is some point to this, but it is not sufficient. The occasion of Melville's remarks was a review of Hawthorne's *Mosses,* and the occasion of Whitman's was the introduction of his own poems.

Their outlook and that of Tocqueville may still be considered reconcilable, however, if it is remembered that American writers, with only their social experience to report, did have a compensatory interest in the first principles of social relationships.[3] If pictures of social life do not abound in their pages, nevertheless they do concern themselves with the terms on which men should combine. If they do not depict American society, they do attempt to predict it.

Finally, however, there are two points of view in limited but significant opposition, and that of Tocqueville was pretty much represented by Emerson (though without reference to Tocqueville). Consequently Emerson was unable to take the novel seriously as a characteristically American art form, since that genre depended upon a social density that was secondary to the idea for which America stood. Indeed, Tocqueville himself finally presents abstractions, or at least projections, of what democratic life means, based on his detailed observation of the beliefs and practices of the Americans. Their society, as he studies it, is not coequal with his subject, democracy, but is a metaphor for its fullest meaning. It is not as yet sufficiently complete to represent rather than suggest, and his task is to amplify the suggestions. In that amplification he did not consider the possibility that the American writer, like himself, might also approach social actuality in some detail as a metaphor for the hidden whole rather than abstracting man from it. Coming from outside America, Tocqueville understandably believed his outlook was available only to the outsider. He did not anticipate the way in which a culture's major writers could themselves become outsiders, at least in point of view. Although very much of the culture, they could develop (or have forced upon them) a persona apart from the mainstream. Man in the abstract was really the man referred to by the politicians and journalists immersed in the American vortex. For all their commitment to what are called the hard realities, these orators and writers were the retailers of generalized figures called democratic man, or common man, or free man, or the American. The great writer, especially the great novelist, would be born into that vortex but would have worked himself into a position apart from it. He would be a native-born outsider.

That Tocqueville did not consider this possibility is not surprising. Although writers, like other artists, have a popular reputation for being different from their fellow men in the way they live as well as the way they work, this, in the main, is a modern notion. In traditional societies the artist had a well-defined place and spoke from within it. But his place in American society seemed to be either no place or the marketplace; either, that is, he was to be a writing preacher, professor, or cobbler, or he was to be a journalist. What was not clear to Tocqueville, or to anyone else in the period, was that, despite the want of established lines of patronage and despite the absence of a finely articulated society, the American writer, too, would struggle to practice his art professionally—free of other jobs and of enslavement to the popular demands of journalism—and that since there was no predetermined place for him in his society, he would make of that necessity a virtue and assume the literary powers of an outsider together with the economic hazards.

None so clearly exemplifies this phenomenon as Herman Melville. As a common seaman he was already on the margin of his society when he began writing *Typee,* the book of adventures that his nascent genius improved into episodes symbolic of America's deepest anxieties about savagery and civilization, mythic location and historical location. Emerson, another widow's child, had drawn some of the same parallels before him:

> In the Fejee islands, it appears, cannibalism is now familiar. They eat their own wives and children. We only devour widows' houses & great merchants outwit & absorb the substance of small ones and every man feeds on his neighbor's labor if he can. It is a milder form of cannibalism.[4]

But he told this to his notebook, and there it existed as a wry comment, shrewd but unresonating. Melville, beginning with experience rather than thought, converted it into symbolic drama, as he did another of Emerson's notebook comments (actually the comment of a friend which Emerson copied with approval): "You send out to the Sandwich islands one missionary & twenty-five refutations in the crew of the vessel."[5] The ideas were in the head of every thinking American, but they achieved expression in the lived drama of a young American who came to the event unstructured by preconceptions. As a result his tale is symbolic rather than didactic. The abstractions it yields are only secondary products of its emotive effect.

When young Melville went east to the Atlantic rather than West to the frontier, he chose, perhaps without much forethought, to accept his bottom position in society rather than contest it. The compensation he most desired for his lot was a sense of social identity—membership in, even solidarity with, a vital community—a sense he had not acquired because of his failures to earn a living on land. This need drew him more strongly than the desire to succeed financially, which would have entailed hard work, competing with others rather than cooperating, or facing enforced solitude and enforced cheerlessness if he went west to Greeley's opportunities. When in late life he looked back on the choice, he reflected that frontier settlers were, in the main, kindly but ungenial in their hard-working existence. Sailors, although they, too, had left home, had done so in acceptance of economic powerlessness and in preference for companionship over success. They frequented the "free-and-easy tavern-clubs" in "old and comfortable sea-port towns," and, more important, they enjoyed comradeship afloat. To work before the mast was to belong to a community that extended its cohesiveness beyond work to all the sociabilities of life. Despite the treacheries that life could visit on us, the flower of life was geniality, "springing from some sense of joy in it."[6] If the price of picking that flower was permanent residence at the bottom, that price was not too much for certain men with certain needs to satisfy. Even when Melville became a known author and developed definite economic ambitions, his literary voice managed always to retain this affability, this sense that being in the lowest layer was not in itself so bad a matter. There were true evils abroad, compared with which a lowly social position was nothing. From this attitude there springs the peculiar air of amiability that plays about even the darkest dramas—the shrug and smile of Ishmael when he is kicked. Men who find too many slender matters inexcusable, Melville seems to say, will not recognize the truly inexcusable when they encounter it.

Before Melville, Richard Henry Dana had embarked on a cruise as a common seaman. Dana, like Melville, was possessed of a social background and education much closer to those of the officers under whom he served than of the crew of which he was a member. Meeting his duties fully and winning his place in the community were challenges that he met triumphantly, a vital test of his worthiness to enjoy the privileged position he did enjoy on land. In that way he foreshadowed the muscular Christianity of Theodore Roosevelt some fifty years later, although in justice to Dana it must be noted that forever after he was sensitive to the plight of abused workers and remembered it in his abolitionist activities and in his legal efforts on behalf of brutalized seamen. Still, he conducted these activities as an enlightened gentleman with an acute sense of how the other half lives rather than as a brother of the downtrodden. In his account of his years before the mast he briefly contemplates the possibility that he will be stranded in California and compelled to remain a mariner for life; when he does so, although he is a laborer, he automatically envisages his career as that of a captain. But none of Melville's sailor-narrators—in *Typee* (1846), *Omoo* (1847), *Redburn* (1849), *White-Jacket* (1850), or *Moby-Dick* (1851)—envy their officers, however much they may resent specific commands, and none aspire to rise above membership in the crew, however much they may desire specific distinction within it.

Since Melville's sailors go to sea principally to find the community denied them on land, they do not fear a loss of identity in becoming members of the ship's society and acceding to its regulations and rituals. Rather, they fear being locked into separateness even there. A major theme of both *Redburn* and *White-Jacket* is that of the protagonist's difficulty and eventual success in achieving the merger he desires. There is nothing like being found a misfit on land to give one a sufficiency of differentness. The sea is for those who find alienation more intolerable than the poverty that caused it.

As a consequence, although the organization of any ship is one of rigid autocratic hierarchy for which there is but one obvious political model—absolute monarchy—ship life nevertheless serves Melville as a microcosm of human society. Political democracy can only with high elaboration be analogized with the way a ship is governed, and before *Moby-Dick* Melville's excursions into this analogy have but slight success. When he concentrates on questions of freedom and authority the voyage theme must be put aside: the ship is abandoned in *Typee;* a mutiny cancels the voyage in *Omoo;* and in *White-Jacket* the theme of political democracy compels a shifting from the narrator's specific concerns to a depiction of the world of the forecastle, where the mate's qualifications are considered to be superior to the captain's. But Melville's primary theme is that of social, not political, democracy, the inherent dignity in the common man and the way communities are shaped by this quality. This theme is served by the crew alone, with the officers functioning as remote, capricious agents of fate who affect the entire community, so that their government does not essentially alter the dynamic of relationships among crew members.

Melville had no model to look to for the rendering in fiction of the democratic man as democratic man. Before him Cooper had addressed the problem, but Cooper did not see that such a theme, new to the novel in English, necessitated a new form. He was content to intrude such a concern into structures that closely imitated the novel of manners. When Natty Bumppo first appears, in *The Pioneers* (1823), he does so as one of a number of minor characters reflecting the range of American society. That novel is presented in the traditional frame of courtship, within which Cooper attempts to demonstrate that even the American village, when it comes of age, will be best organized in terms of social distinctions voluntarily accepted by the lower as well as the privileged classes. His model village, Templeton, requires for its social furnishings examples of each class, from the bottom up, and this hierarchy—from hunter through woodcutter through farmer through craftsman through tradesman through professional man to squire—can be read both spatially as an anatomy of society and temporally as a recapitulation of American history. The classes have a chronological as well as a social relationship to one another, the higher arriving later. Natty is created to fill the dual role of the white man first on the land and the landless man at the bottom of the social ladder.

As he begins to move in the novel, however, Natty displays such virtues of democratic integrity that Cooper, to his credit, allows him greater range than the framework of the plot requires. Having thus discovered him, Cooper returned to him as the central character in four succeeding novels. Even in these, however, Cooper retained the outline of the novel of manners, and even in these he finally patronized Natty from the viewpoint of a squire who recognizes the good stuff of which those lower in society are made. Their virtues are a sound base on which to build a democratic society, but the edifice must be modified by the refinements of civilized life. The plain, democratic man in Cooper is expressive only when filtered through the consciousness of the complicated civilized man who stands firmly on the top of the structure.

Cooper did not, then, offer Melville formal clues as to how to express the democrat as hero. But his Natty parallels Melville's sailors in notable ways, and the parallels, if they do not demonstrate influence, certainly suggest a significant similarity in the way these two authors, concerned beyond their fellows with democracy in the novel, viewed the sources of that system. Although Natty represents a central value in American life, he is not the product of American society nor does he live within it. Rather, he inhabits a middle ground between the settlements and the wilds. That in his simple dignity he is the moral equal of the very best man in society is a result of his having learned from nature and nature's creatures. Inherent value in the common man depends for its ripening on a degree of direct exposure to the natural environment. At the same time, Natty is of European descent, a Christian with an ultimate racial loyalty to the white and an ultimate dread of descending into the pagan behavior of the Indians whom he so greatly admires. He uneasily traverses the territory between civilization and primitivism, too white to be swallowed by the forest and yet too wild to stay in the town. As civilization advances, he flees it; ironically, the path he clears into the wilderness becomes a trail blazed for settlers who will follow.

Cooper's treatment of the pathfinder as the occupant of middle ground between contrasting cultures, whose democratic virtues are learned from nature rather than from his training in a democratic society (which, for Cooper, yields mainly bigots and demagogues), parallels Melville's handling of the common seaman as a truer democrat than any republican on land. Like Natty the seaman has fled the settled regions of his world, and his flight away from civilization, like Natty's, is an advancement of it, since he flees in ships that chart the way for missionary and merchant and eventually carry them as passengers. Again like Natty, he possesses an inherent dignity that has been matured by a life lived in alert response to the voice of nature. That response had been developed for survival and then extended into contemplation, rather than being bred by a political system. And finally the Melville hero, too, is fascinated by and feels an affinity with the primitive people he encounters. Still, despite his distrust of civilization, he has a deeper horror of being swallowed by primitivism.

Such strong parallels do not so much suggest Cooper's influence upon Melville as they indicate the notable fact that the two American novelists who were most concerned with the character of the democratic man both traced this definitive quality to his exposure to nature and his avoidance of established society rather than to American political circumstances. The ultimate relationship of his democratic bearing to the democratic assertions of his society was that he stood as an example of the dignity and worth of the common man, on which a society could possibly be built; he was not, however, its result, and indeed as constituted, that society threatened rather than enhanced him.

The society of the crew was a democratic society because it postponed political questions about the mechanics of government in a republic and gave priority to the question of the social relations to be developed. Men called by the demands of nature into an instinctive selfhood, and yet also by nature gregarious, needed community rather than political power. Melville was concerned centrally with the sociology rather than the politics of democracy, and after *Typee* and *Omoo* he essayed a direct, unliterary approach to the theme. *Mardi* (1849), in title at least, promised to be like its predecessors. Astounded readers discovered, however, that the voyage undertaken in its more than five hundred pages is allegorical, a tour of the modern world in the guise of a cruise among Pacific islands, with each shore visited the counterpart of a civilized nation. Instead of developing appropriate symbolic vehicles for his thoughts on philosophy, art, religion, history, or politics, Melville offered them in extended monologues and lengthy dialogues engaged in by characters who possessed nothing so much as the leisure in which to talk for as long as Melville wished. The book was a commercial disaster and Melville in frustration heeded the warning, for a time at least. He turned back to sea adventures in *Redburn* and *White-Jacket* in order to regain the audience he was losing.

But he was bitter at the failure of *Mardi,* attributing it to the imprudence of trying to tell Americans the truth. He wrote his friend Evert Duyckinck that *Mardi* proved that "an author can never —under no conceivable circumstances be at all frank with his readers."[7] He may have been right, but he certainly underestimated the sheer unreadability of the work. There was indeed matter in the book to offend American readers but few of them penetrated far enough to reach it.

What Melville expressly says about the United States in *Mardi* is that its amazing success stemmed from its possession of abundant natural resources and ample geographical space rather than from its political system. He says that if the country were as straitened in area and natural resources as Great Britain, it is likely that the government would be far more despotic than Britain's. The United States had not yet passed any significant political test. When it reached the end of its space and exploited the last of its cheap resources, then the test would come of its vaunted democracy. Until then Americans might well consider whether other political systems were not better suited to people otherwise situated.

History, Melville suggests, will work against the American idea, most obviously in the exhaustion of the land, but just as effectively in the spread of civilized habits among a once wild or at least imperfectly tamed population. Thanks to her geographical position, America is the savage of civilized nations, and thanks to her savagery, she is the home of equality. But as that equality is the result of savagery rather than of the history Americans are making, they may very well find they have lost their equality once their history has been made. Political democracy is an effect of primitive conditions, not the cause of a free society. If political theory recognizes this, it may be shaped to serve freedom, after literal savagery has passed, by nurturing the savage in each breast.

In order to point the lesson that the essential issue lies in the way men permit one another to exist, regardless of the governmental structure they have established, one of Melville's characters presents to the citizens of Vivenza (the United States) a document, which they shred in outrage. The document proclaims that

> freedom is more social than political. And its real felicity is not to be shared. *That* is of a man's own individual getting and holding. It is not, who rules the state, but who rules me. Better be secure under one king than exposed to violence from twenty millions of monarchs, though oneself be of the number.[8]

When Melville turned in disgust to writing *Redburn* and *White-Jacket* ("They are two *jobs,* which I have done for money—being forced to it, as other men are to sawing wood"[9]), he nevertheless continued to examine in the forecastle the essence of man's freedom, regardless of how domineering the quarterdeck was. He had meanwhile lived through a time of great political disaster, equivalent to the personal disaster of the failure of *Mardi*—the collapse of republicanism in Europe after the revolutions of 1848. In reaction to this he was able, with some good conscience, to provide the chauvinistic fare his countrymen craved, although some pinch of sea salt had to be taken with it. Had not freedom seemed to have failed everywhere but in America, it would be difficult to respect Melville when he contends that the political Messiah has come in the person of the American people: "And let us always remember that with ourselves, almost for the first time in the history of the earth, national selfishness is unbounded philanthropy; for we can not do a good to America but we give alms to the world."[10]

The Americans of whom he speaks are not a separate nation but the advance guard of all nations breaking a path in the wilderness. They are not a particular people but are the potential condition of all people who are ready for freedom, what Emerson meant when he noted that "the Atlantic is a sieve through which only or chiefly the liberal adventurous *America-loving* part of each city, clan, family, are brought . . . the Europe of Europe is left."[11] Watching the "wild Irish" on board his packet from Liverpool, Redburn says:

> Let us waive that agitated national topic, as to whether such multitudes of foreign poor should be landed on our American shores, let us waive it, with the only one thought, that if they can get here, they have God's right to come; though they bring all Ireland and her miseries with them. For the whole world is the patrimony of the whole world; there is no telling who does not own a stone in the Great Wall of China.[12]

Melville's attitude contrasts strongly with the contempt Consul Hawthorne of Liverpool felt for nationalized citizens, based on his belief that only those habituated to America's liberties from birth can make right use of them; others will only make trouble. Hawthorne saw democracy as the earned result of historical process, the product of a tradition that could benefit only those who were born to it. But Melville, although he fled savagery for civilization, nevertheless saw in that savagery a validation of democracy. Having lost his wildness on land, he reacquired it at sea in sufficient measure to temper his commitment to history. He did not discard history as Emerson did; nevertheless he believed, like Thoreau, that wildness preserved rather than destroyed what was best in the world. And like Thoreau, who faced the disappearance of Walden woods with equanimity as long as he could see the woods shining in the healthy faces of immigrant children, so Melville rejoiced in the westward-bound offscourings of the world.

In disgust with the failure of *Mardi* and dislike of the wood-sawing books to which he turned after it, Melville wrote, "So far as I am individually concerned & independent of my pocket, it is my earnest desire to write those sort of books which are said to 'fail.' "[13] And to Duyckinck, editor of the *Literary World,* he wrote, "But we that write & print have all our books predestinated—& for me, I shall write such things as the Great Publisher of Mankind ordained ages before he published 'The World'—this planet, I mean—not the Literary Globe."[14] These are foreshadowings—"loomings" would be Melville's word for it—of *Moby-Dick,* although at the time he made these remarks, in fall and winter of 1849, Melville had not yet settled down to that work. Even when he did so, he at first pursued a false trail and apparently worked on a manuscript that was very much like *Redburn* and *White-Jacket,* treating a whaler as those had treated a commercial packet and a man-of-war. His struggle was not between writing another commercially promising work with which to feed his family and writing another *Mardi* with which to feed his imagination; he no longer sought the self-indulgence of a nondramatic disquisition. Rather, it was the struggle between his sea-novel formula and the larger symbolic values it could be made to convey. For all his expressed contempt for them, *Redburn* and *White-Jacket* had gone some distance toward educating him into the ways in which life among the meanest aboard ship could serve as microcosm of man's historical and cosmic condition.

But the question of audience was a pressing one. He was a democrat, and yet the democratic audience was the chief external obstacle to the full expression of his views in his work. *Moby-Dick* became, among other things, Melville's attempt to define the democratic reader—not to appeal to the populace but to shape the democratic audience through writing democratic literature. Although the projection was different from Whitman's, they shared a proletarian concern to make literature an art that spoke from actualities other than those experienced by the relatively well-to-do. At the same time, they shared an artistic drive toward integrity of vision without compromise with fashion. As a result, *Moby-Dick* could not be a popular work, but it would be addressed to an assumed audience of democratic readers and, with that assumption, shape such an ideal audience even as the ideal of that audience shaped it.

When Father Mapple stands before his congregation early in *Moby-Dick,* he announces that his lesson will be two-stranded: one strand applies to all as sinful men; the other to him alone as a leader of men, as, he says, "a pilot of the living God." The lessons are religious. All men, including Mapple the pilot, must learn to repent of their sins, even if they cannot, as would be desirable, avoid sinning. The special lesson for the leader is that truth must be preached in the face of falsehood, even though acquiescence in falsehood brings temporal comfort and adherence to the absolutes of truth brings woe.

The sermon about preacher and congregation establishes a version of the relation of the one to the many, of the relation of authority to liberty, a subject more fully and ambiguously explored in the consideration of Ahab's relation to his crew. And what is set forth explicitly about the preacher as the voice of the democratic congregation, and complexly about the captain as leader of the democratic crew, plays even more profoundly and more ambiguously over the entire work in terms of Ishmael-Melville and the American readership, in terms, that is, of the American artist (commoner, truth-teller, witness to suffering, sufferer) and the American public, a collection of isolated souls who when massed lacked distinction. They have all embarked on the ship of mortality blown by trade winds to an uncertain haven. What identity will shape them? Are they to be told the awful message that life is pain, and exhorted to kiss the rod, for if it is a dog's life, we should at least know that we are God's dogs and receive our worth from that? Or are they to be coerced into an identity by theatrical demonstrations of the adequacy of their leader to all exigencies, and through the unabating vigor of a keyed-up rhetoric that hums so constantly in their ears that they are persuaded to accept it as the sound of their own voices? These are questions not only about Mapple and Ahab, on one hand, and the congregation and crew on the other, but about Ishmael-Melville, on one hand, and, on the other, his readership in a land with widespread literacy but no wide public for serious literature.

Ahab knows that his primary task in galvanizing his crew of individuals (their separateness emphasized by their being islanders, *isolatoes*) into a unit is to overcome the resistance of the democratic qualities represented in their most civilized form by Starbuck. Starbuck is next in command, as the people are always next in command; Starbuck is married and a father and thus has an interest in life beyond the reaches of the *Pequod*'s savage decks; Starbuck is intelligent and articulate; Starbuck has the true, Platonic courage, based on fear of the adversary's powers, rather than on foolhardy ignorance or reckless disregard of them; Starbuck has a sound, commercial sense of the venture: he kills whales for profit, not in expression of a bloodthirsty nature nor in compensation for the frustrations of life on shore. He is the model democrat who can emerge from the equality of primitive nature: healthy, level-headed, brave, trustworthy, industrious, and modest.

Ishmael feels Starbuck to be so, to be the representative of "that immaculate manliness we feel within ourselves, so far within us, that it remains intact though all the outer character seems gone." Starbuck's is the "august dignity" that "is not the dignity of kings and robes, but that abounding dignity which has no robed investiture." Ishmael says, "Thou shalt see it shining in the arm that wields a pick or drives a spike; that democratic dignity, which, on all hands, radiates without end from God; Himself! The great God absolute! The centre and circumference of all democracy! His omnipresence our divine equality!"[15]

But Starbuck falls to Ahab, falls, that is, to another version of authority than the democratic one Ishmael extols. The ideal man within us all is God within us all. Divinity is a human principle rather than an objectified and therefore opposed power. This divinity falls with Starbuck. The society of the *Pequod* is to be governed by an older form of authority, one that relies on investiture and maintains its power by asserting its ability to protect the common man from trials he cannot endure. If men unite in upholding such authority and submit their wills to it, their recompense for lost self-mastery will come from the unthinking solidarity they gain in the united support of a leader who has persuaded them that his cause is the common cause. They can delegate their weaknesses as well as their strengths to him and sail on.

Why is free man so willing to delegate his freedom? What, in the test, does Melville find wanting in the democratic experience despite his sense of the beauty of the ideal? What, that is, are the sources of Ahab's ascendancy?

Man's experience, says Melville, is more powerful than is his idea of freedom through the merger with a benign oversoul. It is the experience of a suffering in the world for which he is not responsible and which he finds it easier to hate than comprehend. Starbuck had lost a brother and a father in the violence of the whale fishery. And although Starbuck continued brave, he became vulnerable to the man who would play upon his spiritual terrors.

The test of accounting for suffering in the world is political as well as theological, and it is one that democracy cannot face easily. The suffering may be made tolerable as long as the responsibility for it is placed outside the democratic mass. Ahab, the leader, offers so to place it. He can lead, he asserts, because he himself has suffered greatly and therefore representatively. His authority will not reknit the circle, will not again attach the free man's daily reality to his freedom. It will, rather, dismiss his individuality and offer as life's purpose a unified conflict against the source of suffering in this world, describing it as apart from the mass, a malevolence objectified.

That Ahab does not fulfill Melville's vision of the coherence common men require is demonstrated implicitly in the drama and is also stated explicitly. When Ishmael considers the stage devices that Ahab uses to keep the crew steadfast in their (which is to say, his) purpose, he observes: "Be a man's intellectual superiority what it will, it can never assume the practical, available supremacy over other men, without the aid of some sort of external arts and entrenchments, always in themselves, more or less paltry and base."[16] Ahab accepts the baseness with the glory, thereby both advancing his purpose and dooming its result.

Father Mapple saw the break in the circle of democracy, with God at center and God at circumference, as sin. He saw repentance as the source of unity, and truth to sinful experience, which is to say a constant identification of the self as the source of human misery, as the role of the leader. This, finally, is an assertion of original sin, an assertion that suffering proceeds from a shared guilt and is to be redeemed through divine assistance.

But the history of modern democracy begins with a new myth, in which the primitive world without sin is still available to those who grasp the reversibility of time and step out of history as they step into democracy. Belief in the ability of man to rule himself without adherence to inherited, arbitrary rule is based on the denial of any native incapacity in him. When Tom Paine taught the Americans that their war for rights within the British Empire—a historically determined event—was really a war for the reclamation of the independence they always possessed—a mythical event—he told them they were too young for the doctrine of original sin, or, what was the same, had outgrown it. "Government, like dress," he wrote, "is the badge of lost innocence; the palaces of kings are built on the ruins of the bowers of paradise."[17] Reassume your innocence and you need no master over you.

This strain of thought had a powerful appeal for Melville. The most heroic of his earlier characters, Jack Chase, was "a stickler for the Rights of Man,"[18] and Melville himself had grounded America's strength on her savagery. He shared Emerson's fervor for the individual's potential far more than Hawthorne's doubts about it. But he could not slide into an Emersonian acceptance of evil as no more than misperceived good. Something out there resisted. In "Benito Cereno" he was to explore the charmed life led by Americans who, against the manifest evidence of malevolence, acted as if the world were innocent and miraculously got away with it. But he was not the guileless American captain of that tale, and in *Moby-Dick* he sought to comprehend both evil and the rightness of the democratic response. The opposition is dialectic and the containment is within a dramatic world drenched with the ambiguities of the clash.

If man is free and flawless, then man must be the cause of ill as well as good, and suffering can be reduced only through his willingness to take upon himself an almost infinite series of social manipulations and to sink his ego in an almost infinite series of adjustments. The stamina required seems superhuman, but the task by definition is the greatest of human obligations. Wherever the stamina fails, an Ahab stands ready to reorganize the effort along other lines. To follow him may be to surrender liberty, but it is to retain, at least, the precious and delusive source of self-esteem, the belief that one is innocent of the woe that has befallen him. As opposed to original sin, the doctrine of division between innocent self and evil other is Manichaeism. Rather than contemplate his complicity in suffering, democratic man, baffled, accepts a divided world in which a power of evil asserts an independent counter to the good he wills.

Ahab is a Manichaean both in his doctrine and in his trappings. Indeed, Melville risks the dramatic credibility of his narrative in order to underscore the fact at the moment when he produces Fedallah and his Parsee crew. Their function is made plain in one of Melville's reference works, Pierre Bayle's *Dictionary,* in which a discussion of Zoroastrianism occurs in the full and more than slightly sympathetic entry on Manichaeism. Ahab's Manichaeism is not the moral of the tale, but it is the source of one range of symbols that charges the complex world of *Moby-Dick* and is countered by another range, stemming principally from Ishmael's direct perceptions of circularity and merger.

After Ishmael has characterized and to some extent deplored the petty stagecraft of Ahab, he goes on to discuss how political superstition can make a mad man into a mighty man, how the plebeian herds crouch before the severities of a czar because he wears a crown and therefore represents for them "tremendous centralization." Ishmael then remarks, to himself as much as to the reader, "Nor will the tragic dramatist who would depict moral indomitableness in its fullest sweep and direst swing, ever forget a hint incidentally so important to his art, as the one now alluded to."[19] Ishmael, the tragic dramatist, like Ahab, the moral tyrant, cannot afford to neglect the force that will be lent his drama if he centers it on one man and elevates that man to greatness through granting him the trappings of superiority. Although *Moby-Dick* carries as a central concern the nature of democratic man and sees Manichaeism as the paranoid offspring of the failures of the common man to effect his own social and spiritual salvation, the tragedy cannot take that common man as its protagonist, nor can it afford to dispense with theater if it is to reach a responsive reader.

The Ahab who thus receives dramatic focus emerges as the antithesis of the ideal of authority in a democracy. He rules absolutely, holding his mates as well as his crew in awe of him. But we also see that the condition of his leadership existed abundantly in the formless mediocrity of nineteenth-century American democracy, so that Ahab is not untypical of his society. The political paradox his leadership embodies is one that was observed in his day by Emerson, for example, who feared that the populace, in their failure to stand forth individually and realize each his own best self, were vulnerable to the man on a horse who would cohere them as a mass against a fancied objective foe. "The Best are never demoniacal or magnetic but all brutes are,"[20] he wrote. So is Captain Ahab.

The simple, separate person who is the true democrat is also, by definition, unheroic; he cannot achieve the grand effects the reader, interested in a heightened actuality, allows only to the extraordinary—the disproportioned hero. Even Emerson had to talk of Napoleon and Goethe rather than his neighbor Hosmer. But to permit such a hero to gain exclusive control of the drama, as Melville sensed, is to defect from the modern condition. It is the equivalent of the democratic artist joining the opposition and, finding for the common man no identity except that which his leader assigns him, relieving the common man of responsibility as long as he lends his yell to the common outcry. Hawthorne, with a great concern for the common heart of humanity, nevertheless placed at the center of his fictions characters who were deviants from the standard. And Whitman made the common man gigantic by making him contain all men in an idealized presentation perforce abstracted from a specific social setting.

In response to this impasse Melville moves in the direction Whitman also took, although he holds his character to a more detailed actuality than Whitman did. Every atom belonging to Ishmael as good belongs to us. Myself's walking, stooping, peering, listening, suffering, are accomplished by dint of Whitman's breaking the rules and issuing himself a new poetic license. And Melville, too, is unflinching when literary conventions no longer serve in the novel he wishes to write. His narrative is first-person yet it is omniscient. Ishmael sees himself with a cosmic eye, as a man who has been handed a part to play in the world, and yet with a worm's eye, as most like us in his defeats rather than in his triumphs. He is vulnerable because he is good-humored, but when he turns resentful of his troubles, he is again vulnerable. He is clothed only in clothing and is therefore but a savage dressed, yet he is furnished with Shakespeare and the Bible as well as with a seaman's manual and a temperance tract. He is a down-at-heels common sailor, but he is the conscious heir of all that has ever happened on the sea. He has been made by history and he will tell a history, yet he has felt the beginnings and experienced the awesome agony of his captain, who dared to challenge the original contract of the gods, and in his defeat nevertheless took a little bit of heaven with him. Whatever history is, it all comes down to Ishmael, its teller. Without his presence, no history, and without his omniscience, no myth.

As long as the artist is the maker of his art, so long must he speak from and of history, Melville demonstrates. But as long as that art is a created world and he its originator, then so long must he accept the task of giving the cosmic account also. Although he did not, until *Billy Budd,* more than thirty years later, move to direct myth-making, Melville, in all his tales from *Moby-Dick* to the long silence that commenced in 1858, split his point of view. He did not do so twice in the same way, did not again repeat, for example, the combined first-person and omniscience of *Moby-Dick.* But Bartleby and his employer are both necessary lenses for viewing the world in

"Bartleby," as are Benito Cereno and Amasa Delano for viewing the world in "Benito Cereno," while in other tales and sketches other forms of multiple vision are offered, climaxing in the hall of mirrors that is *The Confidence-Man* (1857).

Ishmael the character yields to Ahab on the stage of the novel, but Ishmael the teller encompasses the fall of kings and outlives a Manichaean conflict in demonstration of the view that life brings its woes, but denial of complicity in them is an insane, if noble, mistake. His victory is the limited triumph of a man such as the hero of Whitman's poems, a triumph that enables its undergoer not to crow but to project his hat, sit shamefaced, and beg. We glimpse Ishmael after the *Rachel* has lifted him from the sea, lounging about the ports of Peru, playing the fool a bit as he spins his yarns to grandees in exchange for a glass of chicha. And we also glimpse him with other common sailors in a gam or on a night watch, whispering about the full horrors they have experienced, as survivors of a holocaust whisper intently to one another of what only they can understand. The seamen's muted confidences are obsessively concerned with one or another manifestation of a recurring phenomenon. They have each, at some time or another, been among the nameless in a crew that has been dominated by an extraordinary individual, a cracked prophet escaped from some religious order, an Appollo-like canal man whose presence cowed commanders, a monomaniacal, one-legged Quaker who made his own compass and steered by level log and line rather than by celestial navigation. Somehow they have survived the violence and suffering consequent upon such experience, survived what seemed the eruption of the cosmic into daily life or the temporary flash of majesty in the midst of the crew that darkened the nominal authority of the captain. And here they are again, herded into the forecastle of a ship they do not direct, the anonymous, the survivors, the brotherhood of man.

Melville feels with Ahab, feels along his heart and in his blood, and yet finally has not taken his place with the brilliantly defiant and gloriously defeated. He has, instead, chosen to survive as a lowly figure squatting on the hatches in intense talk with those of us who will squat with him and recognize that the most recent thump we received is not the last that will be dealt us. Our sharing is not one of resentment, but neither is it one of submission. It is, rather, the communion of the otherwise isolated, otherwise lonely undergoers, each too savage to relinquish his self-mastery and each too conscious of his failings to dominate his fellows. It is, that is to say, Melville's practice of literary art in the terrifying void that threatens the citizen of a modern democracy parted from the anchor of traditional beliefs by a rotted cable and adrift in a sea without milestones.

Chapter Seventeen

Abrupt Intermergings: Melville and the Formlessness of Fiction

When J. Inman assumed management of the *Columbian Magazine* in 1843, he confidently announced that "this is the age of magazines. . . . They are the field, chiefly, in which literary reputation is won." The book, he said, "is not of sufficiently rapid production," and the newspaper is too ephemeral, but the magazine hits the happy medium and is the area in which an author can acquire fame. Magazines were read more than any other kind of publication, but whatever promise Inman meant to extend to authors was bound to be dampened by his enthusiastic explanation of why they were read: "They can be dropped into a valise or a carpet-bag as a welcome provision for the wants of a journey by steam-boat or railroad, when the country through which the traveller passes offers nothing attractive to be seen, or the eyes are weary of seeing; they while delightfully the tedious hours of a rainy day in summer, and afford the most pleasant occupation through the long evenings of a winter."[1]

The image of the reader on a journey is an apt one because in America the early dominance of the printing industry by the periodical rather than the book, in contrast to the situation in Europe, was very much the function of national mobility—not just that of the traveler but that of the spreading population. As the historian of the book in America observed:

> In Europe printing was started in settled communities that were centuries old, and as a mechanical means of duplicating, from the accumulated wealth of manuscript collections, the literary heritage of the Classical and Medieval World. In America, printing almost immediately became an instrument of the active westward expansion of a nation, and an important factor of colonization. The European press primarily nourished thought; the American, action. In Europe printing from the very beginning meant "books," in America almost from the start "newspapers."[2]

Certainly Hawthorne, after a trying apprenticeship and a wearying career as a magazine contributor, was happy to focus on books rather than periodical pieces after *The Scarlet Letter* appeared in 1850. He welcomed his hard-earned opportunity to open his ideas slowly, intently, and at length, to address thought rather than boredom. "Experience has taught me," he wrote an editor who solicited periodical pieces from him in 1851, "that the thought and trouble expended on that kind of production, is vastly greater, in proportion, than what is required for a long story." He did not even care to consider prior serialization of his novels, politely assigning the reluctance to his own foibles rather than to his abhorrence of magazines:

> I doubt whether my romances would succeed in the serial mode of publication; lacking as they certainly do, the variety of interest and character which seem to have made the success of other works, so published. The reader would inevitably be tired to death of the one prominent idea, if presented to him under different aspects for a twelve-month together. The effect of such a story, it appears [to] me, depends on its being read continuously.[3]

While Hawthorne in 1851 thus worked his way toward an almost exclusive concentration on book-length fiction, his magazine days happily behind him, Melville, who had commenced with popular novels, saw his book public evaporate after the publication of *Moby-Dick* in 1851, and was compelled to undertake magazine fiction. Although neither knew it, the arcs of their contemporary reputations were intersecting when they met in the Berkshires in

1850, with that of the better known of the two, Melville, beginning its downward curve while Hawthorne's was on the rise. In the same year that Hawthorne declined serial publication, Melville wrote his English publisher:

> This country & nearly all its affairs are governed by sturdy backwoodsmen—noble fellows enough, but not at all literary, & who care not a fig for any authors except those who write those most saleable of all books nowadays—i e—the newspapers & magazines. And tho' the number of cultivated, catholic men, who may be supposed to feel an interest in a national literature is large & everyday growing larger; yet they are nothing in comparison with the overwhelming majority who care nothing about it. This country is at present engaged in furnishing material for future authors; not in encouraging its living ones.[4]

With even the "cultivated, catholic" readers rejecting *Moby-Dick,* Melville had to try the magazines, although he continued to write novels (without a return to profitability) and to experiment with the complexities of split literary presentation. Six years of embittering labor as his artistic vision expanded and his audience shrank, and then silence. In 1892, the world knew Walt Whitman had died. In 1891, Herman Melville died, but few in the preceding decade had known he was still alive.

Melville had arrived at authorship without apprenticeship. Although he was always an avid reader, he had been an aimless one even through his first years of novel-writing. But in 1849, with the increase of his anxiety to write the books for which he felt predestined rather than those for which alone there seemed to be a public, he began to take sharper note of contemporary writers. He disagreed with the optimistic conclusions Emerson drew from his doctrine of man's ultimate oneness with the universe and ultimate capacity to work his way down upon his world, but he did not dismiss the doctrine itself, as did his New York cronies with their worldly-wise contempt for the ethereal emanations from Concord. White-Jacket, the character in search of identity, concludes after his experiences on board a microcosmic man-of-war: "I have a voice that helps to shape eternity; and my volitions stir the orbits of the furthest suns. In two senses, we are precisely what we worship. Ourselves are Fate."[5]

To the eyebrow-raising in New York Melville responded, "Nay, I do not oscillate in Emerson's rainbow, but prefer rather to hang myself in mine own halter than swing in another man's swing." In this letter of 3 March 1849, he told his New York friend, the editor E. A. Duyckinck, "Yet I think Emerson is more than a brilliant fellow," and went on to describe a lecture he had heard Emerson deliver in Boston—the man, he insisted, was no fool. But if, for the sake of argument, Duyckinck wished him to persist in regarding Emerson as a fool,

> then had I rather be a fool than a wise man.—I love all men who *dive*. Any fish can swim near the surface, but it takes a great whale to go down stairs five miles or more; & if he don't attain the bottom, why all the lead in Galena can't fashion the plummet that will. I'm not talking of Mr. Emerson now—but of that whole corps of thought-divers, that have been diving & coming up again with bloodshot eyes since the world began.

If Emerson had a flaw, Melville wrote, it was certainly his cool olympianism, his "insinuation that had he lived in those days when the world was made, he might have offered some valuable suggestions."[6]

In *Moby-Dick,* Melville developed at length the attractions of Platonic idealism and Kantian transcendentalism that were so much the substance of Emersonianism. Although the natural world continually manifested its capacity to erupt in cruelties that belied every comfort this view held forth, still in response to such cruelties, Ahab's belief in a divine malevolence who warred on man and therefore must be warred against was but transcendentalism gone sour. Reality for Ahab as for Emerson resided behind appearances, and man could shake the universe to its roots had he the strength of will. Moreover, although a host of actualities cry no to Ahab's vision and demonstrate his madness, at the novel's close Ishmael finds himself afloat "on a soft and dirge-like main. The unharming sharks they glided by as if with padlocks on their mouths; the savage sea-hawks sailed with sheathed beaks."[7] If Ahab's venture was insane and brought about the death of all who ventured with him save Ishmael, nevertheless ultimate reality was not unaffected. For a day at least, wild nature suspended its laws, in need of rest after the struggle to which Ahab had compelled it.

In *Pierre* (1852) Melville warned against taking any book, and *Moby-Dick* can be included, as a resolution of the conflicts with which it deals—that is, if it treats of fundamental paradoxes such as the nature of God and the contradictory condition of human life, the instinctive drive we feel toward oneness and the objective divisiveness that will not be overcome by love nor by love thwarted into hate. Speaking of a pamphlet that claims to resolve the opposition of God's benign will and His cruel governing of the world (one which, of course, he himself had written and placed in the novel), Melville says:

> To me it seems more the excellently illustrated re-statement of a problem, than the solution of the problem itself. But as such mere illustrations are almost universally taken for solutions (and perhaps they are the only possible human solutions), therefore it may help to the temporary quiet of some inquiring mind, and so be not wholly without use.[8]

The parenthetical remark is the most telling. There is no final answer to the contradictions of existence, and the artist offers the only possible human solution when he provides the fullest illustration.

Melville took with him into the writing of *Moby-Dick* not only a respect for Emerson but also, of course, an acquaintanceship with Hawthorne, both the work and the man. In praise of Hawthorne's *Mosses from an Old Manse,* he had written:

> Certain it is . . . that this great power of blackness in him derives its force from its appeal to that Calvinistic sense of Inner Depravity and Original Sin, from whose visitations, in some shape or other, no deeply thinking mind is always and wholly free. For, in certain moods, no man can weigh this world without throwing in something somehow like Original Sin, to strike the uneven balance.[9]

Certain it is also that Melville did not need Hawthorne for this particular lesson. The Dutch Reform church of his boyhood inculcated it in him early, and his society resounded with quarrels about it. It rivaled politics as a topic of popular discussion at the village store and in the city parlor. The disputes over the meaning of inherent depravity among giants of the pulpit such as Lyman Beecher and Charles Grandison Finney were reported in the press and argued about among the people with something of the delight a later American public was to have in taking sides over the respective merits of baseball teams. The assumption of original sin shaped the outlook of two such different writers as Harriet Beecher Stowe and George Washington Harris, both of whom aimed at an audience of unsophisticated readers. As for Melville, when he seriously considered Emerson's view of man's innocence, he required no special prompting to test it against universal guilt, and in *Moby-Dick* he did so without any solution but the human one of illustration.

The encounter with Hawthorne did, however, profoundly affect Melville. It directed his previously hesitant movement toward producing a work of fiction that would seriously attempt to comprehend the complex of concerns that pressed upon his imagination, concerns he knew he had evaded in his earlier works. In *Mardi* his image of writing had been one of mining. "Genius," he said, "is full of trash. But genius essays its best to keep to itself; and giving away its ore, retains the earth; whence, the too frequent wisdom of its works and folly of its life."[10] From the perspective he had gained after knowing Hawthorne, and as a consequence attempting what he did attempt in *Moby-Dick,* he thought differently. In speaking of Pierre's earliest efforts at writing he could well have been speaking of efforts such as *Mardi:* "No commonplace is ever eventually got rid of, except by essentially emptying one's self of it into a book; for once trapped in a book, then the book can be put into the fire, and all will be well."[11] He went on to maintain that when one encountered an author who had not initially published some rubbish, it was either because the author had committed his earliest efforts to the flames—precisely what Hawthorne gave a fictionalized report of doing in his tale "The Devil in Manuscript"—or had been indebted for his initial success "to some rich and peculiar experience in life, embodied in a book, which because for that cause, containing original matter, the author himself, forsooth, is to be considered original; in this way, many original books being the product of very unoriginal minds"[12]—a version of his own immediate success with *Typee*.

Melville had respect for the apprenticeship Hawthorne had served. Willy-nilly he himself had not burned anything and willy-nilly he had become a successful author, more successful than Hawthorne then was by some measure. But now he saw what it was to be a serious writer, to have apprenticed oneself to one's art regardless of the popular reaction, and to have preserved one's dedication to imaginative truth even after youth had passed into manhood. Until he met Hawthorne, Melville had simply never met a conscious, first-rate artist, and Hawthorne was the best of such in his land.

The "shock of recognition" that thrilled through Melville, producing as one result that very phrase, was not the shock of recognizing in Hawthorne a duplicate of his own responses to the ethical and spiritual questions that bothered him. It was the shock of recognizing that he was not alone in his country and time in believing that such questions could form the center of the novel.

The two men differed in personality and in thought, and no lasting relationship ensued. Melville was far more ebullient and yet at bottom more pessimistic because less inclined to accept the compromise of human capacity that history seemed to dictate. They met, however, at a time when each without selfishness could serve his own need by serving the other. The restrained Hawthorne had emerged from the claustrophobia of his isolated chamber into the limited world of New England social life and a modest literary reputation. Now dedicated first and foremost to remaining a novelist, he welcomed the admiration, conversation, and good cheer of Melville, who was from outside his social circle and represented the brashness of the New York literary scene. For Hawthorne, New England was becoming but a larger dismal chamber, and the exuberant, sunburned ex-mariner who rode over to Lenox to visit him was, in his hearty informality, a door opener. For Melville, fidgeting about whether his new tale of the sea, to be set on a whaler, could possibly become the symbolic novel he had been unable to realize earlier, Hawthorne was a listener whose very silences were pregnant with meaning. When Melville talked about the connection between his drudging experiences before the mast and the large cosmic questions on which he believed his work should rest, his listener, a symbolic artist, was neither incredulous nor politely enthusiastic.

They were not, however, soul mates. Melville's letters to Hawthorne reveal his constant sense of the real possibility that Hawthorne does not agree with him on the nature of existence and may possibly not understand his meanings when he renders them in dramatic form. What Melville took from his encounter with Hawthorne was the perception of the contemporaneity of great writing. He came into a belief that the serious writer wrote from sources shared by other serious writers, so that they were voices of a time rather than isolated, individual creators. At last, it was almost a matter of indifference who was author of the works that demanded expression. The essential reality was that the act of writing was the act of delivering creations whose time had come, not the exploitation of experiences peculiar to the writer nor the revelation of inspiration received from on high.

Melville put his perception thus:

> The world is forever babbling of originality; but there never yet was an original man, in the sense intended by the world. . . . For though the naked soul doth assuredly contain one latent element of intellectual productiveness; yet never was there a child born solely from one parent; the visible world of experience being that procreative thing which impregnates the muses; self-reciprocally efficient hermaphrodites being but a fable.[13]

The perception was confirmed by his encounter with Hawthorne, but its source was an even profounder shock of recognition, his discovery of Shakespeare.

"Dolt & ass that I am I have lived more than 29 years, & until a few days ago never made close acquaintance with the divine William,"[14] he wrote on 24 February 1849. Coming to Shakespeare later in life than had his educated countrymen and far later than had his fellow authors, he blended in his reaction the admiration of the intelligent reader with the literary curiosity of a self-taught writer unaffected by the pious notion that Shakespeare is inimitable. He was not so overwhelmed by the scope of Shakespeare's comprehension as not to scan the plays for the tricks of the writer's trade by which that scope was communicated.

One major problem of craftsmanship that plagued Melville at the time was that of representing the psychological condition of a particular kind of character who lay at the center of the world he reported but who evaded fictional embodiment. This was the man maddened by the contrast between the promise of life and the opposition of circumstances. His outward gestures could only be called evil as he blasphemed or ruthlessly manipulated and scornfully harangued his fellows. But his inward anguish was that of an acutely sensitive, supremely human consciousness wracked by the absurdity and horror of the mean destiny visited upon so splendid a thing as man. The hate that issued from him was founded on a thwarted love for man's potential; the violence he radiated was a crazed assertion on man's behalf in the face both of heaven and of his less sensitive fellows. Melville had given brief essayistic versions of such men in *Redburn* and *White-Jacket,* but lacked the technique to realize them as characters.

Shakespeare showed him the way, and he dared to take the lesson. Although he accepted that the genre of the novel was tied to the account of common men and that their diction, therefore, had to set the tone of his work, he could no longer limit himself by his fervent commitment to the American language or by his respect for the conventions of the novel; he had to attain the extremes of expressiveness available in the full dictionary of historical English. From Shakespeare he developed the perception that a vast part of psychic life was separate from what the reasoning mind could articulate, and therefore that life as it revealed itself was not bound to the words available to the reason of the character who lived it. Rather, the English language at its most eloquent could be made the convention by which the inner character expressed itself. That language, for Melville, was to be found in the plays of Shakespeare and the Bible as translated by Shakespeare's contemporaries. His characters would talk plain English as they talked to the reader or to one another, but when consciousness rather than thought was the substance of their confession, they would reveal themselves in the most heightened and subtle diction the language contained. Shakespeare demonstrated to Melville that to accept the tragic nature of life is to accept also mankind's invention in recompense for this exile from paradise, the language refined by millennia of users since Eden was forsaken.

With his powerful new access to character through language,

Melville reapportioned the balance in his novels between narrative report of incident and dramatic presentation of consciousness. With a full and nervous diction now available to all characters, episodes could be treated as pure drama, even in the novel, with the author's voice yielding to monologue, dialogue, and stage directions.

The result was *Moby-Dick,* which, in addition to taking such major shaping impetus from Shakespeare, also derived from him more apparent techniques: for example, from *Macbeth* a structural rhythm that permits the central character moments of objective recognition of the stages of his mania, so that as his villainies mount, even to the destruction of children (Macbeth's actions against Macduff's family; Ahab's refusal to aid the *Rachel*), the audience is unwilling to relinquish him to death until he himself signals his resignation (Macbeth's "yellow leaf" speech; Ahab's musing on the eve of the chase, "They have been making hay somewhere under the slopes of the Andes"[15]).

In *Moby-Dick,* with the heat derived from Shakespeare and the confidence instilled by the example of Hawthorne, Melville fused disparate levels of reality and clashing signals from the infinite into a mighty whole. But with that achievement—and affected by its commercial failure—he no longer had a sustained interest in the symmetry or cohesiveness of the fictive world. The mysteries that novels solved at last, he said, were only those the novelist had artificially raised at first. Life's ambiguities endured.

In *Pierre* he wrote of a young man with a background drawn deliberately from the world of fiction—a boyhood spent in an idyllic, pastoral setting of wealth and affection. When, however, the dark mystery that unsettles all intrudes, as ever it does intrude into such worlds of fiction, it leads to disaster rather than solution or even tragic defeat, because that mystery at heart is not a puzzle with an answer, but the first sign delivered to Pierre that his world is ambiguous and that no life, even his, actually begins free from inherited complexities nor concludes in a shapely denouement.

The fragmentation of form compelled by such a theme destroyed any practical expectation of a contemporary audience for the novel. Melville knew this, and when talking of Pierre, the character, and the failure of novels read in his boyhood to prepare him for what life was really like, he talked of his own scheme in *Pierre*: "the profounder emanations of the human mind, intended to illustrate all that can be humanly known of human life; these never unravel their own intricacies, and have no proper endings, but in imperfect, unanticipated, and disappointing sequels (as mutilated stumps) hurry to abrupt intermergings with the eternal tides of time and fate."[16] This was not a statement about theme only but about form as well. Melville had lost his tolerance for conventional expectations of beginning, middle, and end, and now, writing for himself and for his art, was concerned with abrupt intermergings.

The same experimental attitude took hold of *Israel Potter* (1855), intended as a routine piece of moneymaking but executed finally to defeat that purpose and achieve a strikingly futuristic rendering of anomie, despite its announced aim of narrating a more literal alienation. Subtitled "His Fifty Years of Exile," the novel treats in detail but a few years of Israel's life and abruptly intermerges the remainder with the "eternal tides of time and fate." Melville transformed a historical tale of accidental exile from America into a parable that foreshadows Kafka in its bleak account of Israel's fruitless search for the way back to himself once he has pushed through a door he wrongly thought could be opened from both sides.

When, once more and all but finally, Melville wrote another long fiction, *The Confidence-Man,* again he served his own experimental needs before the expectations of those who purchased novels in 1857. In so doing, he may have seemed massively and petulantly self-indulgent: in revenge for nobody's caring for his books he appeared to wish to prove he could write a book nobody could possibly care for. The self that was indulged, however, was not that of a wounded author hurtling toward self-destruction, but that of a genius who, having broken through old forms to a new form, now took the step beyond. In pursuit of the ambiguities of life, which yielded no certain meaning, he created a fiction of shifting forms, each cohering only to reveal the greater force of its formless opposite, and so dissolving into formlessness only to be pushed out in another shape, and only again to slide back into the formless void. Appearances became for Melville but the masks put on by the profound facelessness of ultimate reality. He had in *Moby-Dick* explored the paradox that white is both nothingness and the total of every color in the spectrum. He had in "Bartleby" shown modern urban life reduced to so bleak a series of mechanical events that one defeated man achieved his triumph by accepting life as blankness and merging into nothingness rather than resisting. Bartleby's action, however, was surrounded by the lives of others, who found reason for cheer in their monotonous routines and in so doing ambiguously suggested that Bartleby's nihilism was either the excess of a deranged mind or the clarity of the one sane man in an insane world. And he had in *Israel Potter* converted a factual history of an involuntary exile into a fictional parable of anomie and the arbitrariness of modern life. *The Confidence-Man* pressed farther down this road; actuality in it floats up from the hidden depths as a series of shifting masks that might, in their unceasing changes, be all the meaning there is, or might be so connected that an ultimate oneness could be inferred in purposeful operation behind all seeming change.

Set upon a flat-bottomed boat gliding down the Mississippi River, always in sight of land and frequently touching upon it, *The Confidence-Man* requires no lofty main truck to offset the depth of its kelson as *Moby-Dick* did. It consists almost exclusively of talk—cozy chat, gruff bluster, impish extravaganza, treacherous insinuation —all of it informal. In and out of the conversations slide the characters of Shakespeare, named or alluded to, quoted or misquoted, as if they, too, shared the level of humdrum motion toward a constant sameness that prevails on the *Fidèle*. Goneril is now the name of a singularly nasty American housewife, Timon is an ursine frontiersman, and Polonius is talked about as if he were president of a wildcat bank. There is no reference to the positions of Shakespeare's characters within their own worlds, but only to their attitudes toward getting and spending. They are so many commercial object lessons.

Among the vulgar, Melville had pointed out in his Hawthorne review, Shakespeare was a deity. Now aboard the *Fidèle* the Shakespeare canon is handled the way the Bible is: as a commonly accepted account of the human condition that furnishes a treasury of illustrations with which to animate conversations between strangers; a collection of ethical maxims that are agreed to by all in the abstract but that yield contradictory meanings when pursued in the particular. As at times Shakespeare and the Bible appear interchangeable with each other, so at other times they appear interchangeable with the world of the *Fidèle*. Have these two mightiest possessions of English-speaking people been so thoroughly assimilated by Americans that they transfigure daily reality, or has grasping American materialism reduced even these sublimities to its own unimaginative level?

Melville interrupts his baffling drama at one point to talk to the reader about the art of fiction, and specifically about what is involved in the requirement that fiction have a "fidelity to life." Since he has called his fictive world the *Fidèle,* we presume he is talking about his novel's relation to actuality. He sides, he says, with that class who take up novels or sit at plays desiring "scenes different from those of the same old crowd round the custom-house counter, and same old dishes on the boarding-house table, with characters unlike those same old acquaintances they meet in the same old way every day in the same old street."

Not until 1863 did Melville move to New York City, and not until 1866 did he enter upon the drudging duties of an outdoors customs inspector, which he was to pursue for some nineteen years, but already with the last fiction published in his lifetime the mean years on New York's commercial streets are anticipated. Everyday reality is no larger than business transactions: the assessment of rates and payment of tariffs at the customhouse; the consumption of food paid for at the boardinghouse; the routine encounters, as one pursues routine duties, with others in the streets on their own routines. There is, we may protest, also an everyday reality in which the principal business is not business and in which the ritual of taking food is conducted among those one loves without reference to cost and profit. Melville's view of it, however, is of a monstrous, materialistic round.

The passage continues:

> And, as in real life, the proprieties will not allow people to act out themselves with the unreserve permitted to the stage; so, in books of fiction, they look not only for more entertainment, but, at bottom, even for more reality, than real life itself can show. Thus, though they want novelty, they want nature, too; but nature unfettered, exhilarated, in effect transformed.[17]

This is a just description of *Moby-Dick*—exceeding the proprieties in its theatrical unreserve, but even at its most extreme speaking from nature exhilarated rather than spinning a fantasy of escape from reality. Ironically, however, the passage does not describe the work in which it appears, *The Confidence-Man,* which is throughout an acting-out of man's selfishness. If it exceeds reality by giving more reality than real life, it does so by showing people even more cynical, more gullible, more deceitful, and more distrustful than in life. If it unfetters nature, the nature it unfetters is that of the scheming acquisitiveness of social man rather than that of the untutored instincts. The novel is replete with tales of bankruptcy, blasted marriages, and children available for hire on terms designed to make them competitive with that which bids to take their place in the world, machinery.

"Cider-mill, mowing-machine, corn-husker—all faithfully attend to their business," says a character called the Missourian. "Disinterested, too; no board, no wages; yet doing good all their lives long; shining examples that virtue is its own reward—the only practical Christians I know."[18] He resounds a bitter theme Melville had sounded earlier in his magazine tale, "The Tartarus of Maids," an unspoken pun on the machine as "labor-saving" device: it not only spares mankind hard physical work, it also obviates the need for children, so that women are spared the labor of childbirth. Instead of undergoing nine months of pregnancy,the young women in that sketch are freed throughout the year to work in the New England paper mill, serving the needs of one sultan, the machinery that makes its product, a blank roll of paper, in a nine-minute cycle. The industrial images point backward to *Typee,* where the labor of Kory-Kory and the uninhibited sexuality of his society cohere in a blissful world. To be spared labor is to be separated from one's biological essence and to be remade in the image of the machine.

In *Pierre,* Melville had mocked the failure of the novels his young hero read to prepare him for the ambiguities of life. In *The Confidence-Man,* he returned to this theme, now fixing the failure of fiction upon its absolute adherence to the notion that characters must be consistent. Even when an inconsistent character appears in a novel, he claims, the author provides him only for the sake of unraveling the inconsistency at the end (certain of Dickens's characters seem to fit this bill exactly). Novelists universally adopt one or another psychological system to serve the belief that life proceeds according to fixed principle, and so, although life may confuse the living, they can perceive its consistency by reading novels. But *The Confidence-Man,* with wit, complex intelligence, and a vexing fidelity to the perplexities of appearances, never settles psychological inconsistencies but renders them. Characters who observe inconsistency in others frequently debate this among themselves, seeking for the truth behind the shift in appearances, but in so doing serving their own interests, so that they themselves manifest the inconsistency they would eradicate.

The center and symbol of the novel's complexities is the confidence-man himself, whose apellation (confidence) points to the everyday world *(Fidèle)* and to the novel about it ("fidelity to life"). Daily living is a confidence game in that we cannot prosper emotionally or materially unless others have confidence in us, even though to gain such confidence we hide our darker side and so are far from confidential. The novel is a confidence game in that to gain the readers' confidence so that they will read his work, the author offers to unravel all the mysteries in his plot and thus commits himself to falsifying the life he claims to represent. The confidence-man of the title, working the tricks of his trade on the riverboat, is thus a double mirror, reflecting the two-sidedness of literature. As one guise succeeds another and he appeals to religion, philosophy, common sense, history, and sentiment in a ceaseless flow of reasoning and cajolery, the multiplying images go beyond any form acceptable to readers in Melville's day. His theme drives toward pure wordplay; reality may not exist at all except in the words in which it presents itself. This is a direct reversal of the linguistic theory at the base of Emerson and Thoreau, in which thingness creates the word. The possibility of a universe of words separate from and equal or superior to the universe of actuality was later realized in fiction and received a readership after the achievement of James Joyce and the many subsequent changes played on the theme by such as Vladimir Nabokov. They wrote in a time in which belief in absolute ethical truths no longer provided an objective resistance. Melville's experiment, however, was conducted with a lingering yearning for, if not attachment to, a truth beyond appearances. It is more manifestly anguished, more confused, and yet, nonetheless, remarkably impressive.

"It is with fiction as with religion," Melville says, "it should present another world, and yet one to which we feel the tie."[19] Layered between religion and fiction, reality is inexpressible in its own terms. Once it finds words it becomes either religion or fiction, depending on whether it is expressed in terms of the ideals that justify it from above or the motives that it takes initially from nature and then from historical determinants. Emerson, Thoreau, and Whitman took the religious avenue and Poe and Hawthorne took the fictional. Melville sought to straddle the two paths: Ahab's theological views of the whale and Ishmael's abundant provision of scientific and historical data on the species; Benito Cereno's shudder at the blackness at the heart of life and Amasa Delano's cheerful assurance that his chill had been occasioned only by the blowing of the trade winds. But in *The Confidence-Man* Melville no longer sought comprehension through alternate views. Rather, he relentlessly reduced both—symbolized by allusions to the great exemplars of religion and fiction, the Bible and Shakespeare—to the flat level of the deck of the *Fidèle*. The allusions no longer resonated, no longer evoked other worlds to amplify the humdrum commonplace, but were, rather, absorbed and neutralized by the commonplace to function as did other debased counters such as stocks, and bonds, and money. In so writing Melville was not only denying the expressibility of religion and fiction, he was denying the expressibility of life. Silence was the inevitable result.

In the period of Melville's long silence Walt Whitman looked at the troubled, alienated tribe of man and asked, "What is this separate Nature so unnatural?"[20] Americans, too, he saw in 1871, were strangers on the earth, no more content than were their fellows around the globe, restless pilgrims who in their westering were not integrating with the continent but seeking identity with the elusive spirit beyond the sunset. That spirit had first manifested itself in Asia, and America was the penultimate link in the chain that crossed the Caucasus, trailed over Europe, spanned the Atlantic, and now demanded expansion to the Pacific shore and a return to origins. In completeness would be beginning, Whitman affirmed. Meaning resided in the seas of God and awaited the transcendence of terrestrial circumstances to be achieved with the completion of rondure.

Billy Budd, the unfinished fiction found among Melville's papers at his death, also addresses an alienated tribe in terms of a myth that will explain its nature so unnatural. Unlike Whitman's, it moves tactilely through pain and sacrifice; it is the Christian legend. Even in making such an assertion from the resignation of his advanced years, however, Melville characteristically composed a context of detailed history, charged with the social theories in combat at the beginning of the nineteenth century. Although it offers a supernatural explanation of life, *Billy Budd* dramatically renders that historical moment when the doctrine of the rights of man challenged belief in hierarchical society as an organic outgrowth of man's original condition. The tension that seeks adjustment in the tale is one that marked both the American Revolution, which emphasized the rights of man, and the early national period, which, in partial reaction to the French Revolution, emphasized the conservative consolidation of social and political institutions. In his first work, *Typee,* Melville had sounded most of the themes that were to mark the great American works of his day: the one and the many; sexual love and society; the wild and the civilized. He did so with youthful spontaneity. At his death in 1891, he was working on *Billy Budd,* which consciously recapitulated the clash of mythic promise and historical reality that marks the first great body of American literature.

Afterword

At the outset of the 1850s, as we have seen, Henry Hallam, a learned student of world literature, believed that there were no longer any peculiarities remaining to distinguish American from English literature: "There seems nothing in the turn of sentiment or taste which a reader can recognize as not English."[1] He was wrong, in part because he generalized from the writings of such as Longfellow and Prescott, who pursued the continuity he wished to observe, and in part because he believed that the history of literature would be a more powerful shaper of American writing than the history of America itself.

The major writers whose masterpieces were to make the 1850s so memorable had, in the main, announced themselves by the time Hallam made his observation: Emerson's program was fully articulated and Hawthorne and Melville had published remarkable books. Apart from these writers, moreover, Poe had left a body of work that signaled the extraordinary intensity of aesthetic concentration that American isolation could foster. Still, Hallam's mistake is chiefly tied to his failure to conceive that an independent United States was a broad cultural phenomenon rather than merely a political one.

Indeed, the ferment of a society in exuberant recovery from the panic of 1837 was so powerful that it affected the very writers who shared Hallam's views. Their histories, essays, and poems were a reaction to what they regarded as the philistinism of their society. They consciously accepted English standards as a stay against

American vulgarity. The major writers, however, yielded to their untidy America. They did not accept vulgarity, although in its pervasiveness it marked their work occasionally. Rather, they pursued the discovery of the new literary standards they believed were inherent in the organization of American life, although invisible to those who lived that life because literature had never before been democratic.

A respectable number of the first American thinkers to contemplate a democratic literature had concluded that democracy meant the end of high literature as the world knew it. Tom Paine more than suspected that belles lettres was an institution that had been developed by the ruling hierarchy throughout time as a form for its own delectation and as a means to confirm the masses in their acceptance of their lowly lot. Tragedy, for example, trained the proletariat to be fearful of the fall of kings and thus tightened the hold of their masters on them through structuring their feelings to conform to what was. Once men ruled themselves, Paine believed, they would have little use for literature; in a democratic society the perfection of human existence would obviate the need to escape into fantasy. Reason could be addressed directly.

Jefferson, Madison, Franklin, and others were not so extreme as Paine. But they did share his instinct. In a land in which man could accomplish all he willed without the opposition of artificial barriers, what need for a distinct class of men of letters? All who had occasion to write in addition to or in pursuit of their public or commercial vocations would write. The literature of democracy would be the writings of free, active men going about their business. The modern function of the great literature of the past would be utilitarian—it was good so far as it helped free men prepare themselves for lives of practical consequence. The conviction shines through Jefferson's letters of advice to the young or his proposal for the University of Virginia. Franklin's *Autobiography* is sprinkled liberally with observations on his indebtedness to literature as a good teacher of effective writing and thus as a guide to how to influence others to light the streets, buy one's products, vote for paper currency, or build a hospital. His attitude is too easily dismissed when it is branded as lowbrow. It is difficult to locate a highbrow counter to it, because the attitude was not that of a group but of the era, the time of expectant democracy. Jonathan Edwards has been cited to the contrary, but Edwards's highbrow writings were produced as an instrument of his public career, as Franklin's were of his. A minister wrote theological treatises; a printer wrote pamphlets.

Even in the early days of the republic, however, there were men who theorized about American belles lettres, seeing the possibility of such as consistent with the new society. Still, they accepted the unshakable generic definitions of European literature, and considered only what distinctive subject matter Americans could pack into these containers.[2] They habitually made the following bad analogy: American youth is to English age as classical literature is to modern literature; therefore American literature should be epic or didactic in classical ways. The American Revolution, they insisted, called for an epic treatment similar to that given the Trojan War by Homer; the American Indians, they pointed out, cried for literary rendering in parallel with the writings of the Roman Stoics, whom the Indians so greatly resembled. The analogy was bad because the nation, although young as a political entity, was as old as other lands in its literary inheritance. Its residents were the inheritors not only of Homer but of Shakespeare and Milton, of Pope and Richardson. Political infancy did not mean literary innocence.

As Emerson showed explicitly in his essays and Melville implicitly in *Typee,* the idea of American literature had to be tied to the actuality of a culture that was the result of a long history and yet was so undetermined that it could contemplate its future without the restraint of precedents. In keeping with the notions of Paine or of Franklin, the writers of the new literary democracy knew that writing would have to arise from the everyday reality of the republic. But unlike their predecessors, they saw that daily business did not constitute the reality but masked it, and so the practical had to be penetrated rather than served. The American writer could not, then, be just another public or commercial careerist. He had to be apart from the pushing and hauling in order to balance it with his sense of what it meant. The wild, slovenly land was not just the arena for the westward sprawl of Europe, it was a countering influence to European history. The land itself, rather than institutions, was the lifeblood of democracy.

The writers who recognized this also recognized, and of necessity, that they had to abandon traditional genres and create the new forms that would contain the new matter. American literature meant new shapes as well as new themes.

This shift—from the old idea that American literature must be either practical in purpose or classical in form to the new idea that it was the voice of the latent forces in the land—had to be preceded by a redefinition of American society. This came into being in the formative years of Emerson's generation. Literary democracy grew from the new nationalism. In the Federalist period nationalism meant a balancing of sectional economic interests. The United States as a whole was what resulted from the conflict of its constituent parts. It defined itself in terms of Europe and frequently used European political reality to characterize its attitudes: Hamiltonians were pro-British, anti-French; Jeffersonians were pro-French, anti-British. But a consequential change in national self-consciousness began to appear in the War of 1812 and grew to overarching dimensions in the time of Jackson's presidency. The success of the War Hawks in bringing about a conflict with Great Britain was the triumph of a new view of American self-interest. This self-interest was not the residue left after factions had clashed nor did it define America in the passive terms of its relationship to the European powers. Rather it was based on the full and furious admission that what America wanted most was more land. The West defined the new nationalism not by becoming yet another region added to North and South but by gaining the agreement of all regions as to its quintessential American character. It was "more American" both temporally, in containing America's future, and spatially, in being freer of European traces.

However much Emerson deplored the land-greed of the new nationalism from a moral or political standpoint, he built on it culturally. As has been seen, he was certain that the "nervous, rocky west" would provide the ultimate validation of his claims on behalf of modern man. Thoreau, too, deplored the materialism that was unleashed but embraced wildness as definitive of the best in his countrymen. Melville and Whitman were explicit in their early acceptance of "Manifest Destiny," and Hawthorne, despite his personal conservatism and his habitual skepticism, was a member of the Young America branch of the Democratic party. This group aggressively wished to reverse history by carrying western democracy not only to the East but into the heart of Europe, stirring revolutions there. Poe, too, was profoundly affected, albeit negatively. The closed spaces of his theory and practice are a marked reaction to continentalism. The new nationalism was an essential condition for the new literature because it provided a positive, dynamic sense of American identity, however much the artists were to criticize the naked avarice it revealed. The generation we have been observing grew up in a country that had an ebullient sense of its national self—Irving and Cooper did not.

Accompanying this large political development was a significant economic one. In the 1820s and 1830s the growth of the factory system produced two new social classes, the industrial capitalists and the factory workers. Strikingly, the major writers came from the economic groups that were the most threatened by the new classes. The ministerial caste, into which Emerson was born, found itself dictated to by the wealth of its parishioners rather than acting as a censor of it. The middling landed families of Hawthorne and Melville had no power to exert against the new capitalists who preempted their social status. The carpentry of Whitman's father and the home industry of Thoreau's were made marginal by factory processes.

In passing, it can also be observed that the greater number of major reformers in the period—agitators for abolition of slavery, temperance, women's rights, and improved conditions for the poor, insane, or imprisoned—came also from the fading classes. The children of prosperous farmers, rising merchants, and financiers were prominent neither in reform leadership nor in the ranks of the writers.

One is led to the hypothesis that not only did America need to come into possession of a positive nationalism before a native literature could flourish, but that it had to dispossess certain groups in the process so as to free (if not compel) their children to respond with the weapons of thought. To this one must add the observation that the same commercial and industrial developments that dispossessed the classes from which the writers came also provided them with improved means of printing and circulating what they wrote, as well as a widening number of countrymen who had both the knowledge and the leisure to read what they wrote.

F. O. Matthiessen observed that the unique power of the literary flowering of the 1850s could be investigated in several different ways:

> You might be concerned with *how* this flowering came, with the descriptive narrative of literary history. Or you might dig into its sources in our life, and examine the economic, social, and religious causes *why* this flowering came in just these years. Or you might be primarily concerned with *what* these books were as works of art, with evaluating their fusions of form and content.[3]

None of these investigations can be conducted so purely as to exclude the others. *What* happened inevitably overlaps *how* it happened; *how* it happened implies *why* it happened; *why* it happened demands some account of *what* happened. But the distinctions have an empirical validity and Matthiessen's *American Renaissance,* devoted to *what* happened—to, that is, an aesthetic analysis of the great works of the 1850s—is itself a major work of literary criticism.

I have been concerned centrally with a descriptive narrative of *how* a major literature arose in the United States between the great panic of 1837 and the outbreak of the Civil War. In tracing this quickening of the literary life I was drawn inescapably to a degree of literary and linguistic analysis, to a consideration, that is, of *what* happened. And in this Afterword I have also attempted to draw out from their implicit location in my pages generalizations about *why* it happened. But the controlling theme has been descriptive.

As Melville framed my narrative, so he may inform this Afterword. What he observed of the novelist who seeks to be faithful to the complexity of life is true also of the historian. A novelist, Melville said, can assign satisfactory explanations to human behavior only insofar as he first artificially abstracts that behavior from the ambiguous fullness of life that is its vital element. Fidelity to life, he felt, is best achieved through illustration rather than explanation. If illustration offers only part of the truth, that part at least is living.

I have sought to be faithful to the intermergings of life rather than to sever my subjects from them to find easier explanations. The resulting truths may lack a certain symmetry, but, then, life is always less finished than the ideas we can invent to account for it.

Notes

CHAPTER ONE

1. Frances Trollope, *Domestic Manners of the Americans* (London, 1927), pp. 186–87.
2. Henry Wadsworth Longfellow, "To the Driving Cloud," *The Poetical Works* (London, 1912), p. 129.
3. George Ticknor Curtis, *Life of Daniel Webster* (New York, 1872), I:260.
4. Herman Melville, *Typee* (London, 1922), p. 167.
5. Ibid., pp. 149–50.
6. Ibid., p. 150.
7. Ibid., p. 270.
8. Thomas Paine, *Common Sense*, ed. Nelson F. Adkins (Indianapolis, 1953), p. 4.
9. *Typee*, p. 270.
10. Ibid., p. 273.
11. Ibid., p. 310.
12. Ibid., p. 200.
13. Ibid., p. 291.

CHAPTER TWO

1. Ralph Waldo Emerson, "Man the Reformer," *Complete Works*, Riverside Edition (London, n.d.), I:221–22.
2. Emerson, "The Conservative," ibid., p. 303.
3. Nathaniel Hawthorne, *Mosses from an Old Manse*, *Works*, Centenary Edition (Columbus, Ohio, 1974), X:31–32.

4. P. T. Barnum, *The Life* (London, 1855), p. 75.
5. See Ernest L. Bogart and Donald L. Kemmerer, *Economic History of the American People* (New York, 1947), and George Rogers Taylor, *The Transportation Revolution, 1815–1860* (New York, 1951).
6. Alfred D. Chandler, Jr., "Henry Varnum Poor," *Men in Business,* ed. William Miller (Cambridge, Mass., 1952), p. 255.
7. Freeman Hunt, *Lives of American Merchants* (New York, 1969), I:xlvii. This edition is a reprint of volumes first published in 1856 and 1858.
8. Ralph Waldo Emerson, *The Journals and Miscellaneous Notebooks,* 12 vols. to date (Cambridge, Mass., 1961), V:332. Since this is a diplomatic edition I have not reproduced the full punctuation in quotations from it.
9. Emerson, "The Method of Nature," *Works,* I:184.
10. Emerson, *Journals,* V:332.
11. Emerson, "The American Scholar," *Works,* I:82. Subsequent quotations are from this text.
12. Emerson, *Journals,* VIII:319.
13. Ibid., p. 264.
14. Ibid., VII:376.
15. Ibid., III:136.
16. Ibid., V:100.
17. Ibid., p. 462.
18. Ibid., VII:437–38.
19. Emerson, "The Divinity School Address," *Works,* I:144.
20. Emerson, *Journals,* V:197.
21. Ibid., VIII:122.
22. Emerson, *English Traits, Works,* V:110.
23. His reaction to the industrial condition is on pp. 163–64.
24. Ibid., p. 272.
25. See Lewis Perry, *Radical Abolitionism* (Ithaca, N.Y., 1973) for an excellent analysis of these ideas.
26. Emerson, *Journals,* IX:446.
27. John Jay Deiss, *The Roman Years of Margaret Fuller* (New York, 1969), p. 107.
28. Emerson, *English Traits, Works,* V:288.

CHAPTER THREE

1. All quotations from *Nature* are taken from Volume I of the Riverside Edition of the *Complete Works* (London, n.d.).

2. Ralph Waldo Emerson, *The Journals and Miscellaneous Notebooks*, 12 vols. to date (Cambridge, Mass., 1961–), II:197.
3. Emerson, "The Young American," *Works*, I:349.
4. Ibid.
5. Emerson, "Demonology," *Works*, X:12.
6. Emerson, "Fate," *Works*, VI:20.
7. Ibid., p. 13.
8. Emerson, "The Over-Soul," *Works*, II:251.
9. Emerson, *Journals*, IX:113.
10. W. J. Stillman, *The Autobiography of a Journalist* (London, 1901), I:147.
11. Emerson, *Journals*, IX:75.
12. Ibid., p. 121.
13. Ibid., XI:440.
14. Ibid., IX:405.
15. The terms here follow the meaning given them by Mircea Eliade in his *The Sacred and the Profane*, trans. Willard R. Trask (New York, 1959).
16. Emerson, "Circles," *Works*, II:300.
17. Emerson, "History," *Works*, II:43.
18. Ibid., pp. 42–43.
19. Emerson, *Journals*, VIII:398.
20. Ralph Waldo Emerson, *Journals*, ed. E. W. Emerson and W. E. Forbes (London, 1913), IX:7–8.
21. Emerson, *Journals*, XI:528.
22. Harriet Martineau, *Retrospect of Western Travel* (London, 1838), III:231.
23. Emerson, *Representative Men*, *Works*, IV:38.
24. Emerson, "The Poet," *Works*, III:15.
25. Horatio Greenough, *The Travels, Observations, and Experiences of a Yankee Stonecutter* (Gainesville, Fla., 1958), p. 33. Facsimile of 1852 edition.
26. Michael Chevalier, *Society, Manners, and Politics in the United States*, ed. J. W. Ward (New York, 1961), p. 269.
27. Greenough, *Travels*, p. 33.
28. Ibid.
29. Ibid., p. 66.
30. Ibid., p. 187.
31. Emerson, *Journals*, V:150.
32. Martineau, *Retrospect*, III:202–203.
33. Emerson, *Journals*, VII:431–32.
34. James Russell Lowell, *Literary Essays* (Cambridge, Mass., 1890), I:7.
35. Emerson, *Journals*, XI:192.

36. Ibid., VII:51.
37. Emerson, "Give All to Love," *Works*, Vol. IX.
38. "Uriel," ibid.
39. "The Snow-Storm," ibid.
40. "Blight," ibid.
41. *The Correspondence of Emerson and Carlyle*, ed. Joseph Slater (New York, 1964), p. 486.

CHAPTER FOUR

1. George Haven Putnam, *George Palmer Putnam* (New York, 1912), p. 178.
2. Ibid., p. 177.
3. Ibid., p. 176.
4. Frances Trollope, *Domestic Manners of the Americans* (London, 1927), pp. 321–22.
5. *The Journal of Richard Henry Dana, Jr.*, ed. Robert F. Lucid (Cambridge, Mass., 1968), I:102.
6. Ralph Waldo Emerson, *The Journals and Miscellaneous Notebooks*, 12 vols. to date (Cambridge, Mass., 1961–), IX:104.
7. Harriet Beecher Stowe, *The Minister's Wooing* (London, 1859), p. 13.
8. John Greenleaf Whittier, "Among the Hills," *The Writings* (London, 1889), I:263.
9. "The Fruit-Gift," ibid., II:32.
10. "The Last Walk in Autumn," ibid., p. 37.
11. Henry Wadsworth Longfellow, "The Golden Mile-Stone," *The Poetical Works* (London, 1912), p. 311.
12. Henry Wadsworth Longfellow, *Kavanagh, Complete Writings* (Boston, 1904), VIII:426–27.
13. See Theodore Parker, "The Position and Duties of the American Scholar," *Collected Works* (London, 1864), Vol. VII.
14. Parker, "A Sermon of Merchants," ibid., p. 26.
15. Theodore Parker, *Experience As a Minister* (Boston, 1859), p. 93.
16. Parker, "American Scholar," p. 245.
17. W. J. Stillman, *The Autobiography of a Journalist* (London, 1901), I:202.
18. Harriet Martineau, *Retrospect of Western Travel* (London, 1901), II:10.
19. Daniel Webster, "Adams and Jefferson," *Works* (Boston, 1853), I:143.
20. *Memoir and Letters of Charles Sumner*, ed. Edward L. Pierce (London, 1878–93), II:352.

21. James Russell Lowell, "L'Envoi," *The Poetical Works* (Cambridge, Mass., 1890), I:73–75.
22. An incisive description of this class can be found in the opening pages of Volume III of Pierce's *Sumner*.
23. Lucid, *Journal of Dana*, I:234.
24. Oliver Wendell Holmes, *The Autocrat of the Breakfast-Table* (Boston, 1891), pp. 259–60.
25. Thomas Wentworth Higginson, *Cheerful Yesterdays* (Boston, 1898), pp. 70–71.
26. Pierce, *Sumner*, III:7.
27. *Life, Letters, and Journals of George Ticknor*, ed. George S. Hillard (London, 1876), II:258.
28. Edwin P. Whipple, *Character and Characteristic Men* (Boston, 1888), p. 152.
29. Perry Miller, *The Raven and the Whale* (New York, 1956), p. 110.
30. Longfellow, *Kavanagh, Writings*, VIII:425–27.
31. *The Diaries of William Charles Macready*, ed. William Toynbee (London, 1912), II:231.
32. Ibid., pp. 229–30.
33. Herman Melville, "Hawthorne and His Mosses," *Representative Selections*, ed. Willard Thorp (New York, 1938), p. 335.
34. Ibid., p. 337.
35. Ibid., p. 339.

CHAPTER FIVE

1. Edgar Allan Poe, "Ligeia," *The Complete Works*, ed. James A. Harrison (New York, 1902), II:251.
2. Poe, "The Assignation," ibid., pp. 123–24.
3. Poe, "The Domain of Arnheim," ibid., VI:182.
4. Poe, "The Island of the Fay," ibid., IV:194.
5. Poe, "To Helen," ibid., VII:46.
6. Poe, "Some Words with a Mummy," ibid., VI:136.
7. Poe, "Marginalia," ibid., XVI:78–79.
8. Poe, "The Poetic Principle," ibid., XIV:273.
9. Lisa Appignanesi, *Femininity & the Creative Imagination* (London, 1973), p. 12.
10. Poe, "The Colloquy of Monos and Una," *Works*, IV:203.
11. Poe, "Mellonta Tauta," ibid., VI:207.
12. Poe, "Lever's 'Charles O'Malley,'" ibid., XI:97, typifies Poe's references to Burke.
13. Edmund Burke, *Reflections on the Revolution in France*, ed. William B. Todd (New York, 1959), p. 58.

14. Ibid., p. 205.
15. Ibid., p. 71.
16. Poe, "Monos and Una," *Works,* IV:209.
17. Poe, "The Poetic Principle," ibid., XIV:273–74.
18. Poe, "The Philosophy of Composition," ibid., 196–97.
19. Ibid., p. 203.
20. The idea of Poe's relation to the backyard tinkerer is taken from Daniel Hoffman, *Poe, Poe, Poe, Poe, Poe, Poe, Poe* (New York, 1972).
21. Poe, "A Dream Within a Dream," *Works,* VII:16.
22. Poe, "The Tell-Tale Heart," ibid., IV:88.
23. Poe, "Sarah Margaret Fuller," ibid., XV:75.
24. Poe, *The Narrative of Arthur Gordon Pym,* ibid., II:17–18.
25. Ibid., p. 178.

CHAPTER SIX

1. Nathaniel Hawthorne, *The House of the Seven Gables* (New York, 1961), p. 165.
2. Statistics are taken from George Rogers Taylor, *The Transportation Revolution, 1815–1860* (New York, 1951).
3. Freeman Hunt, *Lives of American Merchants* (New York, 1969), I:233.
4. Ibid., p. 268.
5. Details of Philadelphia history are taken from J. Thomas Scharf and Thompson Westcott, *History of Philadelphia,* 3 vols. (Philadelphia, 1884).
6. Ibid., I:688.
7. Facts about Lippard's career are based on the valuable work of Emilio De Grazia, *The Life and Works of George Lippard,* unpublished doctoral dissertation (Ohio State University, 1969).
8. George Lippard, *Adonai, The Pilgrim of Eternity* (Philadelphia, 1851), p. 28.
9. Quoted by De Grazia, p. 328.
10. George Lippard, *The Quaker City; or, The Monks of Monk Hall* (Philadelphia, 1845), p. 4.
11. Ibid., p. 328.
12. Lippard, *Adonai,* p. 82.
13. Ibid., p. 97.
14. George Lippard, *Memoirs of a Preacher* (Philadelphia, 1849), p. v.
15. Ibid., p. vi.
16. Ibid.

17. Fanny Fern, "An Interesting Husband," *Fern Leaves from Fanny's Portfolio* (London, 1853), pp. 301–302.
18. Lippard, *Quaker City*, p. 112.
19. Ibid., p. 352.
20. Ibid., p. 156.
21. Quoted by De Grazia, p. 353.
22. George Lippard, *New York: Its Upper Ten and Lower Million* (Cincinnati, 1854), p. 68.
23. Ibid., p. 64.
24. *The Autobiography of Lyman Beecher*, ed. Barbara M. Cross (Cambridge, Mass., 1961), II:167.
25. This account of the order and its influence is based upon Vernon Stauffer, *New England and the Bavarian Illuminati* (New York, 1967), a reissue of the 1918 edition.
26. Ibid., p. 140.
27. George Lippard, *Constitution and By-Laws of Progress Circle, No. 9, of the Brotherhood of the Union . . .*, p. v.

CHAPTER SEVEN

1. Harriet Martineau, *Society in America* (London, 1837), I:30.
2. Ibid., I:210.
3. Ibid., II:260.
4. Ibid., II:263.
5. Ibid., II:252.
6. Nathaniel Hawthorne, *The House of the Seven Gables* (New York, 1961), p. 31.
7. *The Journal of Richard Henry Dana, Jr.*, ed. Robert F. Lucid (Cambridge, Mass., 1968), II:532.
8. Nathaniel Hawthorne, "The Sister Years," *Twice-Told Tales, Works*, Centenary Edition (Columbus, Ohio, 1974), IX:338–39.
9. Details in this paragraph are based on Louisa Hall Tharp, *The Peabody Sisters of Salem* (Boston, 1950).
10. Thomas Wentworth Higginson, *Cheerful Yesterdays* (Boston, 1898), p. 86.
11. Ibid., p. 87.
12. Tharp, *Peabody Sisters*, p. 161.
13. James T. Fields, *Yesterdays with Authors* (Boston, 1900), p. 113.
14. Ibid.
15. Julian Hawthorne, *Nathaniel Hawthorne and His Wife* (Boston, 1885), I:88–89.
16. *Letters of Hawthorne to William D. Ticknor* (Washington, D.C., 1970), I:54.

17. Ibid., II:96.
18. Nathaniel Hawthorne, *Passages from the French and Italian Notebooks* (Cambridge, Mass., 1879), I:258.
19. Ibid., II:44.
20. Ibid., II:54–55.
21. Ibid., II:80.
22. Nathaniel Hawthorne, *True Stories from History and Biography, Works,* Centenary Edition (Columbus, Ohio, 1972), VI:71.
23. Nathaniel Hawthorne, *The Scarlet Letter, Works,* Centenary Edition (Columbus, Ohio, 1962), I:195.
24. Ibid., p. 127.
25. Ibid., p. 162.
26. Ibid.
27. Hawthorne, *Seven Gables,* p. 129.
28. Ibid., p. 156.
29. Ibid., p. 161.
30. Nathaniel Hawthorne, *The English Notebooks,* ed. Randall Stewart (New York, 1962), p. 45.
31. Ibid., p. 351.
32. Ibid., p. 45.
33. Nathaniel Hawthorne, *Septimius Felton* (Boston, 1879), p. 110.
34. Hawthorne, *English Notebooks,* p. 96.
35. Nathaniel Hawthorne, *Life of Franklin Pierce* (Boston, 1852), p. 31.
36. Ibid., p. 29.
37. Hawthorne, *French and Italian,* II:168.
38. Nathaniel Hawthorne, "A Book of Autographs," *The Snow-Image and Uncollected Tales, Works,* Centenary Edition (Columbus, Ohio, 1974), XI:362.
39. Horatio Bridge, *Personal Recollections of Nathaniel Hawthorne* (London, 1893), p. 189.
40. Nathaniel Hawthorne, "Chiefly About War Matters, *Miscellanies* (Boston, 1900), p. 382.
41. Ibid., p. 384.
42. Ibid., p. 381.
43. Hawthorne, *Septimius Felton,* p. 81.
44. Ibid., p. 30.

CHAPTER EIGHT

1. Nathaniel Hawthorne, *Our Old Home, Works,* Centenary Edition (Columbus, Ohio, 1970), V:3.

2. Nathaniel Hawthorne, *The Scarlet Letter, Works,* Centenary Edition (Columbus, Ohio, 1972), I:37.
3. Nathaniel Hawthorne, *The House of the Seven Gables* (New York,1961), p. vii.
4. Nathaniel Hawthorne, *The Blithedale Romance, Works,* Centenary Edition (Columbus, Ohio, 1964), III:2.
5. Nathaniel Hawthorne, *The Marble Faun, Works,* Centenary Edition (Columbus, Ohio, 1968), IV:3.
6. This characterization of Scott's views is based on his General Preface to the Waverly Novels.
7. Hawthorne, *Old Home,* p. 241.
8. Ibid., p. 242.
9. Nathaniel Hawthorne, *Twice-Told Tales, Works,* Centenary Edition (Columbus, Ohio, 1974), IX:48.
10. James T. Fields, *Yesterdays with Authors* (Boston, 1900), p. 122.
11. James Russell Lowell, *The Poetical Works* (Cambridge, Mass., 1890), III:60.
12. Margaret Fuller, *Memoirs* (London, 1852), I:220.
13. Louisa Hall Tharp, *The Peabody Sisters of Salem* (Boston, 1950), p. 300.
14. Henry David Thoreau, *Familiar Letters,* ed. F. O. Sanborn (Cambridge, Mass., 1894), p. 421.
15. M. A. DeWolfe Howe, *Memories of a Hostess . . .* (Boston, 1922), p. 55.
16. Ibid., p. 58.
17. Nathaniel Hawthorne, "The New Adam and Eve," *Mosses from an Old Manse, Works,* Centenary Edition (Columbus, Ohio, 1974), X:247.
18. Nathaniel Hawthorne, *The English Notebooks,* ed. Randall Stewart (New York, 1962), p. 89.
19. Hawthorne, *Twice-Told Tales,* p. 58.
20. Hawthorne, *Marble Faun,* p. 347.

CHAPTER NINE

1. Julian Hawthorne, *Nathaniel Hawthorne and His Wife* (Boston, 1885), I:260, 262.
2. Nathaniel Hawthorne, *The Blithedale Romance, Works,* Centenary Edition (Columbus, Ohio, 1964), III:47.
3. Hawthorne, *Hawthorne and His Wife,* I:258.
4. Daniel Webster, *Works* (Boston, 1853), II:107.
5. Ralph Waldo Emerson, *Complete Works,* Riverside Edition (London, n.d.), XI:338–39.

6. L. Maria Child, *Letters from New York* (New York, 1843), p.237.
7. In an introductory note dated 15 March 1855 to *Beauties of Fanny Fern* (London, n.d.).
8. Fanny Fern, *Ruth Hall* (London, n.d.), p. 35.
9. Margaret Fuller, *Memoirs* (London, 1852), II:1.
10. Ralph L. Rusk, *The Life of Ralph Waldo Emerson* (New York, 1949), p. 378.
11. Margaret Fuller, *Woman in the Nineteenth Century* (London, 1845), p. 36.
12. Horace Greeley, *Recollections of a Busy Life* (New York, 1868), p. 179.
13. Alexis de Tocqueville, *Democracy in America* (New York, 1954), II:224.
14. Michael Chevalier, *Society, Manners, and Politics in the United States,* ed. J. W. Ward (New York, 1961), p. 294.
15. Tocqueville, *Democracy,* II:225.
16. Harriet Martineau, *Autobiography* (London, 1877), II:73.
17. Fanny Fern, *Fern Leaves from Fanny's Portfolio* (London, 1853), p. 259.
18. Harriet Martineau, *Society in America* (London, 1837), III:106.
19. Edwin Percy Whipple, *Recollections of Eminent Men* (Boston, 1887), p. 216. On this alliance of women and clergy see Ann Douglas, *The Feminization of American Culture* (New York, 1977).
20. Child, *Letters,* pp. 193–94.
21. Ibid., p. 255.
22. Ibid., pp. 235–36.
23. For example, to Frederick Law Olmstead, as he reports in Part II of his *Walks and Talks of an American Farmer in England* (New York, 1852), p. 73.
24. Oliver Wendell Holmes, *The Autocrat of the Breakfast-Table* (Boston, 1891), p. 43.
25. Oliver Wendell Holmes, *Elsie Venner, Writings* (Boston, 1861), V:172–73.
26. Chevalier, *Society,* p. 303.
27. F. H. Hedge in Fuller, *Memoirs,* I:115, 116.
28. Ibid., III:154.
29. John Jay Deiss, *The Roman Years of Margaret Fuller* (New York, 1969), p. 139.
30. Fuller, *Memoirs,* II:133–34.
31. Martineau, *Autobiography,* II:71–72.
32. Fuller, *Memoirs,* III:160.
33. Fuller, *Woman,* p. 138.
34. Ibid., p. 165.
35. Margaret Fuller, *Summer on the Lakes* (London, 1861), p. 212.
36. Ibid., p. 46.

37. Nathaniel Hawthorne, "My Visit to Niagara," *The Snow-Image and Uncollected Tales, Works,* Centenary Edition (Columbus, Ohio, 1974), XI:284.
38. Fuller, *Summer,* p. 5.
39. Deiss, *Roman Years,* p. 47. Mickiewicz rallying the exiled Poles in 1848 included in his manifesto, "To the companion of life, woman, citizenship, entire equality of rights."
40. Fuller, *Memoirs,* III:132.
41. *The Writings of Margaret Fuller,* ed. Mason Wade (Clifton, N.J., 1973), pp. 470–71.

CHAPTER TEN

1. *The Letters of John Greenleaf Whittier,* ed. John B. Pickard (Cambridge, Mass., 1975), I:249–50.
2. Lewis Perry, *Radical Abolitionism* (Ithaca, N.Y., 1973), p. 58. At almost every point at which I touch upon the abolitionist movement I am indebted to this study.
3. Theodore Parker, *Collected Works* (London, 1864), VII:4.
4. Alexis de Tocqueville, *Democracy in America* (New York, 1954), II:169.
5. See Ernest L. Bogart and Donald L. Kemmerer, *Economic History of the American People* (New York, 1947), p. 380.
6. *The Era of Reform,* ed. Henry Steele Commager (Princeton, 1960), p. 53.
7. Michael Chevalier, *Society, Manners, and Politics in the United States,* ed. J. W. Ward (New York, 1961), p. 199.
8. For a full discussion of Webster's position, see Richard N. Current, *Daniel Webster and the Rise of National Conservatism* (Boston, 1955).
9. William Charvat, *The Profession of Authorship,* ed. Matthew J. Bruccoli (Columbus, Ohio, 1968), p. 304.
10. Ibid., p. 301.
11. Carl Bode, *The Anatomy of American Popular Culture, 1840–1861* (Berkeley, 1959), p. 111.
12. *The Journal of Richard Henry Dana, Jr.,* ed. Robert F. Lucid (Cambridge, Mass., 1968), II:487.
13. *Life, Letters, and Journals of George Ticknor,* ed. George S. Hillard (London, 1876), II:286.
14. Harriet Beecher Stowe, *Uncle Tom's Cabin* (New York, 1963), p. 82.
15. Ibid., p. 137.

16. John Donald Wade, *Augustus Baldwin Longstreet* (New York, 1924), p. 284.
17. Ibid., pp. 284–85.
18. Stowe, *Uncle,* p. 160.
19. Ibid., p. 188.
20. *The Autobiography of Lyman Beecher,* ed. Barbara M. Cross (Cambridge, Mass., 1961), I:391.
21. Ibid., II:430.
22. Harriet Beecher Stowe, *Sunny Memories of Foreign Lands* (London, 1854), II:272.
23. The theory is set forth in "The Old Oak of Andover," *Tales and Sketches of New England Life* (London, 1855).
24. Harriet Beecher Stowe, *The Minister's Wooing* (London, 1859), p. 356.
25. Stowe, *Sunny,* I:223.
26. Stowe, *Tales,* p. 166.
27. Stowe, *Minister's,* p. 266.
28. Ibid., p. 211.

CHAPTER ELEVEN

1. Jay B. Hubbell, *The South in American Literature 1607–1900* (Durham, N.C., 1954), p. 261.
2. Ibid., p. 595.
3. John Donald Wade, *Augustus Baldwin Longstreet* (New York, 1924), p. 146.
4. Hubbell, *South,* pp. 346–47.
5. Frederick Law Olmsted, *A Journey in the Seaboard States, in the Years 1853–1854* (New York, 1904), I:154.
6. Ibid., II:379–80.
7. Ralph Waldo Emerson, *The Journals and Miscellaneous Notebooks,* 12 vols. to date (Cambridge, Mass., 1961–), VII:473.
8. For details of his life see Milton Rickels, *George Washington Harris* (New York, 1965).
9. George Washington Harris, *Sut Lovingood,* ed. Brom Weber (New York, 1954), p. 54. The editor of this collection altered the original orthography in the reasonable belief that Harris's attempt to represent the sound of Sut's voice through misspellings was unnecessary for the effect he desired and presents an arbitrary obstacle to the modern reader. In my citations I rely on this edition as well as those that have the original orthography, and fear I may also have unconsciously let

my own spellings intrude from time to time. At any rate, the words are Sut's.

10. George Washington Harris, *High Times and Hard Times,* ed. M. Thomas Inge (Nashville, 1967), p. 150.
11. Ibid., p. 47.
12. Harris, *Sut Lovingood,* p. 19.
13. Ibid., pp. 35–36.
14. Ibid., pp. 37–38.
15. Harris, *High Times,* p. 52.
16. Harris, *Sut Lovingood,* p. 124.
17. Ibid., pp. 178–79.
18. Ibid., p. 77.
19. Ibid., p. 78.
20. Ibid., p. 99.
21. Ibid., pp. 138–39.
22. Ibid., pp. 119–20.
23. Ibid., p. 277.

CHAPTER TWELVE

1. Ralph Waldo Emerson, *Complete Works,* Riverside Edition (London, n.d.), X:429.
2. Ibid., p. 347.
3. Ralph Waldo Emerson, *Journals,* ed. E. W. Emerson and W. E. Forbes (London, 1913), IX:15.
4. Emerson, *Complete Works,* X:446.
5. Ibid., pp. 447–48.
6. Henry D. Thoreau, *Early Essays and Miscellanies* (Princeton, 1975), p. 40.
7. Ibid.
8. Ibid., p. 41.
9. Ibid., p. 110.
10. Henry D. Thoreau, *Familiar Letters,* ed. F. O. Sanborn (Cambridge, Mass., 1894), p. 253.
11. Henry D. Thoreau, *Reform Papers,* ed. Wendell Glick (Princeton, 1973), p. 194.
12. Henry D. Thoreau, *Walden,* Concord Edition (Boston, 1929), p. 357.
13. Henry D. Thoreau, *The Maine Woods,* ed. Joseph J. Moldenhauer (Princeton, 1972), pp. 127–28.
14. *Walden,* p. 108.

15. Ibid., p. 24.
16. Ibid., p. 270.
17. Ibid., p. 367.
18. Henry D. Thoreau, *Autumn,* ed. H. G. O. Blake (Cambridge, Mass., 1892), p. 116.
19. Henry D. Thoreau, *A Week on the Concord and Merrimack Rivers,* Concord Edition (Boston, 1929), pp. 107–108.
20. Ibid., p. 418.
21. Ibid., p. 420.
22. Thoreau, *Early Essays,* pp. 141–42.
23. Thoreau, *Walden,* p. 338.
24. Ibid.
25. Henry D. Thoreau, *Winter,* ed. H. G. O. Blake (Cambridge, Mass., 1887), pp. 405–406.
26. Ibid., p. 264.
27. Ibid., p. 257.

CHAPTER THIRTEEN

1. Henry D. Thoreau, *Early Spring in Massachusetts,* ed. H. G. O. Blake (Cambridge, Mass., 1893), p. 112.
2. Henry D. Thoreau, *The Maine Woods,* ed. Joseph J. Moldenhauer (Princeton, 1972), pp. 22–23.
3. Ibid., p. 15.
4. Henry D. Thoreau, *Reform Papers,* ed Wendell Glick (Princeton, 1973), pp. 174–75.
5. Thoreau, *Early Spring,* p. 337.
6. James T. Fields, *Yesterdays with Authors* (Boston, 1900), p. 110.
7. Ralph Waldo Emerson, *Complete Works,* Riverside Edition (London, n.d.), X:440.
8. W. J. Stillman, *The Autobiography of a Journalist* (London, 1901), I:168–69.
9. Thoreau, *Maine Woods,* p. 71.
10. Henry D. Thoreau, *Autumn,* ed. H. G. O. Blake (Cambridge, Mass., 1892), p. 394.
11. Henry D. Thoreau, *Walden,* Concord Edition (Boston, 1929), p. 350.
12. Henry D. Thoreau, *A Week on the Concord and Merrimack Rivers,* Concord Edition (Boston, 1929), p. 53.
13. Henry D. Thoreau, *Summer,* ed. H. G. O. Blake (Cambridge, Mass., 1884), p. 110.
14. Further on this topic, see Ann Douglas, *The Feminization of American Culture* (New York, 1977).

15. Henry D. Thoreau, *Cape Cod* (Cambridge, Mass., 1893), p. 302.
16. Thoreau, *A Week,* p. 161.
17. Thoreau, *Maine Woods,* p. 229.
18. Thoreau, *Reform Papers,* p. 178.
19. Ibid., p. 64.
20. See Richard N. Current, *Daniel Webster and the Rise of National Conservatism* (Boston, 1955), p. 100.
21. Thoreau, *Maine Woods,* p. 230.
22. Thoreau, *Walden,* pp. 35–36.
23. Henry D. Thoreau, *Early Essays and Miscellanies* (Princeton, 1975), pp. 249–50.
24. Ibid., p. 251.
25. Ralph Waldo Emerson, *The Journals and Miscellaneous Notebooks,* 12 vols. to date (Cambridge, Mass., 1961–), VII:143–44.
26. Henry D. Thoreau, *Familiar Letters,* ed. F. O. Sanborn (Cambridge, Mass., 1894), p. 138.
27. Thoreau, *Walden,* pp. 227–28.
28. Ibid., p. 231.
29. Thoreau, *Familiar Letters,* pp. 187–88.
30. Thoreau, *Reform Papers,* p. 158.
31. Thoreau, *A Week,* p. 341.
32. The story is "The Dustan Family," in Nathaniel Hawthorne, *Miscellanies* (Boston, 1900).
33. Thoreau, *A Week,* p. 343.
34. Ibid., p. 345.
35. Ibid., p. 351.
36. Thoreau, *Reform Papers,* pp. 150–51.

CHAPTER FOURTEEN

1. Ralph Waldo Emerson, *Journals,* ed. E. W. Emerson and W. E. Forbes (London, 1913), IX:401.
2. Walt Whitman, *Leaves of Grass,* Facsimile Edition of the 1860 Text (Ithaca, N.Y., 1961), p. 300. Unless otherwise noted, quotations from Whitman's poetry are taken from this edition. In further citations titles will be identified but not page numbers, and the titles, of course, will be those given the poems in the 1892 edition, since it is by these that the poems are most readily located.
3. Henry D. Thoreau, *Familiar Letters,* ed. F. O. Sanborn (Cambridge, Mass., 1894), pp. 345–47.
4. Ibid.

5. Walter Harding, *Thoreau, Man of Concord* (New York, 1960), p. 63. Harding is quoting from *Anne Gilchrist,* ed. Herbert Gilchrist (1887).
6. "To the States."
7. "A Hand-Mirror."
8. *Song of Myself*
9. "Whitman-Introduction," *Leaves of Grass, The First (1855) Edition,* ed. Malcolm Cowley (New York, 1978).
10. *Song of Myself.*
11. Henry D. Thoreau, *Walden,* Concord Edition (Boston, 1929), p. 4.
12. *Song of Myself.*
13. "Whitman-Introduction."
14. Walt Whitman, *Specimen Days,* ed. Floyd Stovall (New York, 1963), p. 250.
15. Quoted in Roger Asselinau, *The Evolution of Walt Whitman: The Creation of a Personality* (Cambridge, Mass., 1960), p. 75.
16. "I Sing the Body Electric."
17. *Song of Myself.*
18. "In Paths Untrodden."
19. "Whoever You Are Holding Me Now in Hand."
20. "I Saw in Louisiana a Live-Oak Growing."
21. "Native Moments."

CHAPTER FIFTEEN

1. Thomas Carlyle, "Shooting Niagara: And After?" *Critical and Miscellaneous Essays* (London, 1899), V:40.
2. Ibid., p. 43.
3. Horace Traubel, *With Walt Whitman in Camden* (New York, 1961), I:267.
4. Thomas Wentworth Higginson, *Cheerful Yesterdays* (Boston, 1898), p. 230.
5. Walt Whitman, "Collect," *The Complete Writings,* ed. Richard Maurice Bucke, Thomas B. Harned, and Horace L. Traubel (New York, 1902), V:276.
6. Walt Whitman, *Song of Myself, Leaves of Grass,* Facsimile Edition of the 1860 Text (Ithaca, N.Y., 1961). Unless otherwise noted, quotations from Whitman's poetry are taken from this edition.
7. "Song of the Broad-Axe."
8. *Song of Myself.*
9. Ibid.
10. "The Sleepers."
11. "To Think of Time."

12. *Song of Myself.*
13. "As I Ebb'd with the Ocean of Life."
14. *Song of Myself.*
15. "Whitman-Introduction," *Leaves of Grass, The First (1855) Edition,* ed. Malcolm Cowley (New York, 1978).
16. Excluded from *Leaves of Grass* by Whitman but to be found in the edition edited by Sculley Bradley and Harold Blodgett (New York, 1965) as "Great Are the Myths."
17. *Whitman in Camden,* I:212–13.
18. John Greenleaf Whittier, "Robert Dinsmore," *The Writings* (London, 1889), VI:248.
19. In his Introduction to *Leaves of Grass, The First (1855) Edition,* p. xxii.
20. "Whitman-Introduction."

CHAPTER SIXTEEN

1. Herman Melville, "Hawthorne and His Mosses," *Representative Selections,* ed. Willard Thorp (New York, 1938), p. 336.
2. Alexis de Tocqueville, *Democracy in America* (New York, 1954), II:80.
3. This is the argument in Harold Kaplan, *Democratic Humanism and American Literature* (Chicago, 1972).
4. Ralph Waldo Emerson, *The Journals and Miscellaneous Notebooks,* 12 vols. to date (Cambridge, Mass., 1961–), VII:421–22.
5. Ibid., IV:23.
6. Herman Melville, "John Marr," *Collected Poems,* ed. Howard P. Vincent (Chicago, 1947), p. 161.
7. Herman Melville, *The Letters,* ed. Merrell R. Davis and William H. Gilman (New Haven, 1960), p. 96.
8. Herman Melville, *Mardi* (Evanston, 1970), pp. 528–29.
9. Melville, *Letters,* p. 91.
10. Herman Melville, *White-Jacket* (Evanston, 1970), p. 151.
11. Emerson, *Journals,* XI:397–98.
12. Herman Melville, *Redburn* (Garden City, 1957), p. 281.
13. Melville, *Letters,* p. 92.
14. Ibid., p. 96.
15. Herman Melville, *Moby-Dick,* ed. Harrison Hayford and Hershel Parker (New York, 1967), p. 104.
16. Ibid., p. 219.
17. Thomas Paine, *Common Sense,* ed. Nelson F. Adkins (Indianapolis, 1953), p. 4.
18. Melville, *White-Jacket,* p. 18.

19. Melville, *Moby-Dick,* pp. 129–30.
20. Emerson, *Journals,* VII:376.

CHAPTER SEVENTEEN

1. Rufus W. Griswold, *Passages from the Correspondence* (Cambridge, Mass., 1898), pp. 108–109.
2. Helmut Lehmanns-Haupt, *The Book in America* (New York, 1939), p. 119.
3. Griswold, *Passages,* p. 280.
4. Herman Melville, *The Letters,* ed. Merrell R. Davis and William H. Gilman (New Haven, 1960), p. 134.
5. Herman Melville, *White Jacket* (Evanston, 1970), p. 321.
6. Melville, *Letters,* p. 78.
7. Herman Melville, *Moby-Dick,* ed. Harrison Hayford and Hershel Parker (New York, 1967), p. 470.
8. Herman Melville, *Pierre* (Evanston, 1971), p. 293.
9. Herman Melville, *The Apple-Tree Table and Other Sketches* (New York, 1922), p. 63.
10. Herman Melville, *Mardi* (Evanston, 1970), p. 595.
11. Melville, *Pierre,* p. 359.
12. Ibid., p. 361.
13. Ibid.
14. Melville, *Letters,* p. 77.
15. Melville, *Moby-Dick,* p. 445.
16. Melville, *Pierre,* p. 199.
17. Herman Melville, *The Confidence-Man,* ed. Hershel Parker (New York, 1971), pp. 157–58.
18. Ibid., pp. 99–100.
19. Ibid., p. 158.
20. "Passage to India."

AFTERWORD

1. Supra, p. 61.
2. A valuable selection of early theories of American literature is in Richard Ruland, *The Native Muse* (New York, 1972).
3. F. O. Matthiessen, *American Renaissance* (New York, 1941), p. vii.

Index